THE FALCON AND THE SNOWMAN: AMERICAN SONS

Written by

Christopher Boyce

Cait Boyce

Vince Font

The people, places and events described in this book are real. However, in some cases the names and identifying characteristics of certain individuals have been changed to protect their privacy.

Copyright © 2013 Christopher Boyce, Cait Boyce and Vince Font

All rights reserved. No part of this book may be reproduced, stored in a retrieval system, or transmitted in any form or by any means without prior written permission from the authors, except for the use of brief quotations in a book review.

Published by Vince Font LLC

ISBN 978-0-615-90541-9

All photographs and images are the property of Christopher and Cait Boyce, except where noted.

Cover design by Jane Font

Edited by Nancy LaFever

Visit the book website at www.thefalconandthesnowman.com

FOREWORD

I am an old man now, far older than my sixty years. A quarter century in federal prison will have that effect on you. I was introduced the other day to another fly fisherman and I heard his wife whisper in the background, "That old man can't be The Falcon." In truth, I can hardly believe it myself.

When I look in the mirror these days, a young voice in my head asks, *What happened?* This book is an attempt to answer that question. It is for me also a catharsis. I have carried the weight of this thing upon my shoulders since I was a young man. It has, at times, ground me down into the dust, and I cannot do it anymore. I must be done with it.

An introduction is a beginning. Let me try to begin there. When I was a young boy, my father and I would read his history books. He was an important part of the intelligence state in its crude infancy and a lover of history. My father admired the audacious and I admired my father. I read from his books that the ancient Gaels judged a man by the power of his enemies.

When I was off doing boy things, running in the fields with my hawks or fishing in the tide pools, I would dream of these judgments of the ancient Gaels. One day, I told myself, I too would have powerful enemies. I believed that a man's life must be a quest worth living, but these sentiments would one day turn my life into a living

Several years ago, I had an idea to write a book but was stymied by my own need to be anonymous and not rock the boat for others. I went to my mentors for confirmation that I wasn't crazy – my darling mother, Helen Mills, my oldest friend Rick Weedon, and my friend in Australia, Paul Weston. My Mom told me I was only somewhat crazy, Rick thought it sounded like a great idea, and Paul was completely supportive and thought the people of Australia would be, too. And so it began. In the process of writing this book I lost my mother, but I know that she would have been very proud of the finished result.

I dedicate this book with all my love to Helen Patricia Mills and Thomas C. Mills, my parents, for their undying support and love for their rebel daughter.

I also want to thank my brothers and their families – Tim and Lori Mills, Daniel and Imelda Mills, and Tim Jones – for being excited about this project and for their complete acceptance of Chris and our life together.

Thank you, also, to the women in my life who held tight during this time and let me run amok: Sandra Hess, Linda Sheridan, Travis Darby, and Pam Hurley.

And to Chris... (Cait Boyce)

I dedicate all that is mine in this book to my wife, Cait, who rescued me with her love and legal wizardry. (Chris Boyce)

To my wonderful wife, Jane, for believing in me when I didn't believe in myself, and for busting my balls to get me to start writing again. You were right. (Vince Font) hell. Still, it is my life, the only life I have ever known, and though I would now change some of it, I would not change all of it.

When I was fifteen, my father took me to the Custer Battlefield National Monument on the Little Bighorn. I imagined George Armstrong Custer pitching his three hundred cavalrymen into four thousand Sioux warriors and being annihilated. I stood on the ground where he fell. I breathed it all in, the dust, the despair and death, the whole gruesome fight.

I must confess that I walked off that battlefield not thinking thoughts generally associated with baby boomers. I was an incurable quester. I was Don Quixote looking for a windmill. And not exactly a prime candidate to work for a National Security Agency subcontractor. In fact, I was their worst nightmare, a longhair with top secret clearance based on a joke of a background security investigation. This blew my mind. And one day, I meant it to blow theirs.

My enemy, I decided, was the United States intelligence complex. I asked myself a dozen times a day, *What would Thomas Jefferson think of our current government that had somehow morphed out of the limited, balanced, political institutions he had designed?* I decided that if Jefferson still possessed any consciousness at all, the poor old patriot must be spinning in his grave.

In late 1974, I was hired to work in TRW's Black Vault, which was actually an NSA encryption operation supporting satellite surveillance of Russia. The satellites used Pine Gap, in the Australian outback, as a communications "foot." At my first security briefing, the project security director informed me that the NSA was not willing to live up to our agreement to share all information gathered at Pine Gap with our Australian allies. I was told that we were also hiding the new, more sophisticated, successor Argus Project of surveillance at Pine Gap from the Aussies in violation of the Executive Agreement between our two countries.

I was told the elected Labor Government of Australia was a threat to American interests; that the Whitlam Government was socialistic and that their inquiries about Pine Gap were compromising the security of the project. I later read encrypted dispatches discussing the infiltration of Australian trade unions by the CIA, and listened to our project CIA resident refer to the Governor-General of Australia, Sir John Kerr (the man who unconstitutionally sacked Gough Whitlam as Prime Minister), as "our man Kerr."

I watched my government deceive an ally, an English speaking parliamentary democracy who had fought next to us in two world wars. I concede I was naive, that allies deceive each other every day, but still I was disgusted. Without giving it the deliberation it deserved, I decided to do as much damage to the American intelligence community as I could possibly do. And nothing I could think of would bring greater horror to America's spooks than to pass NSA codes to the Russians.

So began my self-destructive descent into hell. I was an army of one, out to damage what I saw as the Great Rotten Republic – at which point, I went to see my old falconry buddy and ne'er do well friend, a smalltime drug dealer named Andrew Daulton Lee. I explained to him what I had in mind. He looked at me in disbelief, but after a few moments I could see dollar signs dancing in his eyes.

I cannot say that at that point we did not often enter the realm of the absurd. We certainly did. We listened to Janis Joplin, ate marijuana brownies, and had clandestine meetings with the KGB. We laughed at Cheech and Chong while photographing crypto codes with a miniature Minox camera. If ever such a thing as longhair, amateur spies could exist, we were it.

One night, half the Palos Verdes police department chased Daulton in their squad cars for twenty minutes all throughout our wealthy neighborhood in what was undoubtedly the greatest road rally of their lives. Meanwhile, my ear cocked to the approaching sirens, I frantically buried secret documents under my mother's daffodils. The hijinks and shenanigans never ceased. Until, of course, they did. As they had to.

In January of 1977, the past caught up. The intelligence complex nailed us. They meant to destroy us. For Daulton, it meant first being tortured within an inch of his life by Mexico's Seguridad Federal before being turned over to the American authorities. For me, it was several dozen FBI agents coming at me from every direction after a day of flying my falcons. It was time to pay the piper. Chains. Humiliation. Incarceration with no end. Waiting to be murdered. They must pay for this, the U.S. Attorneys told my father's lawyers. And we did.

On April 28, 1977, a jury found me guilty of espionage and I was sentenced to forty years imprisonment. Weeks later, my old chum and partner in crime Daulton Lee was sentenced to life for the same.

By the time I made my decision to break out of federal prison or die trying, there was already one book out. In 1985, Hollywood told our story in the motion picture *The Falcon and the Snowman*. I got to watch the movie on a small television set at Marion Federal Penitentiary, seated right next to the guy who portrayed me, Timothy Hutton. When it was over and the credits rolled, a part of me wanted to cry out, *But that's not the end!* The truth was, I was still living the nightmare, long after the lights had gone up in movie theaters around the country.

I would continue to live that nightmare for another seventeen years, until a woman I met by the name of Cait Mills saved my life. She also saved Daulton's. Today, Daulton Lee and I are free men, thanks to the dedication and hard work of a woman I now call my wife. This book, *The Falcon and The Snowman: American Sons*, is the answer to every person who ever asked the question, *What happened next?*

This is what happened next.
(Christopher Boyce, 2013)

THE BODY

Chris
(August 2005)

Christopher Boyce was bleeding. The gash on the back of his hand oozed a dark shade of crimson, mixing with dirt and sweat. He held up his hand, stared at the cut, cursed. There had been seven presidential elections since he'd last tangled so ferociously with a chain link fence, and he decided he liked it no more now that he was repairing it than he did when he was scaling it.

He wiped the blood on his pant leg and inspected the cut again, oblivious to the commotion that was unfolding a mere hundred yards away. He didn't even notice he was being approached from behind until he heard the voice.

"Mr. Boyce."

Chris jerked his head around, startled. His eyes met the sight of two uniformed police officers standing only feet away. They were so close, in fact, that he had no trouble recognizing the symbol on their shoulder patches, the unmistakable logo that identified them as deputies of the county sheriff's department.

How the hell did I let these guys sneak up on me? he thought.

But before he could pursue that internal rebuke any further, Chris froze. He saw that one of the deputies had his hand resting firmly on the pistol grip of his holstered sidearm.

Instantly, his thoughts flew to Cait. Had she been in an accident? Not likely. At this hour of the day, she'd surely still be at the office, buried under a stack of legal briefs a foot high. But even if there had been an accident, that certainly wouldn't explain the pistol-ready stance.

Unless something terrible had happened.

"Mr. Boyce." This time there was a more demanding tone in the deputy's voice.

He stood from his squatting position and faced the uniformed men. It was an almost comical mimicry of an Old West standoff – except in this case, the odds were two to one, and Chris hadn't owned a gun since the bank robbery spree a quarter century earlier.

"Yeah?"

"Did you bury a body in your backyard?"

The words rattled around in Chris's head, seeking purchase but meeting only flat incomprehension. After all, it isn't every day that you get hit with an inquiry of that magnitude. For the absurdity of the question, the cop might as well have asked him to explain his role in the Kennedy assassination.

"What?" His mind was spinning in a thousand directions, trying to figure out what was going on. Although his composure was beginning to fall away, his face was as cool and expressionless as a mask.

"Did you bury a body in your backyard?" the deputy repeated, placing an emphasis on *body* as if the man before him had somehow missed the crucial noun that underscored the gravity of the question.

Chris didn't care much for the tone in the deputy's voice. It wasn't so much a question as it was an accusation. He had heard that voice before, in a life almost twenty-five years past, and it wasn't a voice he'd ever hoped to hear again. A tingling sensation of shock began to radiate downward from the center of his forehead.

"What are you talking about?" The bewilderment in his voice was obvious only to himself. He noticed that the tingling had now radiated to his fingertips, causing them to tremble almost imperceptibly. He could feel his heart pulsing in his temples, and beads of sweat began to run freely down his ribs from his armpit.

"A body has just been dug up in your backyard," the deputy said. "What do you know about it?"

At fifty-two years old, Chris was no longer the tireless athlete he had been in his youth. The days of effortless leapfrogging from one sport to another and racing through the rolling hills and open fields that had once surrounded the outskirts of his childhood home in Palos Verdes, California, were long gone. He wasn't exactly over the hill – not yet, anyway – but he wasn't a young man, either. The years had brought the unavoidable evidence of age; signs that had manifested in the all too frequent inclination to stroll rather than trot, even when headed out for an afternoon of hawking with Zeke, his peregrine falcon. The fact was, he hadn't run from anyone or anything in years. But at that moment, he found himself fighting the urge to bolt.

And he almost did. But the realization that he'd been boxed into a corner between the two deputies and the chain link fence told him it would be impossible to escape if he tried. The deputies were both large men and had the look of ex-athletes. They were also considerably younger and he knew he'd be no match against them. There was no way out.

He struggled to get ahold of himself. *Post-traumatic stress*, he reasoned, almost as if to assure himself that he was okay, everything was fine, that the urge to run was simply the last remaining remnant of an incident long past. *Bad memories, that's all, and these guys aren't doing a very good job of assuring me they don't think I'm guilty of something.*

The thought crystallized in his mind and he held it there, studying it for what seemed like an eternity but was actually only a split second. It snapped him out of his contemplative trance like a slap in the face, with the last spoken words of the deputy still lingering in the air like an unanswered charge: *What do you know about it?*

"Not a damn thing!" Chris answered. The indignation in his voice caused the denial to come off more like a bark than a sentence.

Realizing he'd been standing in a defensive position the entire time, he relaxed his stance and stepped forward – but as he did, he held his hands at his sides, palms out, in the walk of a man who's had his fair share of scrutiny under the eyes of the law.

He cast a quick, damning glance down at his hands and closed them, reminding himself as he had so many times during the course of the last three years that he was a free man, even though the overshadowing memory of twenty-five years spent staring out from behind barred windows would never truly leave him.

His eyes met those of the first deputy, the one who had done all the talking. The nametag on his chest read J WATERS. Chris hoped it was a name he wouldn't become familiar with.

"Show me," Chris said disbelievingly, as if calling the bigger man's bluff.

Deep down inside, he didn't know if he wanted Waters to show his hand. A body discovered near his home could spell trouble. Even though he was no longer behind bars, he was still a parolee of the Federal Bureau of Prisons. A body discovered on or near his property would most assuredly land him back in custody. If being pulled over for driving too fast was an offense great enough to threaten his newfound freedom, then certainly the evidence of a heinous crime within a stone's throw of his front door would be.

Waters made a sharp motion with his left hand, pointing the way. It was more of a demand than an invitation, but it was entirely unnecessary. By now, Chris felt himself being tugged at by a deepening curiosity. He went willingly.

As the three men crossed the sagebrush plain toward the northeast corner of his property, a question rose in his mind, causing him to replay the events of what had started out as a normal day but had quickly detoured into territory of the strange and bizarre: *Who had discovered the body and called the police?*

He recalled that his neighbors, an older couple he and Cait were acquainted with, had recently hired a contractor to build a fence along the property line that separated their lots. It was to be something of a monstrosity, a one-hundred-yard wall of demarcation with little purpose in such a rural area, but Chris had reasoned that what wasn't of any cost to him was also not of his concern.

An hour before the deputies showed up, he had set about the task of retightening the tension wire on a sagging section of the chain link fence he'd installed in an effort to keep Cait's dogs – Lola, Theo, and Chase – from wandering off. Although the house sat on a two-and-a-half acre expanse of land, the majority of the lot beyond the edge of the green lawn was a minefield of sagebrush and stickweed burrs the dogs could seldom resist venturing into.

As he worked, Chris had noticed a small group of men digging post holes in the ground where the fence would be built. *Noticed* was actually an understatement. The racket thrown out by the motor-driven auger had made it impossible to ignore, a sonic blight against the typically serene ambience of the surrounding plains and the juniper woods beyond.

At some point, he recalled now, the auger had gone silent. When he looked back in their direction, the workers were no longer anywhere in sight. He hadn't seen them run for the main road, digging frantically for their cell phones as they beat a hasty retreat to report their ghastly discovery to the police. Now Chris was about to see with his own eyes what it was that had sent the handymen scurrying and had brought the long arm of the law curling around him in a decidedly chilly embrace.

He walked ahead of the deputies until they reached the property line where the auger now sat mute. The hole in the ground was less than a foot across and almost three feet deep. He stood at the lip of the upturned earth and peered down.

There was no mistaking it was a body. Chris had expected to see a neat pile of bones, but what he witnessed instead set his stomach on edge. The auger had struck the body as it plunged into the ground, rupturing the heavy duty plastic bag that encased it. Some of the bag's contents were bulging from the tear, leaking a horrifying stew of hair, bones, and rotted flesh.

He choked as his nostrils encountered the rising stench. Instinctively, he clapped a hand over his mouth and nose, squinting as if to protect his eyes from the odor.

"Shit," he spoke through his hand, to nobody in particular. "Wait 'til Cait hears this one."

"Who's Cait?" Waters asked, and damned if his voice didn't still hold an air of condescending suspicion.

I thought we were over that hurdle, Chris thought to say, but didn't. *Anyway, how many killers do you know who'd gag at the sight and smell of their own deeds?* He decided the deputy probably didn't know the answer to that question any more than he did.

Waters and his partner stared at him, waiting for an answer. But this time he didn't respond at all, only continued to look into the gaping hole in the ground, transfixed by the mystery that was unfolding. Besides, Cait had always reminded him to keep his mouth shut around cops, and if ever there was a time to do that, it was now.

A police siren wailed in the distance. Before long, a dozen police cars had arrived, delivering a small army of sheriff's deputies to converge on the site of the freshly discovered grave. They milled back and forth, taking turns looking at the grisly discovery, spouting conjecture, some joking, others serious, all of them eyeing Chris with stony, suspicious faces.

When the forensics team arrived, they used shovels to dig a trench around the hole. In short time, they had widened it to the point where it now actually resembled an unearthed grave. Chris shuddered at the thought.

He turned and began walking back to the house, but Waters stopped him. He had been standing nearby the whole time, ensuring Chris didn't stray too far, by now convinced he had to be hiding something.

"Mr. Boyce?" he called out. "Where are you going?"

Chris stopped and turned around. He cocked his thumb in the direction of the house. "I have to make a phone call."

Just then, something darted between the two men and lunged at the shallow grave. It was Theo, one of Cait's three dogs. In the whirlwind of events, Chris had forgotten all about the unfinished fence. Taking full advantage, Theo had managed to escape by wriggling around the sagging mesh of chain link a hundred yards behind. It was an act Chris couldn't help but look on with admiration.

One of the forensics officers bagging and tagging the body parts cried out. Chris sprang forward, half expecting to have to pry Theo off. What he saw instead stopped him dead.

Theo had taken one of the bones into his mouth. The forensics officer snatched at it as two more officers closed in from behind, but the feisty dog was too fast. Theo raced away with the newly stolen loot clamped firmly in his jaws.

Dog: 1. Cops: 0.

Chris's face melted into a grimace of disgust and delight as all hell broke loose and a handful of uniformed sheriff's deputies took up pursuit of the dog and the stolen evidence.

No way this day gets any weirder, he thought. *No way.*

The scene erupted into pandemonium. One of the deputies tripped and fell, his plunge punctuated by a cacophony of claps and whistles and voices shouting, "Here boy! Here!" Now there were at least a dozen deputies in on the chase. Automatically, they formed a circle around the dog and began to advance. Realizing he was closed in, Theo dropped to his haunches and started trembling.

That was enough for Chris. He pushed his way through the tight wall of bodies and knelt down protectively beside the dog. He took the bone away and threw it aside. It landed at the feet of one of the approaching deputies with a wet splat. He looked at the jellylike mix of blood and foam on his hand and gagged.

When his stomach finally settled, Chris took hold of Theo's collar and began walking him back to the house. As he went, two eyes bored into the back of his skull. Waters was watching him like a hawk.

THE GREAT ESCAPE

Chris
(January 21, 1980)

Chris ran. In the blackness of the void, he could see only a few feet ahead of him. But the fact that his progress was being slowed by a thickening undergrowth of oak trees told him he was moving in the right direction.

As soon as he was deep enough in the woods to be out of sight of the gun tower, he stopped. He rested his palms on his knees to steady the shaking of his legs and doubled over, struggling to catch his breath.

His lungs breathed fire. Each hitching breath sent thick clouds of vapor dissipating into the cold, wet night. The months he'd spent running miles around the prison track in preparation for this moment had transformed his legs to pistons and his lungs to powerhouse bellows – but once that first breakneck sprint was done, it was all he could do to hold himself up.

He twisted his body south in the direction he had come and peered through the thick growth of trees that hid him from sight. Across the field of fire only two hundred yards from the tree line, Lompoc Federal Penitentiary lay still, illuminated by the blinding lights that shone down on its perimeter. He cocked his head and listened. Total silence.

I did it.

The realization struck him like a hammer, and he almost laughed out loud. But the sudden sight of headlights in the distance brought any premature exultation to a halt. He ducked behind the trunk of an old oak tree and froze to the spot as the perimeter patrol truck drew near.

The truck made a wide right turn and cruised by in its slow, trolling orbit out past the edge of the woods on the small service road that circled the prison. The other patrol truck would be around in another two to three minutes.

He knew he couldn't allow himself any time to rejoice. The improvised *papier-mâché* dummy he'd fashioned after Clint Eastwood's crude masterpiece in *Escape from Alcatraz* had done the job and passed the four p.m. headcount. But he didn't want to stick around to find out if it passed the next. Still on shaky legs, he turned and faced northeast.

He took a single step, then stopped. His legs felt like heavy sacks of flesh.

Easy does it. One step at a time.

But even that was proving almost impossible.

It's not every day you charge blindly to your certain death, he reasoned. *Must be adrenaline. Nerves, or something. This is perfectly normal.* But he was beginning to worry that it wasn't.

It lasted just long enough to raise a tickle of panic – surely he hadn't just pulled off the impossible to go paralytic in the woods like some deer in the path of an oncoming car – but the moment he felt the first faint traces of strength returning to his legs, it subsided.

Better. It's passing. Just take a few more deep breaths.

He ignored the screaming voice in the back of his head, the one reminding him if he didn't move now – and fast – the only walking he'd ever do again would be pacing the length of his cell in a supermax designed especially for escape artists. Instead, he leaned over and massaged the muscles of his legs, slowly coaxing them back to life.

He took a step. *Good.* Then another. *Better.* Then a third... and he was off. Jogging, slowly at first, clutching tree limbs for support, then picking up speed, moving northeast, deeper into the oak forest toward the foothills beyond. His feet soon found their perfect rhythm and his breathing leveled off into that almost hypnotic cadence familiar to all trained runners. He was moving fast now, putting as much distance as he could between himself and the prison before they discovered he was gone.

The advantage didn't last long.

Overhead, a mist of rain that had swept inland from the Pacific Coast was rapidly becoming a full-blown storm. A fog rolled in, thick as pea soup, obscuring his view of the night sky. He had camped these hills countless times in his teens and early twenties, and he knew the land like his own backyard. January in the Lompoc Valley was always wet, but it never got so bad you couldn't make it overnight without shelter. The one thing he hadn't counted on, though, was a downpour.

The deeper he went into the woods the softer the ground became, slowing his progress. The rain intensified, as if some sadistic being had chosen this night to dump the contents of its celestial bucket out over his direct path. His running shoes were punching holes in the mud now, almost disappearing into the ground as he ran. For the first time since he'd landed on the free side of Lompoc's perimeter fence, it felt like the earth had come alive and was conspiring to keep him from going any further.

"Fuck you," he spat, aimed at nothing in particular, but the forest seemed to take umbrage. As if in response, a tree root hurled itself into his path and struck his foot. Or maybe it had been there all along. He staggered and hit the ground chest-first with a grunt.

The rain was coming harder now and the branches of the trees moved with the weight of the water. A cold gust bore down from overhead, pummeling him like a fist. Unmoved, the fog hung in the air. He lifted his head and pushed himself to his feet.

"If you want to stop me," he said aloud, addressing the sky, the night, and anything else that might be looking down, "you'll have to do a hell of a lot better than this."

He readjusted the hood of his soaked sweatshirt, took his bearings as best he could, and started moving again.

***

With every step, he thought of Billy. Did he ever believe Chris could have made it this far? Probably not. *Absolutely* not. Yet in the end, Billy had proven that faith was no prerequisite for becoming the perfect accomplice.

The only other person who knew the details of the plan, Billy had obviously come through on his promise to stick the life-like dummy in Chris's cell bunk for the afternoon headcount. Without that final jigsaw piece in place, escape would have been impossible and the hours they had spent digging his shallow passage to freedom would have been for nothing.

They'd done it all by the light of day, operating right under the noses of the yard guards and gun tower sharpshooters trained to kill on sight. The silt-choked sump drain that lay near the perimeter fence on the north edge of the activity yard had given them the perfect excuse to draw near, setting the stage for his flight to freedom.

It took them three hours to dig the hole. In that time, they had only one close call – when a guard standing lookout came rushing over after watching Chris and Billy roll a wheelbarrow to the drain, stop, and begin prying up its heavy steel grate.

"What the fuck are you doing?" he barked as he approached. The Kill Zone was only feet away, and anyone venturing that close to no-man's land had to have a damn good reason for being there. Just beyond the Kill Zone, the prison's inside perimeter fence rose to a height of eight feet, a chain link barrier with large razor wire coils along its top. Another forty feet beyond was the outside perimeter fence, twice as high and more lethal than the first. Monstrous coils of razor wire choked every square foot of empty space between fences.

Chris and Billy heard the shout and looked up at the same time to see the uniform heading their way. A beer gut swayed over the guard's cinched belt like a bowling ball in a sling as he moved.

"Here we go," Chris said under his breath.

The guard marched up to the two convicts and glared at them. He was unarmed, but that didn't matter. The guards who patrolled the yard never were, for obvious reasons. It wouldn't take much for a motivated convict to snatch a weapon, kick-starting an insurrection that would end in a high body count if it all went straight to hell. Yet despite their lack of firepower, the yard guards hurled their weight with impunity, their nerve buffeted by the presence of the overhead gun towers that surveyed all activity by rifle sight.

"I said what the fuck are you two doing?"

Chris dug into his pocket, pulled out a folded work order, and handed it to the guard. "Griswold sent us out here," he said, referring to the guard who supervised the grounds crew. Chris had been a member of the grounds crew for exactly one week.

The guard glanced down at the work order. Griswold's signature was there alright – Chris had forged it and it wasn't a half-bad job. It was an offense that could have landed him in solitary confinement with another year or more tacked onto his sentence, but he figured it was a gamble worth taking for the possibility of freedom.

"Why do you have that wheelbarrow?" the guard asked.

"Sump's backed up to the grate with sludge." Chris pointed to the drainage ditch at his feet, which sat at the base of a concrete curb that marked the north edge of the activity yard. "Griswold wants us to dig it out and dump it."

The coolness in his own voice surprised him. The guard was standing close enough to have easily read the lie on his face, but even at that close range Chris never lost his composure. Not even when he could sense Billy's flagging.

The guard took a closer look at the at the work order, his eyes zeroing in on the signature line. Chris knew what would come next: a radio call to Griswold to confirm, which would bring the plan crashing down like a shit-storm.

The scheme had taken almost two months to plan. In that time, Billy – who already had a job on the grounds crew – had ingratiated himself to Griswold by showering him with piles of donuts Chris had bought from the chow hall's black market. It also didn't hurt that Billy was an incredibly likeable con who always had a joke and a punch line at the ready. Soon enough, he and Griswold were getting along like old friends. When Billy eventually asked Griswold if he could get his pal Chris a job on the crew, the guard's response was exactly as predicted. "Why the fuck not? Sure." And that was that.

As ludicrous as it seemed, it worked better than Chris or Billy had imagined. Not only did it succeed in getting Chris the job he would need to escape, but the donuts also kept Griswold distracted long enough for the two to steal a blank work order and a pair of pruning shears from the equipment shack. Chris also used this time to fashion a crude, one-legged ladder from a discarded two-by-two and a small block of wood. Now the ladder was stashed under a burlap sack in the wheelbarrow next to the shears, and the work order – forged expertly in Griswold's name – was in the guard's hands.

A bead of sweat trickled from Chris's hairline and caught in his eyebrow. He wiped it away nonchalantly, then shot a glance at Billy. He saw that his friend's eyes had taken on the look of a man about to be caught with his hands fist-deep in a money safe. The guard sensed his unease and was about to speak when Chris decided if ever there was a time to lay it on thick, it was now.

"You know something," Chris said, assuming a defiant stance, "I don't know why the hell we have to be the ones to dig this shit out. So if you think we shouldn't mess with it, that's fine with me. I got better things to do." It was phony indolence, but the guard showed no sign of catching on.

"Why don't you just call Griswold and tell him you're sending us back?" he added. "But I'm not going back empty handed. He gives me enough shit as it is."

Chris met the guard's gaze and waited for him to make the next move. Then, something unexpected happened. The suspicion on the guard's face melted like a snowball on a hotplate. He snapped the work order back to Chris. "Just hurry the fuck up," he said and went back to his post.

Billy and Chris watched him go with the disbelieving relief of a deep sea diver just passed over by a great white.

Thank God for apathy, Chris thought. He turned to Billy, who looked on the verge of throwing up. "You gonna be alright?"

Without a word, Billy dropped to one knee, slid his fingers through the slits in the sump drain's grate, and lifted. "Let's just get this shit over with before I have a fucking coronary," he said. Chris grabbed the hand shovel from the wheelbarrow and jammed the tip under the lip of the grate for leverage.

"Anyone ever tell you that you could win an Academy Award?" Billy asked as they hoisted the grate out of place to expose the fine, damp silt below.

"Anyone ever tell you that you've got a shitty poker face?" Chris shot back.

"Maybe a time or two. You don't get sent to a place like this unless you fuck up big enough to get caught."

"*Now* you tell me."

They set the grate aside and Chris went to work on the silt with the hand shovel. Billy removed the burlap sack and pushed the wheelbarrow in closer.

"Just remember," Billy told him, "you make it to that goddamn fence, you better hit it soft. You tap that snitch wire, it's *sayonara*."

Chris stopped digging and spared a quick glance at the perimeter fence only fifty feet away. He looked up at Billy. "It's as good as done," he said. He forced a cocky grin, but underneath his shirt, his heart was thrumming like a jackhammer.

***

Since his arrival at Lompoc six months earlier, Chris had met only a handful of convicts he genuinely liked. Billy was one of them. Outside in the real world, things would have been decidedly different. But locked in the bowels of one of the worst federal prisons in America, people had a tendency to forge unlikely alliances. Chris was no exception.

The two had gravitated to each other for uniquely different reasons. For Chris, it was Billy's wry sense of humor and exhilarating tales of past escapes, which he listened to with rapt interest. Billy seemed fascinated by the strait-laced amateur whose only crime had sent him so far up the river that he'd surely hit retirement age before ever getting out. He also had great respect for any man capable of pissing that many people off in one deft swat.

Eventually, Chris came to realize Billy was the perfect person to entrust with the full details of his plan to get over the fence. There were other brains he'd picked for useful information – like how to create a false identity with a typewriter and a copy machine, or how to survive in the wilderness for an extended period of time subsisting on nuts and berries – but he never discussed the same topic with more than one person. He held great faith in the infallibility of intelligence compartmentalization. It was a lesson he had helped teach the NSA – and in the irony of all ironies, he was using that lesson to piece together a plan for his escape.

He never talked about where he would go or what he'd do once he got on the other side of the fence, and Billy never asked. Chris needed help gaining access to the prison yard alone and Billy was his best shot. He agreed to take part for nothing in return, except Chris's assurance that if he were ever caught, he'd never bring up his name.

"You don't belong in this place," Billy told Chris after he'd confided his plan for escape. "Shit, even *I* don't belong in this place. But you? No way in hell. You're not cut out for it. No offense."

Chris understood the crime he had committed was egregious. The part of him that had grown to hate himself for shaming his family and breaking his father's heart felt he deserved nothing better. The other part of him, the part driven by the instinct to survive, told him it wouldn't be long before he was murdered.

"None taken," Chris replied. "Believe it or not, in some circles of society that's actually a compliment. You ask anyone on a Palos

Verdes country club golf course if they've ever been in jail, you might as well ask them if they've ever fucked a goat."

Billy grinned, then grew serious again. He was a handsome kid, but sometimes his face hinted at what he'd look like as an old man, and it wasn't a pretty picture. "Talking about the country club elite," he said, "it's a fucking mystery to me why someone like you with no priors gets sent to D Block with the hard cases, but that Lee guy gets put up in the privileged unit."

Chris shrugged. "The animals over here would eat Daulton for breakfast. It was an act of mercy to house him with the upper crust."

Before being transferred from his high-rise prison cell in downtown San Diego, Chris learned through the grapevine that his old friend and co-defendant Andrew Daulton Lee had been sent to Lompoc to serve out his own sentence. At first, the thought of running into his former partner in crime after no contact in almost two years filled him with anxiety. When he finally did see Daulton again, it filled him with a sense of relief. Daulton was a familiar face amid a sea of terrifying strangers. Regardless of how badly things had ended between them, his presence was a comfort.

"Listen," Billy said. The sound of his voice pulled Chris back from his memory daze. "If you want my help getting out of here, you got it."

"Thank you," Chris said.

He admired Billy for his willingness to put his own liberty on the line for someone to whom he owed nothing. With his parole date nearing, Billy was risking everything by agreeing to help. Even the slightest hint of complicity with an escape attempt, successful or not, could delay his parole date indefinitely or add time to his sentence. But Billy was a man caught between compassion and a hard place. He liked Chris and he pitied his predicament. How could someone who'd never even spent a night in a drunk tank survive forty years in federal prison without being killed, or brutalized to the point where suicide would seem like sweet relief?

"Now here's the million dollar question," Chris said. "What do you think my chances really are?"

Billy ran over the details Chris had laid out and angled his chin up as if considering a tough math equation. Finally he said, "I give you one in ten odds. Slightly better the hacks don't find out about it before you even get a chance to try."

"That's not very comforting. I thought you were supposed to be helping me, not trying to scare the hell out of me."

"I call 'em like I see 'em," Billy said. "No bullshit. But just remember that a one in ten chance to make it also means you've got a nine in ten chance of painting the fence with your brains."

Chris suppressed a shudder as a chill ran up his spine, landing at the base of his neck where nine chances out of ten, everything above would soon be obliterated by gunfire.

***

Chris had discovered the way out on the day he followed the security captain and his lieutenant into the prison yard. They had entered unescorted, their position of power making it possible for them to walk safely among the prison population without fear. Few of the inmates even dared make eye contact with them. Those who did simply nodded their heads in deference and got the hell out of the way.

He hadn't been here long, but he knew that seeing the chief guard and his second in command wandering among the convicts was an infrequent occurrence. And so he followed, maintaining his distance, head low as he walked, shooting quick glances from below the brim of his cap.

He was too far behind to overhear any words they exchanged, but their purposeful gait meant this was no leisurely stroll. Unlike the warden, who was the chief enforcer and administrator of all things inside prison walls, the security captain's job held one single purpose: to ensure the impenetrability of the prison's perimeter. Whatever he and his lieutenant were doing out here, Chris reasoned, it had something to do with the prison's security. And that was a subject he had developed a profound interest in.

Ever since his transfer from San Diego MCC, he had been studying his surroundings in search of weaknesses in the armor. It was a hobby he'd adopted without conscious realization, a pastime sprung from the lush ground of fantasy that would eventually evolve into obsession.

Up to this point, he'd found nothing indicating Lompoc Federal Penitentiary was anything but an inescapable fortress. Despite his doubts, one fact remained, indisputable in its clarity: Lompoc had been built by the hand of man. And man, Chris had come to understand in his brief twenty-seven years, was an intensely flawed and often bafflingly inept creature.

The security captain and his lieutenant headed toward the sally port, crossing the concourse that separated the Industry buildings from the prison's north perimeter. The sally port was one of the prison's two main entrance and exit points, a heavily guarded passageway consisting of two large barred rolling gates on either side of a central holding zone. Only one gate would be opened at a time, ensuring that anyone entering or exiting had to pass through two strictly controlled passage points. As the captain and lieutenant approached, the inside sally port gate rolled open and they passed through.

Chris stopped and lit a cigarette, taking up post next to a trash barrel on the edge of the green lawn. For the first time in his life, he was thankful he smoked. A lone man standing stock still was conspicuous enough on its own, but suspicion vanished if he was puffing on a cigarette.

He tilted his head skyward and exhaled a smooth funnel of smoke. At the corner of his eye, the inside sally port gate crawled slowly closed. After a few seconds, the outside gate lurched open and the captain and lieutenant stepped out into the free world. They stopped and looked up.

Standing immediately opposite the two men, across a narrow service road that ran parallel with the prison's outside perimeter fence, was a forty-foot wooden gun tower. Despite its age, it was an imposing presence. It dominated the sally port, giving anyone in it a perfectly clear view of all comings and goings. It also offered a keen vantage point to all activity in the north prison yard. The men stood and stared at the tower, gesturing to it as they spoke.

Chris regarded the old wooden structure. It was basic, little more than a glorified lookout point, but it served its purpose. When he looked back again at the captain and lieutenant, he noticed they'd shifted their focus of discussion away from the tower and were now looking to the northwest.

He followed their gaze and his eyes landed on what looked like a freshly-laid construction site about seventy-five yards from the sally port. He realized he was looking at the cement foundation for a new gun tower, its base protruding from the earth like an enormous impacted tooth. He judged by the size of its foundation that once finished, the new gun tower would stand roughly three to four times the size of the existing one.

"Son of a bitch," he gasped as he imagined the view someone positioned at that height would have. The thought was simultaneously disheartening and intoxicating, a dichotomy almost impossible to process. He was about to let loose with another emotive mouthful when something moved at the edge of his vision.

He turned his head and saw a yard guard coming his way. Although there was no obvious urgency in the guard's movement, the tempo of his steps was accelerated enough to startle Chris into wondering if he'd been staring too long. The last thing he wanted to do was arouse suspicion, and one of the best ways to do that was to get caught spying on the movements of the security captain.

He snuffed the cigarette out on his heel, tossed the butt into the trash, and turned to go. As he did, he cast one final glance at the captain and lieutenant, both still embroiled in conversation, all moving jaws and gesticulation under the shadow of a wooden dinosaur only months from extinction. He started to walk, but then something made him stop in his tracks.

At first he couldn't believe what he was seeing. In his head, he suddenly flashed back to an old paperback he'd had in junior high called *The Great Big Book of Optical Illusions*. Its pages held black-and-white renderings of artfully crafted images, Escheresque optical tricks that challenged your visual perception, shapes hidden within other shapes that only became visible if you stared at them long enough. What he saw now wouldn't ever make it to mass publication, but that didn't make it any less profound: hovering directly over the heads of the captain and lieutenant, in plain view yet masked like a three-dimensional optical illusion, was the way out.

It was a flaw in the sally port's design that may have been part oversight, part outright negligence when the prison was first built. Instead of extending outward, the sally port was recessed so that the secure holding area between its inner and outer gates jutted inward, onto prison grounds. This might not have been an especially grievous architectural blunder if not for the point where the inside perimeter fence intersected with the outer pillar of the sally port.

The intersection of those two points was crucial, because it was the only spot in the prison's entire perimeter not blockaded by a double layer of chain link. In an instant, Chris saw that if he could access this point, there would be no need to traverse the lethal alley of razor wire coils on the ground between the inner and outer fences. There would be no need to climb the outer fence at all. Once atop the chain link barrier that hugged the sally port's cement pillar, it was just a ten-foot drop to freedom and a two-hundred-yard dash to the tree line behind the prison.

That nobody else noticed such a glaring security hole in the otherwise drum-tight perimeter wasn't so surprising. The reality was, in order to take advantage of the opportunity a prisoner would have to become invisible to avoid being spotted by the gun tower guards directly overhead. But if his suspicion held true, and the security captain and his lieutenant were discussing decommissioning the old tower once the new one was in operation, there was a chance he could get over without being seen.

He turned quickly and walked away, struggling to conceal the bounce in his step. By the time he reached his cell, he had developed a tenuous framework for escape.

***

Calvin Robinson bit his lip and stared at the kid. "You're serious?"

"Dead serious."

"Good choice of words. You fuck up, and you will be."

It wasn't the first time in Calvin's life that someone had confided to him their plans for getting free, but this was different. Christopher Boyce was no career criminal or escape artist, and he'd certainly never had to run from the law a day in his life. What's more, he had no connections in the outside world to help him go underground, assuming he made it over the fence without being chopped in half by rifle fire. Although he never said so, Calvin didn't think the kid stood a chance in hell.

"You know what happens to cons who get caught trying to get over the fence," Calvin said matter-of-factly.

Chris did. He had seen it for himself the day two inmates decided to make a run for the fences out by the prison track. The volley of gunfire had continued long after both men were shot down.

"I'm very aware of the risk," was all Chris said.

"So what's your plan after it happens?"

"That's where I'm hoping you can offer me some advice."

Calvin ran a hand through his curly red hair and scratched his beard, an unconscious motion Chris identified as a sign that Calvin's wheels were spinning. They were sitting on the bleachers that overlooked the prison's southwest baseball diamond. Out on the field, a group of inmates were in the sixth inning of a neck-and-neck game.

"Assuming I don't get shafted by some last minute bullshit," Calvin said, "I get paroled in two months. You get your ass over that fence and up into the mountains 'til things cool down and we'll figure out where you go next."

Deep down, Calvin didn't believe it would ever come to that. He pictured the guards extricating Chris's bullet-riddled corpse from the razor wire, hurling it into a body bag and shipping it via pine box back to Palos Verdes. Eventually, he would hear about it through an acquaintance they'd both served time with, or see it on the nightly news, maybe spot the headline in a local rag: INFAMOUS SPY

SHOT DEAD DURING ESCAPE ATTEMPT. Calvin couldn't imagine a different outcome.

Still, he didn't bother trying to talk him out of it. Like everyone else, Calvin Robinson knew that Lompoc was no place for someone like Chris, and that sooner or later the kid would meet his death at the end of some nutjob's blade, or under the boot heels of an Aryan Brotherhood recruit looking to impress. As much as he liked Chris and hated the thought of watching him risk death, Calvin knew it was probably the best of his options. And if the kid somehow adapted, learned to look out for himself in here without help? Calvin didn't want to think what forty years in federal prison would do to Chris. It would make the razor wire and rifle fire preferable by comparison.

"The big question is," Calvin said, "how the hell are you gonna do it?" He decided to humor him – dying man's last wish, so to speak.

Chris spread his hands and tilted his head slyly. "Ah, you see? I could tell you, but then I'd have to kill you." He was the only person in the entire prison population who dared joke with Calvin like that, the only one allowed to. It was a privilege bestowed upon him by a man most inmates regarded with a wary eye and made circles to avoid.

Calvin Robinson was thirty-nine years old and built like a tree trunk. Six-foot-six and not a pound under three hundred, he'd have easily made first string at gladiator or Viking school if he'd been born a thousand years sooner. It was his unfortunate luck that he wasn't. In that long ago world, a man of his physical stature would have commanded adulation and respect, especially factoring in his predilection for drink, thievery and occasional violence. Twentieth-century society, on the other hand, had little use for Calvin's kind.

Their unlikely friendship began three years earlier and 175 miles away in another horrid corner of the world called Terminal Island, the San Pedro port prison where Chris had been sent prior to sentencing. It was here the Federal Bureau of Prisons performed their ninety-day evaluation to determine if he would be sentenced under the Federal Youth Act, a set of guidelines reserved for first-time offenders that would have imposed a dramatically lighter sentence than the one he ultimately received.

Located on a strip of land between Long Beach Harbor and Los Angeles Harbor, Terminal Island Federal Correctional Institution sat just ten miles east of the Palos Verdes Peninsula where Chris had grown up. On days when he received visits from his attorneys, he could gaze into the distance from the visiting room window and see the rolling hills and seaside canyons that were once his extended backyard. If he squinted, he could make out the white stucco frames and orange terracotta rooftops of the Palos Verdes Estates neighborhood where his family still lived, tracing an imaginary route home along winding roads carved into the lush green landscape. He hadn't talked directly to his family since the arrest; the shame he felt for the notoriety he'd brought them was too overwhelming, a nerve too raw to touch. Not surprisingly, he found no comfort being within sight of his childhood home. Only regret.

Due to the seriousness of his crime and the fact that Terminal Island was a minimum security prison, he had been assigned a private cell in the maximum security wing. He soon learned why all the other prisoners called it "The Hole": the dark, dismal cell would be his home twenty-four hours a day, except for the occasional one-hour block of time set aside for exercise in the prison yard. Even his meals were brought to him in his cell.

Each man in The Hole was housed in an eight-by-five pillbox separated by solid cement walls, leaving only the barred cell door between him and complete isolation. Here, Chris's everyday existence had devolved into the slow, torturous murder of time. But the day the cell block door burst open and a shackled Calvin Robinson was led inside, that existence transformed into something resembling bearable.

The first thing he noticed was Calvin's size. The second, that he was barefoot and soaking wet. The guards led Calvin to the empty cell next to Chris, unshackled him, and slammed the iron bars shut. It was a few minutes before Chris finally worked up the nerve to press his face against the bars of his cell to talk to his new neighbor.

When he did, he was pleasantly astonished to discover the imposing giant had something few others in this place had: a sense of humor.

"I tried to catch a ride on Jackie O's yacht," Calvin said, "but it was an invitation-only affair. Goddamn high society gold-digger."

Chris chuckled, the sound striking his own ears like an alien noise. It was the first genuine laugh he'd had in what felt like a hundred years. Calvin grinned, pleased to have finally found a receptive audience. The harbor patrol guys who fished him out of the San Pedro Bay after his failed attempt to swim to freedom hadn't exactly been a barrel of laughs.

"You know Jackie's got that yacht parked right out there on the bay all the damn time, right?"

Chris said yes, even though he couldn't be sure if he was being told the truth or fed a line. It was possible. Terminal Island was a blight sitting in the midst of one of the most attractive areas of the southern coast, and a lot of seafaring traffic sailed past regularly. It wasn't much of a stretch that the ex-First Lady's own personal luxury liner might be throwing down anchor somewhere out there under the sun.

"You wanna know why I think she has them park it there?"

Chris felt like a one-man audience being wound up for the punch line. "Why?"

"I bet she finally got tired of being tycoon poon and she's looking for a genuine outlaw to tame. So I jumped the fence and took a swim. Fuck 'em if they can't take a joke."

Chris laughed. So did Calvin. It was a deep, rolling, unselfconscious guffaw. Usually, sense of humor was the first thing to go when you landed in a place like Terminal Island. To Chris, the fact that his new cell block neighbor had kept his was a sign of his tenacious will to remain human in an inhuman environment.

A fist the size of a small ham reached through the bars of the cell door and unfurled before Chris. "Calvin Robinson."

He angled his body so that he could stick his arm through the bars and watched his hand disappear into the big man's grip. "Chris Boyce."

"Okay, yeah. I've heard of you."

The smile vanished from Chris's face and he pulled his arm quickly back into his cell.

"Fast reflexes," Calvin said. Chris had withdrawn his hand like a man expecting to have his arm torn out at the socket. "But I got no beef. Between you, me and the BOP I have enough shit on my plate without giving a fuck about who did what. Besides, it's not like I haven't done my own share of dancing with Uncle Sam."

The tension in Chris's jaw relaxed. He started to speak, but all he could offer was a weak, "Okay."

Calvin rested his weight against the cold stone wall that separated them and moved his face closer to the bars of his cell door. He lowered his voice and his voice took on a deep, gravelly tenor. In prison, there was no privacy – but that didn't mean he had to make it easy for the bastards around him to eavesdrop.

"Listen, just because I don't have a problem with you doesn't mean there aren't some guys here who'd off you if they got a chance, or do things that would make you wish they would."

Chris felt his blood run cold. This wasn't the first time he'd been warned to watch his back. He'd gotten a high-level overview of the dangers he faced by everyone from his lawyers to the guards that had first escorted him to his cell – but somehow the impact never lost its effect. Not that he needed to be warned.

"If you want some advice, kid… Keep your mouth shut, your eyes open, and don't take food from anyone but the hack who brings it. It wouldn't be hard for someone in here to lace your milk and cookies with lye, know what I mean?"

"Considering the chef's questionable culinary prowess," Chris said, "would I ever even know the difference?"

Now it was Calvin's turn to be taken off guard, and he laughed.

So began a friendship that would grow over the course of the next three months and resume when both men found themselves residents of Lompoc Federal Penitentiary. For Chris, meeting Calvin Robinson was a fortuitous accident, the turn of a friendly card that would play a key role in his escape. It was also an alliance that kept him alive long enough to get his bearings and develop a plan. Other inmates didn't mess with Calvin. They didn't mess with his friends, either. But Chris couldn't rely on that forever.

Out on the baseball diamond, a batter popped a fly ball into a waiting mitt in left field. Calvin barely noticed. He sat fondling his beard unconsciously, contemplating the kid's suicidal ambition. Many men had tried to escape and failed, men who weren't as smart as Chris but who were a lot more practiced at slipping the bonds of captivity. Finally, he said, "Okay. You're right. It's probably best I don't know how you're gonna do it."

Chris nodded his head in a manner that said, "That's settled, then." He reached into his pocket and pulled out a pack of Lucky Strikes. They hadn't been his brand in the real world, but with the Bureau of Prisons footing the bill, he wasn't complaining. He lit a cigarette and turned to Calvin like a student eager for his first lesson.

When Calvin spoke, the look on his face had changed. It was almost imperceptible, but it was there. It was the look of a living man conversing with a dead man.

"First thing you do is research all you can about living off the land. I'm not talking about pitching a tent, cooking hot dogs over a fire pit, that bullshit. I mean *really* living off the land. Up north of here you've got the Santa Ynez Mountains and they're probably full of shit you can eat – mosses, berries, name it."

"I know. I used to come up around this area with my family a lot when I was a kid."

"You're *still* a kid, kid." This time it was in his voice, that sense of witnessing a tragedy in the making and not being able to do a thing about it. *He's just a kid.*

Chris shrugged. "This is the oldest I've ever been, gramps, so pardon me if I don't agree."

Calvin raised an eyebrow. "You paying attention?" Chris nodded deferentially. "Find someone in here who can tell you everything you need to know about keeping yourself fed in the wild, but don't say why. Tell 'em you're writing a book on it. That's step one. The last thing you need is to accidentally kill yourself by eating the wrong stuff."

The thought of anyone making it over the fence and evading death by gunshot only to die a few days later from poisonous berries might have struck Chris as ironic if it had been anyone else's life but his own. He nodded his head, listening intently to every word that Calvin said.

"If you can get over that fence, you head northeast and bury yourself as deep and high in those hills as you can. Hunker your ass down for a solid month, not a day less. If you can manage an extra day or two, even better. Sleep by day, move by night. A month should be more than enough time for them to call off the search in this area. They'll probably have you pegged for heading to Mexico by then, anyway. If you haven't choked to death on a pine cone after a month, make your way down and get yourself to Santa Cruz. I'll give you a number where you can find me there."

A silence fell between them. Out in the activity yard, the rest of the prison population milled about, some talking, others shouting, all trapped in an endless march as time crawled past in infinitesimal increments. Chris stared gravely ahead, looking as if he were considering some inexorable certainty.

"I wonder if you'd be willing to do me one more favor," he said, not looking at Calvin.

"What's that, kid?"

"I'm going to write a letter to my father. And I want you to hold onto it. If they find me and bring me back, I want you to destroy it. But if they kill me or I make it out of here somehow… either way, I'll never see my family again. In that case, I want you to make sure Dad gets my letter." Chris rested his elbows on his knees and his hands came together in a motion that was half prayer, half contemplation. "There're just some things I always should have said. Things I never will. Not while I'm in here."

Calvin's voice softened. He wished there was more he could do. "Alright, kid."

***

The prison cell had been transformed into a charred, hollow shell. Black soot caked its walls. Overhead, the ceiling was scarred with traces of the inferno that had engulfed everything below it. All around the eight-by-ten-foot cell lay heaping piles of ash, where blackened, vaguely discernible shapes left only hints of what had once existed within.

A lone figure sat on a rickety stool in the center of the cell, wordlessly surveying the damage. The stool was the only thing that hadn't been completely destroyed by the fire and he was thankful for that. When he'd come back to his cell and first laid eyes on the destruction, his knees had gone weak at the thought of how things might have turned out if he'd been home when the arsonist came calling. The stool was there just in time, which was a good thing – crumbling to the floor would have made him look even more vulnerable than he already was.

By now, the guards and curious onlookers that had crowded around the scorched cell were gone and he was left to himself again. An enormous metal trash can had been set outside the open cell door by one of the hacks, and a dry mop leaned against it. There were no such things as cleaning crews inside Lompoc. Here, it was DIY or eat shit.

Daulton sucked in a breath and let out a defeated sigh, kicking at a twisted hunk of melted plastic that had once been a cheap transistor radio. Its pieces scattered across the floor and lay still at the foot of what was left of the small wood-shopped desk he'd built with his own hands. A curled pile of ashes that lay on the floor was all that remained of the letters he'd received from home. They were rare, infrequent, precious, lost.

Chris caught the aroma long before he reached Daulton's cell. As he stepped before the threshold, Daulton looked up apprehensively from amid the ruins. Their eyes met. For a flickering instant, that old light of welcome recognition entered Daulton's eyes, but they quickly darkened as a throng of pinprick memories too numerous to contemplate came flooding in. In the space of a second, their multitude receded and something within him wilted imperceptibly. It was always the same each time they met. The two former friends had learned to be civil to one another in their new reality.

"Welcome," Daulton said cheerlessly, feigning indifference, failing miserably at masking the look of terror in his eyes.

"Do you know who did it?" Chris asked, stopping short of adding the words "this time" to the end of his question. It wasn't the first time Daulton's cell had been torched, but now didn't seem like the best time to remind him of that.

Daulton's eyes darted past Chris to the endless row of cells beyond. "Does it even matter? I can name a dozen of those bastards who are probably disappointed I wasn't locked in here when it happened."

Chris sighed heavily and folded his arms. It had been a while since Daulton's last dance with danger, but this time was particularly bad. It looked as if someone had sprayed the cell with lighter fluid or gasoline and let a match do the rest of the work. The last time, the fire hadn't done nearly as much damage. This time, almost everything had been incinerated.

"My chess board seems to have gone up in smoke," Daulton said from his seated position, "and my precious supply of mini-bottles is missing. Sorry if you were expecting a shot of Jim Beam with your game."

"I wasn't really in the mood for a game anyway," Chris said.

In the last six months since Chris came to Lompoc, the two had spent little time visiting one another – but in those dozen or so instances, they'd passed the hours playing chess and sipping from the bottomless supply of mini-bottles Daulton managed to snatch up through one of the prison's black market channels.

The wing of the prison Daulton lived in was reserved for low-risk prisoners, and was called "The Honor Unit" by outsiders who marveled at the noticeably better living conditions that came with residency. The cells were slightly bigger here, and each had a solid door that swung closed and offered at least some semblance of privacy. Daulton's experience as a grade school altar boy had even secured him the enviable job of chaplain's clerk, which gave him access to a small office in the prison chapel where he sometimes spent hours cloistered far from the general population. Often when he left the office, he carried the sweet smell of marijuana on his clothes. Yet despite these minor comforts, Daulton's existence had become – much like Chris's – a game of survival.

"So to what do I owe this dubious privilege?" Daulton asked. He had eventually accepted Chris's presence at Lompoc and had even begun, in his own way, to look forward to their occasional games of chess. But there was always a trace of lingering bitterness he found impossible to conceal. After everything that had happened, he decided there was no reason left to try.

Chris chewed the inside of his lip as he considered his next words. "Something we've talked about before," he finally said. The lowered volume with which he spoke told Daulton precisely what was on his mind.

"That again," Daulton said. "Well, if I ever had any motivation to trade this scene for a Costa Rican beach resort, you've caught me at the right moment."

Chris moved another step closer and leaned in. "I found a hole and I've made up my mind to move on it."

Daulton let the words sink in, studying Chris's face to ensure he was serious. He didn't need to study long. When you know someone as well as he knew Chris, honesty is as easy to spot as a bald-faced lie.

"Well unless you're planning on hiring a helicopter pilot," Daulton said dismissively, "I can't imagine what you could have come up with that would work better than what's already been tried."

Both knew that previous escape attempts from Lompoc had lacked creativity and stealth. But up to this point in their casual discussions of escape, they had only ever talked about what others had done wrong, not what could be done right. Now it occurred to Daulton that Chris had been plotting all along. Not just daydreaming, but actually planning.

Chris continued, choosing his words carefully. He didn't want to provide too many details. They had known each other almost all their lives, but the bond of trust had long since disintegrated.

"Inevitably, it'll require climbing up through the razor wire. But if we move under cover of darkness, it's possible."

Daulton looked startled. "*We?*"

"If we do this the way I see it, we've got the advantage. We have the element of surprise; they have nothing. They're simply defending a line. But they have no way of knowing if we're coming, when we're coming, or where we'll be hitting."

Daulton stood suddenly and the stool rocked backward, landing with a dull crack when it toppled. He pointed a finger sharply at Chris's chest and his voice spat venom despite its purposefully hushed tone. "If you want to get yourself killed, that's your business. But I'll be goddamned if I let you talk me into another of your glorious ideas, especially after seeing how well the last one worked out."

Chris lifted a hand and gestured around the firebombed prison cell. "You mean to tell me you want to stay here? I hate to tell you this, but this décor doesn't suit you. And it doesn't look to me as if your neighbors like you very much."

Daulton said nothing. His size made him a natural target, just as Chris's lack of street smarts made him a marked man. Each of them had witnessed things more horrible than they ever thought they would. Murders happened all the time here. In the space of a week, the inmates on either side of Chris's cell had been brutally slaughtered. He had heard it all – the screams, the death gurgles, the pitiless laughter of the assassins as they retreated from their heinous deeds. These things haunted every moment of his existence.

Chris stared into the face of his old friend across the deep, dark chasm that lay between them. Somewhere far below in that awful darkness, the evidence of all that had transpired since the beginning of their shared nightmare roiled and churned. It was a wound far too ugly to examine, yet much too painful to ignore.

"The truth is," Chris said, then stopped. He knew anything he said would be taken with a fistful of salt, but he was determined not to end the conversation until he'd said everything that needed to be said. "The truth, is I don't want to leave you behind in this terrible place."

Daulton rolled his eyes in a biting mix of outrage and amusement. But when he tried to feign a laugh, his breath caught and he swallowed audibly. His face had gone ashen, and he gazed at Chris from behind two eyes the size of eight-balls. He looked like a man contemplating the certainty of his own death.

"I'm not saying we ride off into the sunset together," Chris said. "Once we're over that fence, we go our separate ways. But at the very least we can help each other get out of this…" He searched his vocabulary for the right word to encapsulate it all. In the end, he chose the only word that would suffice: "Mess."

Daulton leaned over and righted the fallen stool. He placed it back in the center of the cell and sat down again, staring at Chris with cold contempt. "You got me in enough trouble already. I don't need you or anyone else to save me. I can handle myself."

It wasn't the words he spoke, but the expression on his face that told Chris everything he needed to know. Daulton didn't only believe escape was impossible, he had also resigned himself to his fate. There was no cowardice in the decision. If anything, there was a frail courage in his resolve that Chris almost admired. The part of him that felt he deserved to suffer for everything he'd brought upon himself coveted that tenacity. But it was a road Chris was unwilling to take. Not while there was still a feasible – albeit potentially fatal – alternative left to try.

Chris nodded his head slowly, surprised by the disappointment he felt. But amidst it all, he also felt a liberating sense of relief. The reality was, the plan he'd concocted only left room for one passenger. If Daulton had committed to go, it might have still remained viable but it would have undoubtedly ramped up the risk factor. It might even have required a totally different approach that would have forced Chris to put his own plans on hold. He had come here to offer Daulton an opportunity to come with him. Now that Daulton had made his decision, whatever consequences lay ahead, Chris would face entirely alone.

He turned to leave, but Daulton's words stopped him. "You'll get yourself killed." There was a faint, barely perceptible urgency in his voice that could almost have been taken for concern. But the darkness in his eyes belied any trace of sentiment and revealed his words to be half warning, half wish.

The two childhood friends faced one another for the last time. Chris spread his arms and let them fall to his sides. "I'm already dead," he said, and walked away.

***

The afternoon sun clawed its way across the January sky. Somewhere far below, a hole in the earth began to deepen. Chris dropped into the widening pit and began digging at the silt with an empty Folgers can.

Using a coffee can to dig in close quarters was a trick he had learned a lifetime ago planting trees with his father outside their home in Palos Verdes. Bitterly, he wondered how either of them would have reacted if they'd known that one day he would end up using the very same practice as a means of escaping from prison.

When the hole was deep enough, he checked his watch. A quarter to four. In fifteen minutes, the yard would be cleared and the prisoners would be locked back into their cells for the afternoon headcount. Through close study, Chris had learned that just the tip of a prisoner's head poking out from beneath a blanket on his cot qualified as accounted for in the eyes of the apathetic prison staff. It was an observation that had led him to sign up for art class, one of a handful of activities offered to inmates as a way to channel their aggressive tendencies. It was there he studied methods of creating a replica bust of his own head using wet strips of newspaper and flour, an idea he'd latched onto when the entertainment department arranged a special videotape showing of *Escape from Alcatraz*.

He lifted his head above the rim of the hole and looked around. Forty feet away, the guard had turned his back and was talking to one of the sally port sentries. Out in the activity yard, prisoners chased balls, lifted weights, sat along steel benches and conferred in huddles of two and three.

Chris handed one final can of silt to Billy, then assumed the position he'd practiced for hours in his cell. It was a curious fusion of self-taught yoga poses and what fitting into the miniscule hole would require: ass to earth, back to wall, knees to chest, and head down. He double-checked that the pruning shears and ladder were in the hole with him, then looked up and gave Billy a nod goodbye.

Instead of returning the nod, Billy slid the grate into place over Chris's head and whispered, "Good luck." Then he gathered up the rest of the digging tools, tossed them into the burlap sack atop the mound of silt in the wheelbarrow, and wheeled away. They never saw each other again.

Minutes later, the yard emptied. After another forty-five minutes, the "all clear" whistle signaled the end of the four o'clock headcount.

The relief that washed over Chris at its sound was overwhelming. Instinctively, the muscles in his arms and legs, which he now realized had been taut with tension the whole time, relaxed. His heartbeat slowed and for the first time in nearly an hour, he sucked in a deep breath and let it out slowly. Step one, accomplished. He tried not to think about the next step – getting over the razor wire fence.

As the sun sank into the western horizon and the light seeping in through the steel grate vents dimmed, he saw the image of his father before him. What awful shame had he brought him? And to his mother, and his brothers and sisters? What impossible chain of events had led him to this place, the ex-altar boy, ex-son and brother, now poised on the precipice of certain death or life as a fugitive?

Whether he succeeded or failed, he knew he'd crossed a threshold over which he would never return. By dawn, he would either be a dead man or a free man – but either option was preferable to a life of constant terror.

Chris closed his eyes and the image of his father faded into darkness.

DIAL 'P' FOR PANIC (THE BODY, PART 2)

Cait
(August 2005)

The call came in to the office at around two o'clock in the afternoon. It was Chris. His voice, usually cool and reserved, was pitched up a notch and his words spilled out in a mix of urgency and excitement: "They found a body on our property!"

Although I wanted desperately to believe this was some sort of horrible joke, I could tell right away that it wasn't. He sounded like he was in full-blown panic mode. Or close to it, anyway.

Before I had a chance to digest what he'd just said – shouted, actually – he raced ahead in what sounded like one of those irritating vocal impressions of machine gun fire you sometimes hear kids do. The only difference was for his rendition, he threw in a few words for context.

"The place is swarming with cops! The cops are all over the place and there are police cars!"

I damn near dropped the coffee mug I was holding and might have sent it crashing to the floor if my office desk hadn't intercepted its descent. I ignored the splash that licked up over the lip of the mug and doused my hand in black fire. I lowered myself down onto my desk chair and pressed the phone even closer to my ear. Right now, a ruptured eardrum was my last concern.

What the hell has he gotten himself into?

"Calm down and tell me what's going on," I said. I closed my eyes and stared down the backs of my eyelids into that old familiar tunnel, focusing intently. I was already slipping into damage-control mode. That's not a brag. It's how I'm built.

He took a breath. I was grateful for that. The last thing we needed was for him to land himself in the hospital for maxing out too suddenly on the freakout scale. The second to last thing we needed were cops swarming the house. Not that we had anything to hide – I just don't like cops. Never have, never will. And after everything Chris had been through, I felt he'd earned that right, too.

This time when he continued, his volume knob had come down a few notches and his delivery was a bit more composed. But not much. That tangible air of near-panic wasn't yet far enough away for my taste. He said, "The people building the fence next door went to dig a post hole, and they hit something."

I remembered the discussion we'd had the week before about our neighbors, Gary and Jeri (yes, really), and their plans to erect a fence on the border of our respective properties. I hadn't minded the decision, if for no other reason than a fence would serve to keep their two enormous geese from wandering into our backyard and hurling their obscene honks in the direction of our bedroom window at ungodly hours of the morning.

He continued. "When they looked to see what they hit, they found a body wrapped in plastic and they got up and ran out into the street. Then they called the sheriff."

The mental image of an armada of cop cars screeching to a halt on the frontage road outside our home was bad enough. The idea of a body being dug up on our land was even worse. Chris was, after all, a two-striker in a three-strikes state. In the first six months following his release from federal prison, spitting on the sidewalk or failing to find work would have been enough to get him yanked back into custody from the dubious comforts of the San Francisco halfway house he'd dubbed "Chateau of the Damned." Of course by now, his parole restrictions were more lax and that was no longer the case – he could spit away with impunity and all he'd face would be a reprimand and a fine. Yet I had a sneaking suspicion that being dragged in for questioning over the discovery of a dead body wouldn't look so hot on his parole officer's report.

I knew I was getting ahead of myself. These days, with forensics and DNA evidence, it's not as easy as it was in the old days to lock up an innocent person for a crime they didn't commit. But then most innocent people aren't named Christopher Boyce, nor do they share his history – and the thought of him home alone, surrounded by police, most of them very likely knowing exactly who he was and what he'd done thirty years ago, made me nervous. Strike that. It terrified me.

My train of thought had wandered so far off the rails that I almost didn't register when he continued, relaying the story about the sheriff department's sudden arrival and the ensuing accusation-laced inquiries. Then he told me about Theo and the bone, and I almost laughed at the absurdity until he said, "It could be a leg bone! Who knows?"

The gravity of what he said hit me like a gut-punch. "Chris," I said, then asked the obvious question: "Is it human?"

"They won't say and I can't tell. They're being very secretive. They're digging it up and taking it with them."

All the better, I figured. The last thing I wanted to do was spend the night within sniffing distance of an unearthed corpse surrounded by crime scene tape. I knew the tape would probably still be there when I got home from work, but it was something of a comfort to know the body – whoever's body it was – wouldn't be.

"I have to go," he said suddenly. "I'll call you later when I know more." And he was gone. He's never been one for graceful goodbyes.

I held the phone to my ear long enough to get a dial tone. When I set the receiver down, I looked up to see the entire office around me had come to a standstill. They were all staring. Apparently, Chris isn't the only one who speaks too loudly when he gets excited.

"What's this talk about a body?" It was Edwin, the attorney who owned the law office and the guy who signed my paychecks twice a month, but at the moment I was too stupefied to worry how this fiasco might influence his decision to keep me in his employ.

I relayed the story. Edwin shook his head incredulously and his partner, Dean, uttered a nervous chuckle. Maxine, the front desk receptionist, noticed the small puddle of coffee on my desk and ducked into the kitchenette, returning with a paper towel in hand.

As she handed it to me, she said, "You know, this could have nothing to do with it, but I remember hearing that back in the eighties a young wife disappeared in that very same area."

I stopped daubing at the coffee spill and stared up at her.

"She was married to a Marine," Maxine continued. "They think he killed her, but they could never find her body."

The thought that Chris and I had quite possibly been living above the corpse of a murder victim sent a cold chill racing down my spine.

"There's so much open land out there," she said. "He could have buried her anywhere. What if that's her?"

LETTER HOME

Chris
(February 1980)

Charlie Boyce closed the door to his study and sank into the leather chair behind his desk. In one hand he held a drink. In the other, an unopened envelope.

He set the whiskey tumbler down beside a clock whose hands announced it was only 2:05 p.m. He stared at the clock for a long moment, as though struggling to determine if the situation at hand warranted having a drink three hours earlier than the rest of the responsible denizens of Palos Verdes.

"I think you're okay on this one, Charlie." It was the voice of George Chelius, his old friend and lawyer, arriving like the answer to his unasked question.

George took a seat opposite Charlie and squinted through the semi-permanent blue haze of cigar smoke hanging in the air, eyeing the envelope he'd hand-delivered just moments earlier. It had arrived at his office in today's mail, a small envelope sealed inside a larger "dummy" envelope bearing a fake name and a nonexistent return address. The words "To Charles Boyce" were the only thing written on the outside of the smaller envelope, but the handwriting was unmistakable. Even George had instantly recognized Chris's distinctive scrawl.

Charlie looked at the paper package between his fingers, sighed, took a drink. Before he set the glass back down, he took another. He reached into his desk, pulled out a letter opener, and drew it across the envelope's top edge. He removed the folded piece of paper from within like an archaeologist handling an ancient manuscript. His hands trembled. It had been a full two weeks since his firstborn child had disappeared over the fence of Lompoc Federal Penitentiary, and the sleepless nights had begun to take their toll.

Charlie unfolded the letter and began to read.

Dear Dad,

Hello from long lost me. It seems strange to start this letter out with the old cliché "If you're reading this letter I'm either dead or escaped," but I keep racking my brain and they're the only words that seem to fit. No wonder people use them all the time. So anyway, here it goes.

If you're reading this letter, it probably means I'm either dead or have successfully found my way to freedom. Regardless of whichever fate I've met, please know that none of this is your fault.

That's the one thing I regret the most, out of everything that's happened. Not even my crime (as awful as that must sound to you, I know), not the loss of my freedom, and not being able to ever come home again. What I truly regret is that somehow and for some reason you've found a way to blame yourself for this whole mess. If there was anything I could do to take that away, I would – even if it meant losing my life... which I may or may not have already done.

If I have, please know that I acted willingly and that you, Mom, and the whole family were in my thoughts. I know I've made a horrible mistake and that I deserve to be punished for my stupidity. I never thought for a moment that I'd get off scot free and I'd have been just as shocked as anyone if I had. But Dad, I never dreamed that prison could be as horrible as this.

If I give in to my lot and stay, I'll die. Either by someone else's hand or over the natural course of time. With every day, I can feel the humanity bleeding slowly from me. I'm terrified night and day. With my own eyes, I've witnessed levels of depravity and violence so shocking that all of my preconceived notions of "rehabilitation" for criminal offenders have been destroyed forever. There is no rehabilitation in these places, just as there is no justice. There is only death and darkness, cruel and merciless. And if I don't escape it soon, it'll eventually consume me.

Better to die fighting for my freedom than to let all sense of humanity be sapped from me. Better to succeed and have to say goodbye to everything and everyone I've ever known than to bring those things with me into a hell on earth. Those memories are far too precious for a place like this. They don't belong here, just as surely as I don't. And so I've decided to leave. Whether I live or I die, Dad, I just can't stay here any longer.

And now I can't believe that I've written all these words and they're still not what I wanted to say. I guess the simplest things are the hardest to voice, even on paper, and if I had known that life would turn out this way I would have told you that I loved you a lot more often than I did. But I guess some emotions are just so strong that they're impossible to express in language.

Please tell Mom I love her, and all my brothers and sisters. I love you all and saying goodbye is the hardest thing I've ever had to do.

Chris

"Charlie?"

It was George, calling to him from a thousand miles away. Charlie felt a hand on his shoulder and realized he'd been staring into the spaces between the letters of his son's handwritten name. His vision blurred over with tears, but his face remained dry.

"What does it say? It's from Chris, right?"

Without a word, he handed the letter to George and took another drink, his point of focus now fixed on some distant, unseeable place.

When he was done reading the letter, George said, "He gives no indication where he is, which is a good thing. Even the postmark here – Santa Cruz – is probably just a red herring. He's too smart for that."

George paused and looked at his old friend. He sighed deeply, aware that no matter how he tried he'd never be able to fully understand that pain. A tiny, guilty part of him was thankful for that.

"Charlie, you know we're required by law to turn this over to the FBI."

Charlie leaned forward and took the letter from George's hand. Carefully, he stuffed it back into the envelope and reached across his desk to the large ashtray that sat perched at its edge. He drew it in front of him and retrieved the engraved Zippo lighter from the cigar box that he always kept in the top drawer of his desk.

He flicked the wheel of the lighter and it burst to life. Yellow flames touched the bottom of the envelope and the paper began to blacken and curl in his grip. When he could no longer hold it, he set the burning envelope down into the ashtray and watched it burn.

George said nothing. He knew he would have had to fight Charlie to stop him, and he didn't particularly feel like doing that. Besides, Charlie Boyce had been his boss for years at McDonnell Douglas. Habits among the old guard died hard.

Once the flames had died and the letter was reduced to ash, Charlie lifted a fresh cigar to his lips and lit it. For the first time, his eyes met George's troubled gaze.

"Let us speak of this no more," Charlie said. He finished the rest of his drink in a single swallow.

THE FLIGHT OF THE FALCON

Chris
(January 1980 – July 1981)

Wings spread out on the wintry gust; eyes survey the endless expanse of foliage below. The falcon tenses, flexing one wing and relaxing the other, and the ripple of that subtle motion alters its direction, turning its body into the eastward wind. Winters in the Santa Ynez Mountains are cold in January, and the air two thousand feet above the earth even colder, but the falcon bears the frigid chill with strength and determination.

It is a male peregrine in adult plumage, just beginning its northward migration back to the tundra. It tarries nowhere long, a wanderer driven by the instinctual pull to return to its nesting ledge in the high Arctic thousands of miles north.

Sensing movement far below, the falcon plunges. Immediately, the winter brown forest explodes in size and tapestries of gold and rust rush upward. Within seconds, the hunter is skimming over the canopy of trees, its breast raking over the occasional warm patches radiating up from the two-legged creatures who inch their way through the dense undergrowth.

They arrived at the break of dawn, an ear-splitting screech more powerful than a thousand eagles heralding their rushed exit from the large structure of straight lines and angles that has existed like a blight at the periphery of these woods and mountains for generations. Like a solid wave, the men push their way deeper into the brush, led by dogs on leashes that sniff the ground as if in search of something that should not be here.

In the distance, an unnatural, repetitious thumping draws near – the sound of the men's steel bird of prey cutting a gradual, deliberate path through the sky. Its sound radiates in all directions and is absorbed by the wooded hills, until soon it seems the entire forest is pulsing in unison with its thunderous breath.

The falcon pumps its wings in rapid bursts and flies north, putting distance between itself and the intruders. When the steel bird's rhythmic growl has finally receded to a dull hum, the falcon resumes its meticulous search for prey. Driven by pangs of hunger, it circles high above a meadow alive with twittering horned larks.

They do not hold its attention long. From out of the woodline, twisting and turning out of the scrub oaks, a western tanager flies into view, a brilliant flash of yellow, black and orange. The falcon rockets downward in a stoop, snatching the tanager out of the air in a dazzle of yellow feathers. It alights on a boulder with its prey held firmly in its beak and severs the tanager's spinal column.

Wary of foxes, the falcon struggles back up in a flurry of wing beats and comes to rest on a branch, clutching its kill in one foot. Slowly, it begins to pluck the plumage from the dead bird's breast. Exquisite yellow feathers dance in the breeze and cascade to the ground.

Now, from the corner of its eye, the falcon sees movement again. It is a man, pushing his way through the dense undergrowth, moving with the speed and urgency of survival. He is alone, clothed in a combination of mud and threads that cling to his slender frame as if placed there by the elements. He breathes heavily as he moves, clutching at wild shrubs with bare and bloodied hands as he carves a narrow passage through the tangle of oak forest.

The man casts a glance over his shoulder once, as if to ensure the other human predators are not close behind, then halts in his tracks as his eyes fall on the falcon. For a moment their eyes meet, two creatures more alike than not regarding each other in the midst of the vast chaparral.

"Falcon," the man calls out, "thank you for taking the tanager today. I will remember that always."

The man turns away and resumes his hurried journey. The falcon watches him disappear into the scrub oak.

When the falcon can no longer hear the man's footsteps on the tangled ground, it springs upward and pumps its wings into the sky. Below it, the predatory apes are abandoning their hunt, withdrawing to their fortress as dusk settles in. With their retreat, their great hovering steel bird of prey also disappears and the world falls silent again. Deep in the embrace of the woods, cradled by the earth, the fugitive takes shelter in the brambles and sleeps.

***

The dogs are drawing near. Up until a moment ago, his first forty-eight hours on the other side of the prison fence have been relatively uneventful. The search party has never actually come dangerously close, and so far the chopper's only done so once – but the deafening thud of its rotors gave plenty of advance warning, more than enough time to camouflage himself against the forest floor until it passed by.

Tonight is different. The baying of the hounds, at first almost too faint to be heard, is moving closer. Crossing through an acre-wide clearing on the north forty of a cattle ranch some thirty miles northeast of Lompoc, an unsettling thought occurs to him.

They've picked up my trail.

The very implication of the words, spoken as an internal whisper, are a sobering slap to the face. His feet, which had begun to move slowly with the weight of continuous motion, are startled suddenly to life. It's been hours since he last rested, and even that had only lasted long enough for him to swallow one of the dozen packets of vitamins he brought with him. But the closer the howling of the dogs comes, the faster he moves – at first at a brisk walk, then a jog, until he is running full speed through the dark.

Now they are so near that he thinks he can actually count the number of dogs on his trail – maybe half a dozen, closing the distance fast. Their speed and their apparent freedom of movement tells him one thing: the dogs are not on leashes. Which also means they're very likely not bloodhounds. But if not that, then what? A roaming pack? He reasons this could be the case, but decides otherwise the moment he looks behind him to see headlights bounding over the uneven terrain a quarter mile away.

At the very same moment, a patch of clouds over the face of the moon moves away and the light reveals a series of low, dark, moving silhouettes. It is the dogs, now plainly visible in the revealed landscape, racing for him at full speed. They are a mix and match pack of bluetick and redbone hounds – scent dogs – but in the dark, the eyes and ears play tricks. To the running man, they look like a bloodthirsty pack of wolves.

Is this how it ends? In all of his planning and preparation, and through all the sleepless nights he's contemplated everything that could go wrong, he has never once imagined his end could come like this. Gunfire was one thing. Recapture was another. Being attacked and torn limb from limb by animals, on the other hand, had been a fate too terrible to even entertain.

The first dog to reach him moves in close and brushes its nose forcefully against his calf before darting away again. The man nearly falls, but regains his balance and continues to run. The feel of the dog's hot breath makes his legs move even faster, but he's no match for the speed of the pack. Another dog moves in from behind and boldly launches itself into the space between his feet with a vicious snarl. The two of them – man and dog – come down in a tangled blur of flesh and fur.

He scrambles to his feet and cries out in anticipation of attack. The rest of the dogs close in, snouts contorted in mournful howls, feet dancing, tails shaking madly. He balls his hands into tight fists and readies himself to swing, then stops when he realizes the dogs are no longer advancing. Instead of attacking, they form a circle around him, their piercing howls alerting all within earshot of the stranger in their midst.

"Go home!" he shouts at them. "Get the fuck out of here!" But he knows even before he gets the words out they'll do no good. Unwavering, the dogs continue circling excitedly in their victory dance, some barking, others howling. Drawn by their cries, the headlights move closer.

He darts desperately in the opposite direction and the dogs follow. He stops again and spins a full 360 degrees, searching the darkness for any sign of cover. In the moonlight, his eyes land upon a discoloration in the treeless earth, a black band extending from left to right like a false horizon. Believing it's the crest of a ridge, he shoves his way past the circle of still-baying hounds and races for it, the dogs following at his heels.

The vehicle is now so close that he can hear the sound of its engine and feel the vibration of its approach under his shoes. With one final burst of speed, he aims his body for the ridge like a runner after home plate, no longer measuring his steps but hoping his feet won't stumble across some unseen mound or rabbit hole, each capable of breaking an ankle. By the time he reaches the tip of the ridge he's almost moving too fast to stop himself from flying over the edge.

Somehow he brakes just in time, arms pinwheeling for balance, and looks down the steep grade. The near vertical descent that extends beyond the field of visibility lies before him like an eternal black hole, and yet he drops immediately and begins sliding down the incline, flat on his back, arms spread, legs splayed, body tensed for impact through a minefield of jagged rock and crumbling earth.

He reaches the bottom in a heap on his knees, concealed in darkness. Two hundred feet above and behind, headlights stare out into the night. The cacophony of dog voices continues, but now he can hear another sound up there. Human voices. Two, maybe three.

The fugitive climbs to his feet and takes his bearings. The back of his pants and sweatshirt are shredded and the skin beneath them torn, but all of that is forgotten when he sees where he is: only a stone's throw from the bank of a river no less than fifty feet wide.

It's the Santa Ynez, he thinks, and his spirit lifts at the irony that the dogs have inadvertently ushered him in the right direction. The river is illuminated by moonlight and he knows he'll have to emerge from the shadows to cross it, but he's confident even if the dogs do decide to follow him down – and he doesn't think they will – he can lose them easily by wading to the other side. Without another thought or hesitation, he runs to the river and pitches himself waist-deep into its icy water.

The sensation of shock lasts only long enough to cause him to gasp once, and then the report of rifle fire from the top of the ridge pushes all else from his consciousness. Suddenly the water doesn't seem too cold, the night too dark to navigate, or the weariness of his legs too overwhelming to push on across the slow, swirling waters of the river. Moving cautiously to prevent the muddy bottom from sucking his shoes from his feet, he sloshes through the freezing, chest-high water. In less than a minute he's at the other side and dashing for the cover of the tree line.

Up at the top of the ridge, the rancher engages the safety on his rifle and turns his attention back to the dogs. There will be rewards aplenty for their good deed, and this he promises with encouraging words and pats. Perched on the branch of an ancient oak atop a rocky crag overlooking the valley of the Santa Ynez River, the tundra falcon sleeps with its head tucked under its wing. By the time the dogs have finally shut up, Christopher Boyce has long disappeared.

***

The next time they meet, it is the man who sees the falcon first. Days have come and gone, perhaps a dozen, and in that time the presence of the intruders has gradually diminished. In the beginning, they sent their steel hawk and their dogs to rake through every crevice and depression of the vast expanse. But as each successive search returned nothing, their numbers decreased until finally the oak forest lay still once more.

From under a canopy of trees where he sits camouflaged by the brush, the man's voice rises suddenly. "Well, hello there!"

At the sound of the man's voice, the falcon tenses itself for flight. But when it sees the familiar, nonthreatening human stepping into the clearing, it merely bobs its head in curiosity.

"If I'm not mistaken," the man calls up, "we've met before."

This time, there is something markedly different about the man's demeanor. Even his voice has grown lighter. There's almost a sense of music about its sound, and the movement of his body as he extends his arms upward is strangely relaxed for one so far removed from his natural habitat.

"I recognize you," the man says, bringing his arms down by his sides and staring up from the foot of the tree that separates the winged from the earthbound. "And, don't take this wrong, but I do wish you were mine. In another world not far from here, your cousins and I hunted birds together. Hard to imagine that world now."

The falcon is a stocky creature with long, pointed wings and a short tail. It is the embodiment of speed and power – the perfect aerial hunter. Its back is gray-blue and the sides of its face sport a dark, mustache-like bar that serves to deflect the sun's glare from its telescopic eyes.

The bird's face is expressionless; it is not imbued with the same musculature that is the intrinsic trait of human beings. And yet the man believes that he can read a sense of familiarity in the falcon's eyes, which seem to stare down in an expression of constant surprise.

"Something tells me," the man says, this time in a voice far more subdued and reflective, "that you just might recognize me, too. Of course these days, I talk to the wind. I'm probably not the best judge of these things."

The man laughs. The bird stares. Many thoughts pass between them.

"Don't worry. I'm not here to muscle in on your action. Just passing through."

He reaches into the front pocket of his mud caked pants and pulls out a small handful of shelled and peeled acorns, popping one of the kernels into his mouth. "Besides, I'm on a strict diet of nuts and moss. I've given up fowl for the time being and the deer are too damn fast. Even the possums in this neighborhood don't have to worry about me."

The man has grown gaunt since the falcon saw him last. It is an observation that only a seasoned hunter can make, one that spends the majority of its days sizing up prey for the kill. And even though man is not on the falcon's menu of potential sustenance, it perceives all through the same prism.

It sees the man's clothes now hang loosely about his frame, and despite his otherwise vibrant demeanor, the tendons of his neck stand rigid when he speaks and his cheek bones have grown pronounced. The flesh of his face, once smooth, is framed with a growth of beard. All about him is the sense of a danger not yet passed. And yet despite his bedraggled appearance, his voice remains unmistakably alive.

"I'll make you a deal. Fly me outta here and I'll feed you fresh bluebirds every day for the rest of your life. All-you-can-eat buffet. How's that grab you?"

He watches the falcon closely, almost as if anticipating a reply, but it only stares back in observation. A sigh breaks from the man's lips. His eyes, bloodshot from lack of sleep – even after twelve days, he still hasn't grown accustomed to the floor of the earth as his bed – narrow slightly. He cocks his head to one side and holds it there, peering up through narrow slits at the ring of diffused light that obscures everything but the falcon itself.

He is dreaming again, as he so frequently does in his new environment, rising quickly into the air as if the faster he moves, the easier it will be to untether himself from this point in time and space. His mind is tumbling backward, willing the invisible calendar in the sky to do the same.

It wasn't long ago that he was here, he thinks. Maybe not this very spot, but certainly these woods. Six, maybe seven years ago? Not knowing the next time he returned, it would be like this. A fugitive. The hunted.

Certainly the chain of events during that not-so-distant past – the theft of the documents, the rapidly disintegrating relationship with

Daulton, the anger, the betrayal, the confusion – had caused him to consider the very likely possibility of finding himself in grave trouble one day. But in his mind, that trouble had always had a different face.

Perhaps it had only been a vague concept of what might come to pass, minus the terrifying detail that real life had a way of bringing into crisp focus. In that imagined or presupposed reality, his worst-case future had always been one shade paler than all of this, one degree less horrifying, one decibel less deafening. That dreamed-of future had never included this place, or the concrete hell from which he'd fled.

Back there, it was complete captivity. Not only of the body, but of the mind and soul. Even your dreams were haunted by the presence of the bars that kept you confined. Out here in the wild, on the flipside of that great cosmic coin, absolute freedom. But out here also existed another horrifying freedom: the freedom to die. Of starvation, of exposure, of illness, of miserable loneliness.

Up above, the falcon stirs. Down below, the earth spins. Trapped between the two, Christopher Boyce sways dreamily and prays to wake from the nightmare.

***

The tundra peregrine is a nomadic creature. It travels south in fall from the high Arctic, flying as far as Central America before turning back again. Its environments are as diverse as the northern tundra, coastal marshes, and even the skyscrapers of modern cities. It is remarkably intelligent, with an intensely curious nature that, once piqued, may lead it to cross continents before it has been fully satisfied.

When Christopher Boyce walks out of the Santa Ynez Mountains and makes his way north, the falcon in the chaparral follows, migrating northward on its instinctual route. Never so near as to be considered a traveling companion, it exists at the fringes of perception, making its presence known through a faintly heard cry, or the sight of an indistinct shape flying far above the earth.

Sometimes, it rides on spirals of wind and rings its way into the clouds. Other times, it plummets earthward in a stoop to strike its passerine prey, reaching speeds that boggle the mind and terrify songbirds. Ruthless, it lights upon rocks and telephone poles and launches slashing attacks on the unwary, or sits high atop mankind's concrete creations and gazes down on the works of humans. And like the earthbound fugitive, it sleeps the fitful, restless sleep of the hunted.

***

In an unpaved sand and stone pullout of Highway 1 just north of Morro Bay, not far from the roaring sea, a Volkswagen Bus slows to a stop. Its windshield is covered in a layer of salty film and its body spotted with flecks of mud. At first glance, there is nothing to indicate that any living thing dwells within – and then the van's passenger door opens and a woman steps out, her long silver hair flying up around her head in the brisk coastal wind.

She gestures to the man standing by the side of the road with his thumb extended and a dilapidated bedroll at his feet. The colors of the clothes he wears – a ragged pair of denim jeans, a loose-fitting hooded sweatshirt, a pair of mud-crusted sneakers – seem almost to blend in with his surroundings. Together with the month-long beard that hangs from his face, he is little more than a ghost in the background, a faded image still clinging to existence. It is his eyes, piercing blue in their intensity, that make it impossible for him not to be seen.

The hitchhiker and the silver lady exchange words, their voices muffled by the sound of the surf that even at this distance threatens to drown out all else. The driver of the van, a balding man with a pure white ponytail almost to the middle of his back, leans across the passenger seat and with a motion of his hand makes the invitation official. The hitchhiker picks up his bedroll and approaches, climbing into the back seat.

The van resumes its northerly route, following the road in a zigzag pattern that mimics the Pacific Coast's imperfect profile.

They stop frequently along the way, all three passengers breathing in the astonishing beauty – the mists that play above the gently swaying horizon of water, the sudden revelation of some foam-spattered shore against a rocky bluff – and each time they stop, they are convinced it must surely get no better than this. Then another five miles up the highway, it does.

They travel together for most of the day, speaking little. When they reach the Monterey Peninsula 120 miles north, they part ways. After warm handshakes and well wishes, the hitchhiker resumes his journey up the coast and the van and its passengers head inland, bound for a place called Morgan Hill. Jack Kerouac wrote of it, they tell him, as if to offer some justification for not delivering him to his destination, but within an hour he's picked up again, this time by a bleary-eyed truck driver thirsty for conversation.

The eighteen-wheeler snakes its way up the Cabrillo Highway. On a seamy strip of town within walking distance of downtown Santa Cruz, the hitchhiker disembarks; the truck sputters and spits, then keeps on rolling on. In the deepening dusk, the peregrine falcon takes roost atop a power line as the hitchhiker finds shelter below an overpass.

Hours later, in a parking lot in the early light of day, the hitchhiker climbs into the front seat of an awaiting car. Seated behind the wheel, an enormous man with a flame-red beard throws his head back in laughter and grabs the hitchhiker by the scruff of the neck in a playful embrace.

"How the hell are you, kid?"

"I made it, Calvin."

The car pulls away.

***

Many times during his eighteen months of freedom among the people of Bonners Ferry, Idaho, Christopher Boyce spotted falcons that reminded him of the magnificent creature he'd first seen in the thick of the Santa Ynez Mountains. And although the sight of them delighted him, seeing them also destroyed any illusion that he had successfully eluded his pursuers. They were still searching, still trying to pick up his scent, still determined to return him to the bonds of captivity.

On the surface, the life he led during that fleeting period of time gave little indication of where he'd come from, or where he would eventually find himself. Everywhere he went, he walked like a free man and spoke like a free man. He moved about in public with a relaxed, peaceable liberty, the kind rarely afforded to fugitives of the law. But on the inside, the fissures were beginning to form.

When he lay on his pillow at night with his thoughts, it wasn't only the past he felt catching up with him, but also that great blank slate where the future had always lived. He calmed this unease by drinking too much. Then when the booze supply was tapped, he'd take extended hikes into the wilderness, sometimes staying gone for months, long enough for those who knew him by his alias to wonder if he'd ever return. The border into Canada could be easily crossed up here, and anyone seeing Christopher Boyce passing through on his way past the forty-ninth parallel north with his backpack and his hiking gear would assume he was only another local.

But on these treks, the indecision that had plagued him since his successful leap over the razor wire fence a thousand miles south always prevailed. He never lingered long in that place he referred to as "the Canada side of the world." Invariably, he would always return, as if reeled in by some imperceptible tether. In all of the times he crossed over that unmanned, unmarked border, he never once ventured any further than the woods themselves, even though it would have been effortless to do so. Each time he returned to Bonners Ferry, it was always with the thought, *Next time I'll go further.*

Had he known that even now, the hunters were drawing near – tightening the circle – he may not have hesitated but continued north without looking back, may never have given in to the adrenalin rush of walking into crowded banks with a gun in hand, emerging minutes later with thousands of dollars at a time.

Instead, he stayed – rooted, taken hold by a growing idea. One so brazen that if it worked, it would make everything that had happened in the last eighteen months pale in significance.

***

A battered pickup makes its way down a long dirt road in the northern woods of Bonners Ferry. It stops in front of a large, three-story log cabin that probably never looked new, not even the day it was built. A large man with a red beard steps out of the truck as a smaller man emerges from the cabin. They shake hands in the driveway.

"News from the world has it that the fugitive spy Christopher Boyce is definitely in South America," the big man says, "and the feds and the U.S. Marshals are closing in fast on his trail."

They laugh. "I thought it was Australia," the smaller man says.

"Who the hell knows?" Calvin Robinson reaches into his back pocket and pulls out a wad of folded papers, hands them to Christopher Boyce, and says, "Here's that information you wanted. Had to go clear out to Port Angeles to pick 'em up."

"Thanks." Chris unfolds the brochures and thumbs through them, scanning them methodically, as if seeking something specific. After going through each a second time, he settles on one with a decisive tap of his forefinger. The bold lettering at the top of its glossy front page reads PORT ANGELES AVIATION SCHOOL. "This is what I'm looking for. Right here."

"Is now a good time to ask why you've suddenly got a bug up your ass about learning to fly a plane? It ain't like you can apply for a job with United."

"Not a plane. A helicopter. But I figure you have to learn to master one before you can move on to the next." He shrugs. "I have a book on aviation, but what I really need is hands-on experience."

Calvin looks confused. "I don't get it." He gestures in the general direction of the Canadian border, which lies amid the thick greenery and rising summer forest growth just a few miles away. "If you want to get across the border, you can walk it. Forget flying. And if that doesn't get you far away enough, all you have to do is get down to Mexico and hop a flight to Havana. They can get you to the Motherland faster than you can spell 'defector'."

Chris gives him an incredulous look and lifts his hands. "Why does everybody think I'm so hell-bent on going to Russia?"

"Who's *everybody*? And you better not be lumping me in with The Man."

Chris winces, even though he can hear the humor laced in the accusation. In the shared dialect of all convicts, both ex- and escaped, such a comparison is tantamount to an unspeakable slur. "Of course not. Anyway, I had the opportunity to do that once and I turned it down. Would you want to live there?"

"Fuck that."

"That was pretty much my answer, verbatim."

"So why do you want to learn how to fly a chopper? Aren't you satisfied with what you're pulling down at the banks? Don't tell me you're planning to drop in over Fort Knox."

"Not exactly. But you're warm."

A midsummer breeze rustles the leaves of the trees that encircle the cabin. Overhead, hidden in the foliage of a giant cottonwood, a resting falcon blinks unseen. Down below, the two men stare at each other – one with curiosity, the other with knowing.

Chris drops his voice to a near whisper and speaks the name that's been on his mind for months. "Daulton Lee."

The words sound funny on his tongue, an alien utterance in his new life, but a notion that's been kicking around for the better part of a year kindles his senses. A light behind his eyes shimmers.

"Kid," Calvin says, "you're fucking crazy." There is no mistaking the expression on his face; he means every word, and he repeats himself to make sure he's understood perfectly. "Absolutely, 110 percent off your goddamn rocker."

"Could be," comes the nod and reply, then after reconsidering: "I probably am. But you know I only gave him one chance to get out with me. And I didn't give him enough time to think it over. Daulton's never been what you call impulsive. Everything's calculated."

Calvin looked incredulous. "And you think that if you told him about your little plan to drop a helicopter in there like Charles Fucking Bronson that he'd go along?"

"Maybe."

"He might also cut a deal for a lighter sentence and use it to lasso your ass. Ever think about that?"

"Of course," Chris admits. "It was one of the first thoughts to enter my head. And if I end up not going through with it, that'll probably be the deciding factor. Or not being able to learn how to fly a helicopter in the first place. In that case it doesn't matter anyway."

Calvin folds his arms and leans his considerable weight against the bed of the pickup. The body dips and the suspension squeals. "Why the hell would you want to put yourself in that position anyway? You got out. You're here. You don't owe that guy anything."

"We grew up together. Daulton's not any more innocent than I am, but that doesn't change the fact he's there because of something I started. And things got bad for him after I jumped that fence. They transferred him back east. Made it pretty much impossible for his family to visit. That only lasted about a year, but he probably didn't appreciate the isolation. He's back at Lompoc now. It shouldn't be too hard to get him a message."

"Sounds like somebody's been keeping tabs."

Chris shrugs. "You know as well as me how easy it is to find out where someone is in the system just by making a call. And you probably also know it's illegal for the guards to open fire on a helicopter over prison grounds."

"Don't bet on that. Some eager rookie just might blast you outta the sky."

"But there's a chance."

Calvin shakes his head. He is standing with hands on his hips, looking at Chris as if he wants to say more, knowing further words will be ignored. After a moment, he simply shrugs.

"Whatever you say, kid. It's your life. Now let's go inside and get a beer."

Far above the heads of the two men, the falcon takes flight.

Chris and Calvin sit and drink and talk until the early hours of morning. At dawn, Chris drifts off to sleep and dreams of the biggest olive branch in the history of mankind. One the size of a helicopter, big enough to carry Andrew Daulton Lee to freedom.

SNOWMAN MELT

Cait
(July 1981)

There are two ways to get into Lompoc Federal Penitentiary. By breaking laws, or breaking barriers. In my case, my ticket in consisted of the latter – although by the time all was said and done, I couldn't say with any certainty that I'd taken the easiest route.

The drive from San Diego to Lompoc is mostly gorgeous if not wholly grueling – a five-hour, 270-mile trek that hugs the coast from Del Mar all the way up to Capistrano Beach before lurching inland for an unpleasant yet necessary detour through LA County. By the time you hit Camarillo, you're praying for a wayward big-rig to come along and smack you out of your misery. Then just when you think you can't possibly take any more, the Pacific comes hurtling back into view and you forget what the hell you were so pissed off about. At Gaviota Beach, Highway 101 veers sharply north and Mother Pacific bids *adieu*, only to be replaced by lush greenery as far as the eye can see.

It was July, 1981. The day I drove to Lompoc for my first face-to-face meeting with Andrew Daulton Lee had been long in coming and by all rights should have taken place as early as March. But they don't call red tape "red" for nothing: by the time you're done tangling with it, if all you see isn't crimson-hued, you'd better check your pulse.

I'd left San Diego at four a.m. and by the time I turned onto the mile-long dirt road that served as entry to one of the biggest bitch prisons the system had to offer, I was ready to eat glass and shit nails. But the closer I drew to the enormous cement watchtower that overlooked the prison, the more I wished I still had another twenty miles to go. The disembodied voice that shouted from a speaker at the entry gate didn't make my arrival any more pleasant.

"Please state your name and the purpose of your visit," it blared. The voice was coming from a two-way security call box fixed to the end of a red and white striped post.

"My name is Kathleen Mills," I answered, leaning out of my car window to be heard. "I'm here to visit Andrew Daulton Lee." I reached for the legal pad that sat beside me in the passenger seat and read aloud the eight-digit code that was Daulton's official federal brand: "Inmate number 19485-148."

After a few seconds of silence, the voice returned. "Are you carrying any drugs or firearms?"

I knew the question was standard protocol – at least I hoped it was – but it still didn't put me any more at ease. "No," I answered, wondering if the person on the other end had heard my voice shake as clearly as I had.

The silence that ensued for the next five minutes was the worst part. Were they running my name and license plate through a central database to determine if I was on someone's watch list up on high? Probably. Calling the FBI and CIA to inform them that one of the country's most notorious spies was about to receive a visitor? Possible. Then again, it was entirely likely that the person on the other end of the receiver just enjoyed making people squirm. In those interminable five minutes, I did plenty of it.

When the call box finally erupted into noise again, I almost jumped out of my skin. "Park your car in the spaces to your left. Wait at the first sally port for admittance." Although there was no audible trace of emotion in that voice, I could swear I detected a condescending snicker hidden in there somewhere. For someone who detests prisons as much as I do, it never occurred to me that maybe I was in the wrong line of work.

I pulled into the large, half-empty parking lot and killed the engine. The lot was big enough to fit about a hundred cars, but at this early hour of the morning, the only other cars in evidence were those reserved for the Lompoc employees. Up above, the morning sun was warming fast, predicting a waiting oven of plastic and upholstery and a miserable drive back in the oppressive summer heat. I went to roll down my driver's side window, figuring this was probably the last place on earth I'd have anything stolen from my car. That's when the blue rectangular sign screaming ALL VEHICLES MUST BE SECURELY LOCKED BEFORE ENTERING BUILDING flew into my line of sight.

"Wonderful," I said. "We'll be serving roasted Irish lass on the drive home."

I crossed the parking lot in the direction of the sally port, the dry land equivalent of a fortress moat. Its outer gate yawned open as I reached it, then rolled slowly closed again as soon as I stepped within its maw. I stared up at the menacing coils of razor wire that adorned every inch of the prison's high fences, wondering how the hell Daulton's co-defendant Christopher Boyce had negotiated his way past them. Boyce had made a clean getaway and was still on escape status, so he must have known what he was doing. It wasn't until later that I learned the prison had tripled up on razor wire after Boyce's disappearing act – but that didn't make it any less a miraculous feat. Prison fences are a strange paradox. You can read all about them, you can study photos and diagrams, you can see them on TV in crisp, clear focus and you can even close your eyes and use your powers of imagination. But until you've actually stood before one in person, you have no idea just how forbidding they really are.

With the sally port's exterior gate now closed securely behind me, the interior gate began to roll open. I walked through its threshold toward the huge cement steps leading to the visitor's building. Getting my first good look at the various structures that

The Falcon and The Snowman: American Sons

made up the prison compound, I saw this was a place that gave Auschwitz a run for its money with respect to attractiveness – but in that beauty contest, Lompoc took the blue ribbon by a fraction. There were armed guards everywhere I looked, and the hair on the nape of my neck prickled to attention as I pictured their weapons trained on my back, promising a volley of gunfire for every false move I made.

Once inside the visitor's building, my bag was searched and my ID scrutinized. I filled out a visitor's form and was handed a temporary pass and a locker key, then told to stow everything but dollars and loose change (quarters only, for some reason I'll never figure out). The metal detector was next, an experience that came complete with its very own personalized pat down as an encore. When that was over, I was shown a chair and told to wait.

Thirty minutes passed. By this time, other visitors had trickled in, many no doubt familiar with the molasses speed at which the Lompoc visiting hours operated. At the forty-five-minute mark, mercy arrived in the form of another indiscernible, unsmiling uniform who led us all into a large room filled with rows of tables and hideous orange chairs. These were flanked by a wall of windows on one side and a block of vending machines on the other.

I found a coffee machine and pumped a quarter into it. It spat out a pungent brew to match my grim surroundings. I took it anyway. Beggars can't be choosers when the addiction must be fed. I picked a chair closest to the window that offered a view of a well-maintained garden outside and sat.

Coffee in hand, I reflected on the last four months of letters and brief phone conversations I'd had with Daulton. During that time, the Federal Bureau of Prisons hadn't made communication easy. As a matter of protocol, all telephone calls were monitored and every piece of mail was read, making the formulation of a plan for his appeal nearly impossible. Even when everything's above board, you can't exactly strategize your game with the opposition looking on. Ultimately, the hoops I'd had to leap through just to meet the man in person would serve as indication of the mountain of bureaucracy that lay ahead in the coming twenty years.

I choked down the bitter swill and tried to marshal my thoughts into clear and concise questions. I knew almost nothing about Andrew Daulton Lee. Without that knowledge, there was little I could tell the parole commission on his behalf. I remembered the first phone conversation I'd ever had with him; pleasant if not extremely guarded, peppered with occasional flashes of the dry wit and charming personality I would eventually come to know much better than I ever thought I would.

What little I had gathered about Daulton was that he was someone who'd had his fill of people trying to get close. Most of the relationships people had tried to form with him after his incarceration usually came to a screeching halt the moment they tried to steer conversation in the direction of Christopher Boyce. Daulton was wary of betrayal, but I knew this wasn't my concern. I was here to do a job, not meet a pen pal. I'd been asked to represent him, and once that was done, that was precisely where I planned to leave this strange relationship.

Thirty more minutes passed. I sat in silence, dividing my attention between the garden and the others in the waiting room. Many stared, no doubt curious about the six-foot redhead in the linen business suit and high heels trying not to gag on what passed for coffee in this dark corner of the universe. The place was full of children, most of them racing up and down the aisles between chairs, begging their parents for spare change and merrily sprinting to the vending machines to spend their loot, oblivious to the fact that elsewhere there were kids just like them who didn't have to come to places like these to visit their fathers, uncles, or brothers.

The desire to be somewhere else – anywhere else – didn't come crashing down on me at once. Instead it simmered and stewed, and as the sum total of time I'd spent waiting since my arrival neared eighty minutes, I decided that I'd had enough. I stood to leave. Almost as if on cue, the prisoner entry door swung open and Daulton Lee walked into the room.

Our eyes met and he gave me an appraising look. From the perspective of a man only five-three, I must have looked like a giant in my heels. His first three words to me confirmed that.

"Jeez you're tall!" A disarming smile broke over his face.

It's not often you can keep from laughing when you're caught off guard, and apparently today was my turn in the hot seat. I laughed out loud and sat back down.

Daulton approached with his arm extended. "It's good to finally see you in person," he said. We shook. He sat. We talked. For hours.

***

When I first contacted Daulton via telegram – the preferred "rapid" method of communication back in the dark ages of the early eighties – all I really knew about him was that his legal representation had been a joke and the life sentence he'd received for his crime had been severe, bordering on outrageous. Beyond that extremely opinionated view (hey, at least I'm honest) I didn't know much else about the guy or his case. Apparently, I wasn't alone.

The media buzz that had surrounded Daulton Lee and Christopher Boyce at the time of their arrests in 1977 had been more of a flash tempest than a full-blown storm. The evening news talking heads did their duty and reported on the story in a perfunctory manner while the blowhards in Washington used the incident as a soapbox for whatever ideology or programs they were peddling. But it wasn't the scandal that it probably deserved to be. By 1981, the majority of the country had begun to forget all about the two kids from Palos Verdes who'd traded in their freedom for a chance to play secret agent games with the Soviets. Boys are stupid sometimes, but the populace is always amnesiac.

I had to know everything I could about Daulton if I was going to do a halfway decent job of representing him for parole. The brief phone calls and handful of letters we had exchanged in the four months leading up to our first meeting had only given me so much to work with (which was nothing) and so while I sat waiting for the wheels of bureaucracy to turn, I picked up a copy of *The Falcon and the Snowman*.

It was the image of Daulton on the page that basically told me what to expect when we met – the one portrayed by the book's author as a dark, angry, egotistical sociopath. But the person I met that hot July day in 1981 was nothing like that. Sure, there were glimpses of the arrogance that I'd read about in the book. But there was also a deeply human, funny, lonely side to him that I hadn't expected. When the time came to wrap up our first meeting, it dawned on me with a fair amount of shock that I'd actually enjoyed myself. And so I vowed to come back again.

The next time, I didn't find the drive as grueling as it had been that first go-round. But that's the way it always is, isn't it? I eventually came to love that miserably long drive – if it's possible to love anything that's miserable and long, that is – and surprisingly it was Lompoc itself that was the reason. Not the prison, but the city. Back in those days, Lompoc wore the crown of "Flower Seed Capital of the World" for the miles of flower fields that lay on its outskirts and perfumed the summer air with the aroma of carnation, stock and phlox. Cutting a swath through those vast fields of brilliant colors and scents was what I came to associate with Daulton in the beginning, and I genuinely looked forward to those times.

Oh, what a difference a few decades can make.

***

On my second visit, I decided to make a weekend of it. I left San Diego on a late Friday afternoon and found a room at the Lompoc Motel, a far quieter and more comfortable alternative to the Motel 6 which sat just off the noisy downtown strip in the middle of bustling Lompoc. Of course, I use the word "bustling" with extreme sarcasm. Aside from the two motels, the whole of the town consisted of a Circle K, a bowling alley, and a Chinese restaurant I'd eventually come to frequent and appreciate for being the only place open on Christmas Day. In a nutshell, that was all there was to Lompoc in 1981. But the two-lane road that ran through the center of town and served as its main artery to the outside world seemed constantly alive with moving cars.

The motel where I decided to stay was further from the main road and closer to the prison by a few miles. It was owned and run by a couple, newly emigrated from Pakistan, who spoke barely a word of English but made up for the language barrier with a welcome hug, a cup of Chai tea, and cookies. Try asking for that the next time you hit a Motel 6 and see how far it gets you.

By the time I stepped into my room and was greeted by a decidedly retro, orange and avocado green motif complete with tri-colored hanging lamps, I was convinced I'd somehow sidestepped back in time to 1965.

Would that it were, I mused. *I'd buy stock in IBM, stop a few assassinations, and sleep with Jim Morrison before he went belly-up.*

I was asleep the moment my head hit the pillow.

***

"Can we talk about Boyce now?"

It would become a mantra I detested having to repeat.

Daulton looked away and sipped at his coffee, hiding his face behind the paper cup. Sometimes he would use this as a method of avoiding a question he didn't have any interest in answering. Other times, he'd just politely refuse.

It was already the second day of my weekend visit and to this point we'd done little more than talk about life in general. Daulton told me his mother had remarried, and that she'd managed to do it under the radar. I learned his younger brother was still living in the house in Palos Verdes, his oldest sister was in Georgia, and his youngest sister had moved to Shasta County. We talked a bit about his case, but nothing that would send me back to San Diego satisfied that we'd done anything more than shoot the breeze. I was determined not to leave without something to work with.

"Daulton," I said. "There's only so much you can give me that'll help me put together an argument for the parole commission. I know you don't like to talk about Boyce—"

"For the sake of propriety," Daulton broke in, "can we refer to him as my 'co-defendant'?"

I stopped, dropping my hands into my lap. "Your co-defendant, then." I spoke the words with only the faintest hint of a patronizing tone. The fact that I was comfortable enough giving him even that much was evidence of how at ease I'd become in his presence; the fact that he flat out refused to talk about Christopher Boyce was evidence of how little he trusted me still.

"We have to explore every possible option," I told him. "And you've got to be willing to talk to me about certain things you're not comfortable talking about. That includes... *your co-defendant.*" The sideways glance he shot me had corrected me before I inadvertently spoke what had become, in Daulton's lexicon, "The Unspeakable Name."

I understood why. At least I sort of did. Daulton blamed Boyce for the position he was in. Daulton was no angel, and his arrest record for drug dealing and the stack of bench warrants that were already out on him at the time of his arrest for espionage pointed strongly in the direction of a young man headed for some heavy-duty prison time. But in Daulton's eyes, it was Christopher Boyce alone who was responsible for his new life behind bars.

During their bifurcated trials (which is just a fancy way of saying that the case was divided into two parts so that each defendant could be represented by his own lawyer and sentenced separately), the two old friends had turned on one other in an effort to save themselves. Daulton aimed the finger of blame squarely at Boyce, insisting he'd lied to him by telling him they were working covertly for the CIA disseminating counterintelligence to the Soviets. In turn, Boyce did his own fair share of finger-pointing, claiming Daulton had blackmailed him into handing over the sensitive spy satellite intel that had eventually landed them behind bars.

I thought both claims were steaming piles of shit. Just as the juries had when they'd returned their guilty verdicts and as Judge Robert Kelleher had when he'd sentenced them. Of course, I didn't bother mentioning this to Daulton, partly because it would have only pissed him off, but mainly because I didn't care if any of it was true or not. I wasn't interested in retrying his case. All I was looking for was a foundation on which to build an argument for his parole.

"There's nothing to be gleaned there," Daulton said dismissively, and leaned back in his chair in a manner indicative of having already dropped the subject. "We already know that my sentencing statute entitles me to an early parole. I don't see why we don't just pursue that avenue and forget about him."

"Forget about who?"

Daulton squinted at me suspiciously. "My co-defendant," he replied, his words cautious and deliberate. Then, relaxing again: "And trying to make me slip by accidentally uttering his name was a cheap ploy."

I snapped the fingers of my right hand, making an "Aw, shucks" gesture. Daulton smiled. "Games like these will not earn you another cup of that miraculous joe," he said, gesturing to the cup 'o horrors planted on the empty seat beside me.

I shrugged. "It tastes like stump water anyway."

Daulton shifted gears again. He was always doing that. "Back to issues of grave import – the aforementioned sentencing statutes."

I sighed, certain I'd already explained this part to him before. Maybe I had. Sometimes, talking to Daulton was like a tennis match. "First of all, your use of the word 'entitled' is a bit strong. There are no guarantees. The statute you were sentenced under is the technicality that might just get you a seat in front of the parole commission. But it's what I'm able to give them once we're there that makes all the difference in the world."

Looking back on it, my plan to stand before the parole board and extol Daulton's virtues as argument for his early release must have seemed an idiot's ploy to everyone, including Daulton. Even though his words indicated he felt his parole was a foregone conclusion, I don't think Daulton ever truly believed that he would be a free man again. But in my mind and the way it was all spelled out on paper, I thought it just might work.

Judge Kelleher had sentenced Daulton to life imprisonment under statute 18 USC 4205(b)(2), which specified that a federal prisoner serving a sentence longer than one year could be granted early release at the discretion of the parole commission. In plain English, this meant Daulton was eligible for parole immediately, as long as the parole commission approved his request. And since the sentencing guidelines prior to 1987 required that he be given a parole hearing every twenty-four months, I figured it was worth a shot. But the last thing I wanted to do was get up there in front of that stiff group of suits empty handed.

I could produce evidence that in the last four years Daulton had been a model prisoner, but I knew that wouldn't be enough. There was also that pesky little fact of the crime that got him there in the first place. Legally, there's a big difference between being found guilty of espionage and being found guilty of treason, and despite the fact that the prosecutors in the case never sought the death penalty, there were still a lot of people in the country who felt Daulton and Christopher Boyce had gotten off extremely lucky. Sit just one of those people on the parole board, you're sunk.

And so I was piecing together an arsenal from scraps. I needed to probe Daulton for information that would help me present his side of the story and somehow paint him in a better light in the eyes of the parole board. How much influence had Boyce exerted over Daulton during the commission of their crime? Had Daulton made any attempts to change the course they were headed on? But through all of my attempts to pick his brain for anything that would help his case, Daulton remained closed-lipped.

It was starting to become clear to me there was more in his resistance to involving Christopher Boyce than any festering issues of resentment, but I couldn't quite put my finger on what that was. Could it be that Daulton so desperately wanted to separate himself from Boyce – in life as well as in the eyes of the parole commission – that he was willing to risk leaving some critical stone unturned? Maybe, I thought, he was trying to play the "innocent by complete non-association" card.

Boyce's escape from prison had impacted Daulton gravely. The fact that they were both inmates at Lompoc when it occurred cemented Daulton as "Person of Interest Number One" to the FBI and the U.S. Marshals Service, both of whom were embroiled in a bitter custody dispute over ownership of the manhunt.

Even after the authorities were convinced he knew nothing about Boyce's escape plans or where he'd planned to go once he landed on the other side of the fence, orders were put in for Daulton to be transferred to the federal prison in Terre Haute, Indiana. Not only did the move disrupt the small life Daulton had built for himself at Lompoc, but it also situated him too far away from Palos Verdes, where his mother and brother still lived.

In all the time Daulton was housed at Terre Haute, he never received a single visit from family. Eventually, he was transferred back to Lompoc in a rare gesture of mercy by the Bureau of Prisons so that visits from his family members could resume. It was his brother who came most often; David Lee was Daulton's biggest supporter.

In the end, I put Daulton's desire to avoid any conversation about Boyce down to something much simpler than anger, and something far easier to sympathize with: to Daulton, Christopher Boyce was bad luck. And like someone who's been burned too many times by walking under ladders or straying into the path of wandering black cats, Daulton had become superstitious. Christopher Boyce wasn't exactly his boogey man, but he hadn't been his lucky charm, either.

I glanced at the clock on the wall, which announced the second day of my weekend visit was rapidly coming to an end. But there was still one question I couldn't let go unasked. It was the one thing that had been most present on my mind the entire weekend.

"Daulton, did you know anything about Boyce's escape before it happened?"

He stiffened. "If you really want to know the answer to that question, you can ask the U.S. Marshals and the FBI. Or didn't you already talk to them?" His tone was grim, his face set.

I rolled my eyes, worrying that my abrupt question had set me back to square one with him. "I didn't talk to them."

"Are you sure?"

"Yes," I said. I suddenly felt like a teenager being given the third degree by an overbearing parent. I resented every second of it. "I'm sure. It's a legitimate question and an issue we have to discuss."

"So you're telling me you weren't sent here to determine if I know anything about my co-defendant's whereabouts?"

My patience, already on a short fuse, was starting to wear thin – and when that levee breaks, God help anyone standing in front of it. "No, Daulton," I said, accentuating every syllable sharply, "if that were the case, I would have asked you the first time we met and saved myself a repeat visit to Bumfuck Egypt."

"Because if you really want to know, all you have to do is ask."

I stared at him. Although his poker face held strong, I was starting to think that maybe – just maybe – Daulton had ventured past the point of mistrust and was now having fun at my expense. I decided to humor him.

"Okay then," I said. "I'm asking."

"So ask."

"Did you know anything about Boyce—" I started, then stopped abruptly. Daulton's eyebrows lifted at my grievous misstep, but then the eyes below lit up and he nodded enthusiastically like a proud teacher when I corrected myself: "…about your *co-defendant's* escape?"

Daulton didn't miss a beat, shifting into deadpan mode. "Shit no. Next question."

I laughed. Daulton smiled. It occurred to me at that moment that a part of him wasn't here to talk about getting out of prison. I was probably the first woman he'd talked to in years that wasn't a relative, and he was enjoying my company. Maybe a bit more than he should have.

"You're a lot easier on me than the feds were about that," Daulton admitted. "I probably had to say 'no' more times than a virgin on prom night before they left me alone. The fact is, my co-defendant would never have discussed his escape plans with me."

Daulton straightened in his chair and began to regain the formal, almost cold composure I'd eventually learn not to take personally. The Lees were cocktail-hour socialite bluebloods, after all, and Daulton's aloof reserve was evidence that some forced childhood behaviors never really go away.

"You're positive about that?" I asked, resolved not to drop it until I'd given him every chance to come clean.

He looked me square in the eye. "Two-hundred percent. If he had, I would have gone right to the warden with it and scored *beaucoup* points for saving taxpayer money on that feeble manhunt."

Feeble was the right word. It had been close to a year and a half since Boyce's escape, and from the occasional news blurbs I'd managed to catch here and there, the authorities were nowhere near finding him. Did I secretly root for Christopher Boyce? You bet your ass I did. Did I let on to Daulton that I did? Answer that one yourself.

"True," I said. "But if he had hinted at it and you didn't take him seriously, or if you suspected he might be serious but didn't snatch up the opportunity to catch a ride out of *Le Chateau Lompoc*, it could look equally good for you as someone just interested in paying your debt to society."

Daulton shook his head and shrugged. "Wish I could lay claim to that one, but I can't."

And that was that. Daulton had a way of making things sound completely plausible and totally unquestionable. He had an incredible ability to look you straight in the eye, gently touch your hand, and tell you anything he wanted you to believe. And you would. At that moment, he could have told me "I have a giraffe in my cell – we play chess together" and as much as I'd like to think not, I probably would have bought it. At least for a minute, anyway.

It would be another thirty years before I learned what Daulton had really known about Christopher Boyce's escape.

GOING SOUTH

Chris
(July 1981)

Chris banked wide over the Strait of Juan de Fuca before turning back toward Fairchild Airport in Port Angeles. He was deep in thought. He had still not resolved the ultimate question: to make the attempt or not.

Nothing else he could conceive of would stir up the federal beehive more than a helicopter snatch out of a Bureau of Prisons penitentiary. But did Daulton have it in him to climb into a copter, probably under gunfire, and fly out of that hell?

He didn't know the answer to that question.

The Cessna touched down lightly on the runway. He was getting better with each landing. He taxied slowly across the grass airfield to his tie-down spot and cut the engine. Soon, he would have his pilot's license. After that, he would begin taking helicopter lessons.

He sat in the Cessna's pilot seat and stared out the windscreen. *I should be somewhere else,* he thought. *Why not just pack up my things and move to Wisconsin somewhere? Or even better, farther. Maine. Start all over again.* But the one thought that always prevented him from doing so was Daulton. His escape had ensured his old friend would never be released. As long as Chris was free, Daulton would remain imprisoned.

A helicopter snatch wouldn't be that difficult to pull off. He had been around airports enough now to know how easy it was to "borrow" small planes and helicopters. If the keys were not actually under the aircraft seats, they were unsecured in the offices of the airfield managers. Small airfields had virtually no security systems. It was simple to know which aircraft were fueled and which weren't. Obtaining the skills and documentation to enable him to swipe a helicopter was the easy part.

There was one other thing he had going for him. He knew Lompoc – the prison and the surrounding land – like the back of his hand. He was sure he could come in low and fast at treetop level, grab Daulton, and be gone in seconds. He could even use smoke to make himself a difficult target. He was confident he could pull it off. The danger lay in communicating with Daulton. He would have to trust the little bastard not to rat him out.

His brain told him he didn't owe Daulton a thing. But his heart felt sick knowing that the best friend of his youth, the boy he had grown up with, would be forever condemned to that hell. If it could be done, he would do what needed to be done to free Daulton. And he would revel in the consternation it would bring to the federal bureaucrats. Just the thought of it made his heart sing.

He climbed out of the Cessna and stood leaning against the strut. He closed his eyes and breathed the sea air, going over the information he had. It wasn't much. He knew Daulton had been moved back to Lompoc. Finding out had just taken a call to the BOP inmate locator number. It was a good start, but he needed a contact. Someone who would visit Daulton and pass him a message. Someone he could trust.

They had hundreds of mutual friends from childhood living in the South Bay, but none he felt he could really trust. He pondered over it for another minute, then put the thought out of his head. It wasn't a decision that needed immediate attention. What he needed to do first was scout the penitentiary; to return to the hellhole from which he'd escaped. To sit down with binoculars high in the woods and watch it like a hawk. Although the thought of returning there revolted him, he didn't see much danger in it. It was surely the last place anyone in their right mind would expect to find him.

He thought it over for the next few days as he gathered his equipment. He bought a cheap VW Bug from a student in Seattle for $400. Finally, late one afternoon in July of 1981, he stowed his backpack, bedroll, water bottles and binoculars into the old Bug and headed south into California.

It was a homecoming and a horror show, all at the same time. California was his home, but going back was also like venturing into the lair of a beast. He focused on the drive and tried to put everything else out of his mind. At San Jose, he cut across Highway 17 and drove out to the old Pacific Coast Highway. He camped on the beach at Big Sur and fell asleep listening to the surf against the shore. He tried to forget that the prison was only another four hours south.

In the morning, he stripped down and jogged along the beach. The wet sand squished between his toes. He paused and looked back at the tracks behind him. No one followed. Above him, herring gulls swirled, circled and called in their rasping *kaaws*. Terns whistled and flashed down the tide line. He ran on, warming his blood and opening his lungs.

It was cold and grey and his flesh shivered. The waves surged past him up the shore. He waded out into the sea and let the surf rush around his chest. It made him strong. He dipped his head in the foaming heave and felt invigorated. It was good to be cold and naked and wet and alive. It shrank the scrotum and concentrated the mind.

Dripping with salt water, he walked back to camp and toweled off. His teeth chattered. He pulled on a sweatshirt and lit a cigarette. He knocked the sand from his feet and threw on his Levis, then warm socks and boots. He fried eggs and hash browns on his camp stove. When he was finished eating, he climbed into the VW and drove south.

Just before noon, he passed Hearst Castle. At Morro Rock, he took out his binoculars and watched the peregrine falcons stooping at sandpipers on the spit. Not long after, he arrived in the tiny town of Lompoc. The penitentiary was there, just down the road. It was a malevolent monstrosity he didn't want to face again. He dreaded it and was drawn to it. He wanted to kill it. Knowing that was impossible, he decided he would settle for breaking Daulton out of it.

***

The oak woodlands of the California coast in summer are a drab place of browns, tans and dull greens. On a two-track just off San Lucia Canyon Road, Chris parked the VW deep in the trees and changed into khakis and camo.

At dusk, he stepped off into the woods with his bedroll, backpack and binoculars. In his right hand he clutched his Roger Tory Peterson *Field Guide to Birds*. His pocket held a compass. He wasn't armed; he intended neither to be seen nor confronted. This was only a look-see expedition. He was a birder, after all.

Lompoc Federal Penitentiary was only a half mile away.

***

Soon after midnight, he came to a small clearing in the scrub oak and found the penitentiary. It emitted a colossal glow above the forest top that obscured the twinkling of stars, even the lights of passing airplanes. He stood there in the darkness, feet frozen in place, contemplating the far-off glare of billions of candlepower emitted from the federal surveillance lights.

He remembered the despair of being pinned nightly under those despicable beams. He started to turn away, but stopped himself. The lights were all turned in upon the beast itself. They would not shine on him as he watched from the woods.

I'll be safe out here.

He moved slowly in the dark, one step at a time, constantly pausing to look and listen. As he closed the distance, he began to hear the great, sickening electrical hum that powered the glow. It was a thing he remembered, a thing he had run from. He struggled to overcome the fear. Returning to this place wouldn't be a walk down memory lane. He knew this going in. But he also hadn't imagined it would be so unnerving.

He continued through the darkness toward the glow until he could see the entire thing – not just the lights, but the whole structure itself – through the chaparral. The sight of it stopped him in his tracks. It seemed so alien to the night all around it, so devoid of any semblance of humanity or nature. To his eye, it was the personification of evil. He knew all about the nightmare world that existed within.

Slowly, he crept forward. One foot at a time, stepping gently. More than once, he stopped to watch the prison as if to ensure it wouldn't come alive before his eyes. Except for the obnoxious humming, it was eerily quiet. He moved forward again, determined that the dawn would find him under cover, close enough to see all the comings and goings in the prison yard.

Hours later, he found himself on a small, scrub-covered knoll looking down onto the north side of the penitentiary. He was about a half-mile out, far enough away that he wouldn't be seen. He sat down in the brush with his back against an oak and half-slept, watching the constant circling of the outer perimeter patrol trucks until the sun came up and the great work whistle sounded, summoning prisoners to their drudgery.

It was only the second time he had seen the penitentiary in daylight from the other side of the fence. The first time had been when he was delivered here in chains. If anything, it was even more ominous now.

He watched the prison through the binoculars all morning, keeping his hand movements slow and deliberate. Prisoners, alone and in small groups, straggled on and off the yard. These were the lucky ones who had somehow avoided the prison sweatshops. They were the bankers, the janitors, the disabled. Some jogged, some worked the weight pile, and others walked endlessly around the yard. Every single one of them stared longingly toward the fences, toward freedom. Watching the inmates reminded Chris of visiting the old Los Angeles Zoo – except in the zoo, the animals didn't regularly kill each other.

After observing for hours, he saw nothing much had changed security-wise that would obstruct a helicopter snatch off the prison yard. The only difference he could detect were the perimeter fences themselves, which had apparently been given an extra two layers of razor wire since his escape.

The sudden crack of automatic gunfire jolted him. It was directly behind him, to the north of the knoll. For an instant, he cursed himself for not having brought a gun. Then he remembered that the prison target range – the place the guards went on a daily basis to practice their killing skills – was back there somewhere. It had been placed there to intimidate the prisoners.

He had always loathed listening to the sound of that gunfire. This time was no different. It lasted for what seemed like hours, coming and going in sporadic bursts, but it gave him the opportunity to get a fix on its location. He made a mental note to fly a wide arc around it when he flew in.

Late in the afternoon, he saw a foursome of prisoners enter the yard together. They looked and acted different. Each was dressed in a neat white shirt and shorts and carried a tennis racket with him. They moved with carefree grace, seemingly oblivious to their surroundings.

He remembered that the tennis players at Lompoc had not been average convicts. Most of them were upper-echelon drug dealers. Through the binoculars, he could see that one of the men stood a head shorter than the rest.

It was Daulton. Although Chris was too far away to see his face, he recognized his old friend from his height and from the signature two-handed racket swing he had developed just a couple of years earlier. Prison had revealed several of Daulton's hidden talents. One of them was tennis.

Chris suddenly saw how the helicopter breakout could succeed. He would simply plant down right there in the middle of the tennis court. He would come in low, from the northeast, then exit by flying over the cell blocks and the front gate to the south. Hugging the treetops, he would swing southeast in a ten-mile-long arc before veering northeast, up and over the La Panza Range to Painted Rock

Ranch. He would stash a car there in the brush in advance – maybe two, so they could go their separate ways.

But stealing a helicopter and flying it in would be the easy part. Even the getaway could work. The hard part would be making contact with Daulton.

When he got back to the Bug, he kicked it to life and headed out of the woodlands into town. The city of Lompoc was home to several hundred prison guards and other assorted Bureau of Prisons employees, but he felt confident nobody would recognize him there.

First, he had to make a phone call to Calvin. Then it was time to do a bit of snooping.

YOU WILL MEET A TALL DARK STRANGER

Cait
(August 1981)

The sign above the door of the Rice Bowl café was tacky, and the chef's handiwork left something to be desired, but the place met with three criteria that would transform me into a bona fide regular over the course of the next twenty years: it was open Christmas Day, it offered booths the size of Cadillacs, and it was close to the Lompoc Motel. Which all meant on weekends when I came north to meet with Daulton in that horrid orange visiting room, the Rice Bowl also served as my office away from home and feeding table at the end of a long day of jawing with my friend, the condemned.

In the short month since my first meeting with Daulton, I had managed to knit together the delicate strands of an argument for his parole. Working around the inaccessibility of the disappeared Christopher Boyce was like trying to pull together the pieces of a jigsaw puzzle without an important corner piece or knowing if there was one missing at all. I figured to wait for his return would be a waste of time. So I pressed on.

It had been almost nineteen months since Boyce's escape. So far, not a single alphabet soup organization had caught up with him. Despite occasional rumors and news blurbs proclaiming a "tightening of the circle" – PR-speak, as far as I was concerned – neither the FBI, the U.S. Marshals, nor Interpol had pulled jack shit. I had a feeling that they probably never would.

I won't lie. Christopher Boyce's escape from prison was an issue of great conflict for me. There was a big part of me that wanted him back in custody so I could rummage his brain for something that would make my job easier – helpful clues, missing facts, or lately-birthed desires to take full ownership and absolve Daulton of any wrongdoing in their crime together. Not that doing so would have changed things, but it couldn't have hurt. On the other hand, there was a small part of me that secretly rooted for Boyce with every single "nope, nothing yet" progress report that found its way to broadcast on slow news days.

I kept these thoughts from Daulton. Lately, the extent of any conversation about his "co-defendant" (or "He Who Shall Not Be Named," as I mockingly referred to Boyce in my internal voice) was limited to passing mentions, or the frequent snide remarks he always had ready to ascribe to his estranged old friend when it became necessary to acknowledge his existence.

On some days, I was convinced Daulton understood the futility of demonizing Boyce. Other days, I had no doubt he would go to his grave refusing to take his share of the blame, forever clinging to Christopher Boyce as the embodiment of his earthly woes. Then there were days when he would come to our meetings with black eyes, or split and swollen lips, or with an agonizing limp in his walk, and I would again be reminded he was coping with things in the only way he knew how.

It was always the same. No matter how many times I asked, he would never give me the details of how he'd received his injuries. At first I thought his evasiveness was driven by some sense of personal shame, maybe the feeling that he should have been able to protect himself more capably, and so I let it lie. Eventually, a far simpler answer occurred to me. For Daulton, our time together in that visiting room drinking bad coffee and plotting his parole was a reprieve from a world where the threat of death lurked around every corner. The last thing he wanted to do was sully the experience by bringing all that fear and horror with him.

I did my best to mask my outrage. Whether or not my attempts were successful is another story. The closer he and I became, the more each incident threw me for an emotional loop, after which I would emerge even more resolved than I had been before. In that way, his terrifying predicament became one of the greatest weapons in my arsenal, and I allowed myself permission to use it frequently. Any time I grew weary, or saw his cause as hopeless, or perceived my abilities as just not good enough, I'd simply remind myself of the imminent danger he faced on a daily basis. If there ever was a kick in the ass more effective than that, I never discovered it.

None of this was to say I thought Daulton deserved a pass for what he'd done to get where he was. A crime had been committed and a judgment rendered. But if you asked me if I thought he was completely out of his depth doing life in a federal prison like Lompoc, my answer would have been an unequivocal "hell yes!"

One thing was indisputable: he had been a well-worn traveler of the road to ruin long before our paths crossed. And yet of all the spectacular mistakes he'd made in his young life, it was stupidity and greed that had led him to this place. The truth was, he was no more a Communist than I was a Republican. But I supposed it was far too frightening for anyone to conceive that an amateur without a single complex motive could have caused so much purported damage to national security – least of all Judge Robert Kelleher, who had sentenced Daulton to life because he didn't have the authority to give him the death sentence.

"Egg rolls. White rice. Lemon chicken."

The arrival of my dinner on the table broke my contemplative spell with the force of a dull hammer – only instead of striking me between the eyes, it caught me square in the gut. My stomach, incensed at having been forced to endure hours of vending machine coffee without food, cried out. I was just about to lower my face into a steaming dish of lemon chicken when I heard a voice utter my name.

"Cait?"

I looked up and locked eyes with the waiter who'd set the food down. He was a five-foot-zero Asian guy in a collarless white shirt and black pants, with a widow's peak that made him look like an ageless caricature. A wave of shame hit me when I realized I had been so completely wrapped up in thought that I'd ignored his presence; the fact that he apparently knew my name but I had no clue to his made me feel even worse. So I offered up my best humble smile – probably some instinctual remnant of my teenage years – and filled the air with a jumbled stream of apologetic babble that came out: "Oh... sorry, I... thank you. I'm sorry. Yes. Thanks."

He looked confused and said, "Phone."

"Huh?"

"Phone call." He motioned to the pay phone on the wall by the entrance. The receiver was off the hook, dangling from its coil cord like a dislocated arm.

"For me?"

"You Cait?"

"Yes. I'm Cait."

"Phone call. He ask for you."

The crazy image of Daulton ringing me up, begging me to smuggle him a bag of egg rolls rose before me, then dissipated of its own absurdity. Who the hell could be calling me here? It was the first question I asked when I put the phone to my ear. The voice that answered sounded a million miles away. "Is this Cait Mills?"

"Yes. Who is this?"

"My name is Guy Blake. I'm a staff reporter for the *Lompoc Record*."

I recognized the name of the town newspaper. I wouldn't call it a rinky-dink operation, but the name didn't exactly carry the same esteem as, say, *The New York Times*. Or the *Sacramento Bee*, for that matter. I remember being impressed a newspaper that small could have a staff resourceful enough to pinpoint my identity and where I was in their little town.

"Okay," I said. "What do you want and why are you calling me at a pay phone?"

"I would have called you at your motel room, but the privacy of that line can't be guaranteed."

Great, I thought. A nut. The only difference was this one claimed to have a job, and with the local paper, no less. Maybe the city of Lompoc was a lot weirder than I had first thought.

"Well thanks for the warning," I said, and was moving my hand to hang up the phone when the man on the line said: "This is about Daulton."

I pulled the phone back to my ear. My visits to Daulton were no secret. It wouldn't take much for someone to grab my name from the visitor's roster, do a little bit of digging about who I was and what my intentions were. I had nothing to hide. But that someone had gone to the effort of tracking me down was a shade threatening.

Instinctively, I looked around to see if I was being watched – a stupid thing to do, knowing full well that if the person calling me didn't want to be seen he would have ways of accomplishing that.

"What about Daulton?" I asked. I did nothing to hide the impatience in my voice. I wanted to make it clear that if my caller wanted the conversation to continue, his next words had better be good.

"I'm interested in talking to him. I think there's something I can do to help out his situation."

"Like what?"

"That's a conversation I was hoping to have with him, but you're invited to be there. Do you think you could arrange for me to meet with him?"

I released a heavy sigh. "I don't think so. Honestly, I can't see how getting his name in the paper again can help him."

"I don't think you understand. I'm not interested in writing an article. I have some information that could get him out of prison."

The guy had my full attention now. I knew the case against Daulton like my own life story and there was nothing there to suggest he was innocent. But it was possible I might have missed something. After all, I wasn't looking for evidence of guilt or innocence. I was building a case for his parole. But the remote possibility the person on the phone might know something I didn't intrigued me. Still, I needed to know for certain before I took it to the next step.

"If you have evidence that could lead to that, why talk to me about it? I'm not his lawyer."

The caller – Guy Blake, or whatever he said his name was – made a weird swooshing sound with his lips as if he were considering my question. "It's not exactly the kind of thing that would go down well with the DA," he finally said. "If you know what I mean."

"Actually no, I don't know. If you have something to share, spit it out. My lemon chicken is getting cold."

"Not over the phone."

"Then this conversation is over."

I had hoped my approach would get Blake talking, but it didn't work.

"Think it over and I'll call you again tomorrow," he said and hung up.

I walked quickly back to my booth and sat down, no longer as ravenous as I had been moments earlier. The steam was still rising from my lemon chicken, but instead of reaching for the chopsticks I grabbed one of the fortune cookies and snapped it in half.

The scroll that came out read *You will meet a tall dark stranger*.

"Let's hope he's rich and well-endowed," I muttered, then snatched up an egg roll and sank my teeth into it.

***

Back in the dark ages before cell phones and GPS tracking and social media check-ins, getting a call from someone while you were in public was a freaky experience. Especially at a pay phone. As it is, there are few things that can make you feel more watched. But the mysterious Guy Blake had a way of making it even weirder. I almost didn't take his call when it came in again the following night at the Rice Bowl. But of course, I did.

"Did you have a chance to think it over?" Blake asked. When I didn't respond, he added, "There really isn't a lot of time left."

"Time for what? I'm still not even sure who you are. If I give the local paper a call tomorrow, would they even be able to confirm you work for them?"

The next five seconds of silence told me everything I needed to know.

"Listen," I said, "I'm a busy person. I don't have time for phone games."

"I understand this is totally off-the-wall. But if you agree to talk to me in person, I'll tell you everything. Then you can decide for yourself if it's something you want to pass on to Daulton."

The way Blake spoke Daulton's name had such a familiarity about it that I became convinced I was talking to someone who knew him. Besides, most outsiders didn't know he preferred to go by his middle name and would have called him Andrew instead.

"Can you at least tell me how you know him?" I asked.

"Not on the phone, sorry."

"Okay. Where?"

I almost couldn't believe I was agreeing to it, but damned if my "no stone unturned" instinct wasn't kicking in. Hard. There was also an urgency in Blake's voice that had me convinced he was sincere. He may have been a little paranoid, calling me at a pay phone, but that didn't rule out the possibility that he might have genuine information to share. Although the intellect half of my brain knew much wiser people had flown headlong into some dreadful fates based on far more information than I had in front of me, still I agreed.

"You know the Hyatt in Santa Barbara?" he asked.

"Yes. You're kidding."

"I'd rather meet on neutral ground. There's a parking lot across the road from the hotel, on the beach."

"Alright," I said. "When?"

"Tonight."

I looked at my watch and saw it was a quarter to seven. It was about a forty-five-minute drive south to Santa Barbara. If I ate fast and drove faster, I might have enough time to get there before dusk – the last thing I wanted to do was meet up with a perfect stranger in the dark, public place or not – but by the time I finally did arrive, the sun had already extinguished itself on the rolling black horizon northwest of the Channel Islands.

The parking lot was practically deserted when I pulled in. It was also dark, but the backsplash of light coming from the streetlights on the main street offered some sense of safety. It was a good place to meet and not be seen.

I parked my car and looked around, half expecting some sign telling me where to go – an X taped to the trunk of a palm tree, or an idling car parked in a corner of the lot with its lights off. The sensation of being watched was strong. Stepping out of the car into the cool night breeze, it was unmistakable. I was seconds away from saying the hell with it and climbing back into the driver's seat when someone called out.

"Hello."

I turned my head and caught sight of a figure about thirty feet away, a shadow outlined against the light cast by one of the sodium streetlamps. The figure raised a hand in greeting, but didn't come any closer. I decided to move fast, closing the distance between us before I lost all nerve. In a few seconds, I was face to face with Guy Blake.

The first thing I noticed was his height. The guy was no Billy Barty, but he wasn't the tall drink that goddamned fortune cookie had brought me to expect.

So much for tall.

The next thing I noticed was the fake mustache glued to his upper lip in an effort to disguise his appearance. I didn't know who the hell the guy thought he was fooling, but it certainly wasn't me. He wore a baseball cap down tightly over his forehead, forcing tufts of hair out around his ears. A pair of thick-framed glasses sat on his nose. Although the orange-yellow glow of the sodium light cast everything with an odd hue, I could tell he was Caucasian.

So much for dark.

His clothes were just as bizarre. Everything about him – from the oversized corduroy jacket hand-me-down, to the wrinkled chambray shirt he wore buttoned to the collar – looked like an undercover cop trying to pass for civilian. And failing miserably.

I was about to let him know, but he spoke first.

"Cait? Guy Blake."

"That's what you say, anyway."

"Thanks for coming," he said, ignoring my not-so-subtle challenge. "I wanted to make sure we could talk without anyone listening in."

Behind the glasses, his eyes were dancing faster than the eyes of any hopped-up speed addict I'd ever seen. But I could tell by his body language that he was clean. He was just nervous. Very nervous.

It was contagious. I reflexively tucked my car key into the space between my forefinger and middle finger – a trick my mother taught me, although she was always more partial to a corkscrew than a key – and balled my hand into a fist, holding it down by my side. I wasn't taking any more chances. I had already waded out farther than I was comfortable with, and it was usually then that the bottom dropped out from under you.

"It's a lot easier these days for the CIA or FBI to listen in on private lines," Blake went on. "And, you know meeting face to face in Lompoc was out of the question. Too many eyes a little too close."

I didn't want to stand here all night listening to a discourse on paranoia. But at the same time, I didn't want to upend the guy's mental apple cart. So I considered my angles of approach. I could humor him, speak calmly. That would be the smart thing to do. But then there'd be no guarantee that he would show his hand. I'd just driven fifty miles and had another fifty back to Lompoc. I still had the motel room for another night, with plans to visit Daulton in the morning. If I came all this way for a clandestine meeting, my take had damn well better be worth it. I decided for a mid-range approach.

"How long have you been following me around?"

"Not long. I just had to make sure I could trust you." A nonplussed response. Maybe the guy wasn't as off-kilter as he looked.

"Uh huh. Still, that trick with the pay phone in the restaurant. Pretty good."

He shrugged, but said no more.

"So what did you mean when you said you had some information that could help Daulton?"

Blake hesitated, then glanced around the parking lot again. He was easily the most paranoid person I had ever met. And I'd met some doozies.

"I'll get to that. First, how long have you been… representing him?"

"Not long."

"And you're petitioning for his parole?"

His knowledge of my business with Daulton was unsettling, but I had plenty of time to ponder the possibilities later. Right now, I was more interested in what the guy had that I could use.

"It's a long shot," I said, "but yes."

"Is he as optimistic?"

"Of course not." What I didn't say was it was a lot easier to be optimistic about the future when you weren't locked in prison surrounded by a bunch of killers.

Blake let out a sharp chuckle, then set his face straight again. "You know, Charles Manson had a parole hearing a couple of years ago. Just because it's on paper doesn't mean it'll ever happen. Do you honestly think…"

"Daulton's no Charlie Manson," I fired back. "And the one thing he's got going for him is that I'm experienced enough to help him out and green enough to believe anything's possible." I shrugged. "Maybe that's two things."

At this, Blake's demeanor shifted. He lifted his hands to chest level and brought his palms together, almost imploringly. He looked like a man about ready to impart some kernel of wisdom he wasn't sure would stick.

"Just ask yourself this question," he said. "If they were willing to plant Daulton's fingerprints in that vault at TRW, what makes you think they'll ever let him go free?"

Blake's words were slow and deliberate, grave in their delivery. Which only made their impact more resounding when I realized he had a damn good point.

In my review of the court transcripts of Daulton's trial, I had come across only one piece of evidence that I could never get my mind around – a solitary fingerprint, lifted from a piece of equipment inside the Black Vault at TRW. It was identified as Andrew Daulton Lee's.

The Black Vault was the restricted communications den where Christopher Boyce had worked, the place he had gained access to the top secret Pyramider documents he and Daulton sold to the Soviets. The discovery of Daulton's fingerprint putting him inside the Black Vault was incontrovertible evidence of his guilt, just as twenty-five of Boyce's fingerprints all over the compromised Pyramider documents had been evidence of his. It was the nail in the coffin that had sealed the case against Daulton. It was also utterly inexplicable.

Entry to and exit from the Black Vault had been so strictly controlled at TRW that there was no way in hell Daulton could have gotten inside to leave accidental evidence of his presence – and yet there it was, as clean and unambiguous and as damning as the security camera photos of him entering the Russian Embassy in Mexico City. The implications were chilling. When I'd asked him about it, he had given me a look so troubled that I knew he wasn't hiding a thing.

"And even if you do succeed," Blake continued, "what makes you think he won't just die mysteriously in his cell the night before he's set to walk free? It happens, you know."

I was starting to feel like I hadn't given as much thought to that fingerprint as I should have. Up to this point, all I'd really been focused on was Daulton's parole. But now, I felt like an out of breath mountaineer who realizes halfway up the mountain that she's left her oxygen cylinders at base camp. And I felt stupid to have missed a sign that had been before me the whole time.

"How do you know about that?" I asked him. "The fingerprint."

"It's no secret."

"No. But I don't know very many people who'd go to the trouble of reading all twenty-thousand pages of court transcripts. Unless you attended the trial?"

"What's the difference? What matters is that we both know it's true and we know that fingerprint was planted. Maybe by the FBI, maybe by the CIA. Whoever did it, it was done to guarantee a guilty verdict."

There was a curious inflection in Blake's voice. The way he said the word "we" made me wonder to whom he was referring – him and me, or he and Daulton.

Blake gave me a long stare. Then he said, "Look, I know I called you out here to talk about issues that could help free your friend. But I'll be honest with you. It's nothing that will be of any use to you. Not the way you're going about it."

Inside, a tiny pinprick hole formed on the surface of my hope bubble. I already knew what would come next: the all-too-familiar rush of disappointment as yet another curtain was lifted to reveal nothing but an empty stage.

"Then why the hell are we even talking?"

"Because as far as I can determine, you're closer to him than anyone else."

He was right. I'd been making the drive up from San Diego to Lompoc every weekend for the past two months. You get to know a person well when there's nothing else to do but sit and talk.

"Okay," I sighed, and crossed my arms. "Then why don't you just lay it on me and let's cut the bullshit?"

Blake took a small step forward and leaned in close, as if he were about to drop the secret of the century. I held my ground, but my grip around the car key tightened. When Blake spoke, it was in the tone of someone imparting a vital secret.

"Has he ever talked to you about helicopters?"

"Helicopters?"

"Helicopters. Has he mentioned them before?"

I stared at him blankly. "No. Why?"

Blake began to move his hand to the inside breast pocket of his jacket. For the first time since the start of our conversation, I felt a sense of alarm as a single thought came over me: *Nobody else in the world knows where I am.*

"If I asked you to pass something on to him," he began, but never got a chance to finish his sentence.

A blinding light splashed over us. In an instant, the parking lot was illuminated in white light. I turned to its source and shielded my eyes. A Santa Barbara PD cruiser was making its creeping approach, spotlight ablaze.

As I stepped toward the light I noticed the entire parking lot had emptied, except for my car. The cruiser pulled up beside me and shut off its spotlight.

"This lot's closed after dusk," the cop said. "Is that your car?"

"Yes," I answered. "We're leaving."

The cop threw me a quizzical look, then put the cruiser back into gear and rolled away. He flipped the spotlight on again as he drove the length of the parking lot, casting a beam of light out across the rising tide.

When I turned back to face Blake, he was gone.

"Fuck," I hissed.

I lingered another full minute, waiting to see if Blake would emerge from wherever he had disappeared. By the time the PD cruiser finished its circuit of the parking lot and began moving back in my direction, I knew our rendezvous was officially aborted.

I walked to my car, got in, and headed back to Lompoc.

***

The next morning, I dialed the *Lompoc Record* from the phone in my motel room. I asked if they had a staff reporter named Guy Blake. The lady I spoke to said she'd never heard the name before.

"I didn't think so," I said, and thanked her.

For the next half hour, I stared out the window of my motel room and wondered who the hell I'd actually met in that parking lot in Santa Barbara.

I decided if he contacted me again, I wouldn't consider anything he had to say until he came clean on who he was. I didn't get that chance. I never heard from Guy Blake again.

FALCON CAGED

Chris
(August 21, 1981)

Christopher Boyce tapped his foot to the rhythm of the music and wished he were dead. He might have preferred a nice John Philip Sousa march to Kool & the Gang's "Celebration," but it wasn't the song driving him to despair – it was his newfound company.

The movement of his foot was an unconscious action, more motor reflex than anything. The thoughts of death, on the other hand – the ones that raced through his brain with a speed and weight that nearly blotted out his vision – were purely conscious.

He considered ways of doing it himself. He could ask to use the bathroom, then shatter the mirror with a single fist-pump and have a shard of glass through his jugular sooner than they could break down the door and stop him. He could launch himself headfirst like a missile through the hotel window that even now peered out onto a depressingly dreary Port Angeles night, but he wasn't sure a fall from two stories would kill him, even if he did land on his head. In the end, Chris knew he could no more take his own life than that of another human being. And so he sat and stared, and tapped his foot and prayed for a swift and merciful death. Instead, he got more music.

It was radiating from the adjoining hotel room, where a team of more than a dozen U.S. Marshals and FBI agents had transformed their task force command post into an impromptu party zone. The rest of the crew – there were twenty-eight of them in total who had been sent to this small corner of the continent, each of them chosen for their expertise in finding people who didn't want to be found – were either on their way or already packing their bags in preparation to be shuttled to their next assignments. Work in the service of the law meant no rest for the weary, many of them had come to learn.

The mumble of voices played like an incessantly looping bass line, and the shouts of laughter that erupted from the other side of the door struck his ear like cymbal crashes. At one point, a hollow pop and a ricocheting WHAP against the ceiling signaled champagne. Chris wondered numbly if the faceless partiers had cleaned out the local bubbly supply on his account. He also wondered how the other residents of the hotel were appreciating the racket.

Chris raised his shackled wrists and motioned to the two marshals who were seated across from him at the hotel room table, playing cards. From his seated position on the edge of the room's bed, Chris looked like the most dispassionate spectator in history.

"I don't suppose there's any chance we could do without these?" he asked them. They were the first words he'd spoken since they'd brought him here.

One of them, a twenty-something guy with meaty shoulders and a military flat-top, wrinkled his nose and gave Chris a considering look. "I seriously doubt that," he said, and the tone in his voice had a genuine note of regret. "But I can ask Denny." He looked at his partner, who only shrugged.

It hadn't been a serious request, just an attempt to shatter the depressing silence. But before he could tell the marshal to forget about it, the guy was up and walking for the door. He looked almost eager to get away, something Chris couldn't blame him for. He wasn't exactly conversational company. Besides, it sounded like the guys next door were having a lot more fun.

The marshal cracked the adjoining door and poked his head through the threshold. As he did, the muffled sound of voices and music came spilling in with treble clarity, landing like an unwanted ray of sunlight on a scene of perfect gloom. He wished suddenly that he'd kept his stupid mouth shut.

Beyond the open door, he could see the dial of a bedside radio tuned to the local FM hit machine and shadows moving on the wall. There must have been close to twenty people in there now, probably standing elbow to elbow. From the sounds of it, they were having a great time.

Someone he hadn't seen before – obviously another marshal or FBI agent – poked his head in from the party room and lifted a plastic cup brimming with champagne. "Hey, Chris!" the man said. He looked like a New Year's Eve partier just getting revved up. "Cheers!"

The familiarity in that complete stranger's voice was disconcerting, as if he'd known Chris for years. Realizing that it had been longer than eighteen months since his escape from Lompoc and probably just as long that some of the people here had been assigned to track him down, he figured the guy probably did know him. And pretty well, too. Forcing a grim smile, he nodded and watched the man throw his head back, swallowing his drink.

A moment later, the flat-topped marshal who'd been conferring with someone in the other room was swallowed by the din and Denny Behrend entered the room in his place. He was still wearing the same flannel button-up he had on an hour earlier when they'd arrested Chris at the Pit Stop, a drive-in burger joint around the corner.

The U.S. Marshals' point man for the Port Angeles leg of the manhunt, Denny had spent the last three weeks canvassing town alongside a small undercover army of fellow marshals and FBI agents, all looking for Chris. Tonight, Denny had a smile on his face that said it all: he'd caught his man and all was right with the world again.

"Sorry, Chris." Denny shut the door behind him and the sound of the festivities receded mercifully. "The cuffs stay on." He sat down at the table next to the other marshal, who was now shuffling the cards with expert dexterity.

"As you can imagine," Denny continued, "you've got everyone here thinking you might pull a Houdini and disappear right in front of our eyes. So until we can get you outta Dodge, you don't leave our sight and the cuffs don't come off."

Denny held out a half-empty pack of Marlboros to Chris. "Will these do? Not sure if they're your brand. I don't smoke, myself, but the guys next door are feeling pretty charitable tonight."

Chris bowed his head gratefully and picked a cigarette out of the pack gingerly, holding his handcuffed wrists together as he did. The action of having to do so put a knot in his gut and reminded him that soon, it would come as second nature. His heart darkened at the realization.

Denny sat back in his chair and looked Chris up and down. "Is everything good?" he asked. It was as if he sensed Chris fading into some dark mental recess and was trying to keep him tied to this reality. He had about a million questions for Chris, none of which could be answered if his newly acquired guest sank too far into himself. "Everyone treating you okay? You hungry? We didn't exactly let you finish your dinner."

Not a half hour earlier, Chris had been sitting behind the wheel of his Oldsmobile in the Pit Stop parking lot, just sinking his teeth into the last half of his cheeseburger when the sudden appearance of a dozen men with handguns froze him in place.

It was Denny's voice that he heard first. Those two simple words – "Hi, Chris" – were the first time in more than a year and a half anyone had addressed him by his true name. During that time he'd gone by a handful of aliases: Jim, Jimmy, Anthony, Tony, even Kid. But never once Chris. The sound of his name being spoken aloud struck him with an odd combination of terror and relief. He didn't have time to process the emotion. A second later, they were on him.

One of the marshals had climbed into the car and slid across the Oldsmobile's enormous bench seat without him even realizing it, and when he grabbed hold of Chris's elbow to slap the handcuffs on, he found the arm stiff, unyielding. "Drop the hamburger," the marshal ordered. Almost in defense of the absurdity of his words, he added, "I don't want to get grease on my cuffs."

Chris obliged, and that was that. It was a textbook arrest. No standoff, no shootout, no proclamations of never being taken alive. It was also the last way he had ever envisioned being recaptured.

He shook his head and took a deep drag from the cigarette. "I'm okay, thanks." Then, noticing the earnest expression on Denny's face: "I appreciate it, though. Thank you."

Denny Behrend was a United States Marshal with a reputation for two things: going after his man like a dog after a bone, and treating that man with the utmost respect once the chase was up. Now that the hard work was done, it was all magnanimity and pleasantries from here on out.

"I know you probably don't exactly feel like celebrating," he said to Chris, "but I hope you don't mind. There's standing room only next door." Denny tapped the marshal still performing fifty-two-card theatrics. "Go next door and get yourself a cup of champagne. Tell the guys they can spread out in here."

Denny turned back to Chris and smiled. "I can't tell you how good it is to see you in the flesh. You get so used to staring at a wanted poster that you become amazingly familiar with a person's face after a while. I'm happy to say you look exactly like your photo. And a little surprised."

"Sorry if I'm not as enthusiastic to see you fellows," Chris replied dryly.

Now there were people spilling in from the adjoining room, bringing their drinks — and the party — with them. One of them bumped into Chris and nearly spilled his drink onto his lap, then clapped a hand on his shoulder apologetically.

"Sorry about that, buddy."

Someone pulled out a camera and the marshals took turns posing with him like a prized catch. Denny let it go on for a moment, then waved them away.

"Do you know we had people as far as South Africa and Australia looking for you?" Denny asked. He had to raise his voice to be heard. "Turns out you were up here the whole time."

That last sentence was spoken with only the slightest hint of a question mark at the end, but Chris caught it. He thought Denny looked and sounded like a man poised to launch a volley of questions, and decided to indulge his new captor. After all, what harm could come now? Just as long as he kept Billy, Calvin and Gloria out of it. They were the people who had helped him the most and he swore to himself that he'd do everything he could to keep them out of it, even if it meant getting a stiffer sentence. As far as he was concerned, he would never be a free man again. Might as well go down in flames.

"Actually, I wasn't here the whole time," Chris said. "I was in and out. I spent a lot of time in Idaho. Robber's Roost area. You know, the first place anyone on the run would go? And apparently the last place the feds or marshals would think to look."

Chris thought about the innumerable times he'd spent hiking the wilderness of northern Idaho in the last eighteen months, drifting across the border into Canada and back again with unbelievable ease. Now he wished more than anything that he'd simply kept on moving.

"So much for solid leads," Denny said. He checked his wrist watch. In about forty-five minutes, he and his team would escort Chris to nearby Fairchild Airport. From there, a U.S. Coast Guard helicopter would fly them to Seattle where the long process of arraignment would begin.

"I've got one question I've been burning to ask you for about a year and a half now," Denny said.

Chris lifted his eyebrows. "Just one?"

Denny shrugged, took a sip of champagne, and hit Chris with a smile bright enough to dazzle a dentist. "It might require a multi-part answer."

"Ask away." Chris sounded tired.

Denny scooted forward in his chair and set his elbows on his knees. "How in the *hell* did you get out of that place?"

Some of the others gathered around, U.S. Marshals and FBI agents alike, all looking at Chris with the interest of a captive audience.

My captors, my captives.

He could have laughed, but didn't. Instead, he cleared his throat nervously and began.

"Well, getting into that hole was the easy part." He knew he didn't have to explain. The newspaper articles that reported his escape had made a great deal of the uncovered sump drain and the tools he'd left behind. The marshals and the FBI would have been well studied on the mechanics of his escape preparations, but as yet nobody had figured out exactly how Chris managed to get over that fence without being seen. It was time to set the record straight.

"Climbing out of that hole and getting over the fence," he continued, "was the hard part. The yard gets deathly quiet after dark..."

THE INVISIBLE MAN

Chris
(January 21, 1980)

. . . It's sort of like being in a church, only worse, if you can imagine. If you make a sound inside a cathedral, you get stared at. Make a sound in a prison yard after dark, you get shot at.

So I waited. I sat in that hole for hours with my head just inches below the sump drain grate until the sun was down and I knew I couldn't wait any longer. Just as I getting ready to make my move, I heard a sound.

I held my breath and listened. It sounded like quiet whistling, the kind you do when you're on some mindless chore, but out in the deserted activity yard it sounded almost ghostly.

It was one of the night guards doing his rounds. He was out there by the perimeter fence with his flashlight, looking for anything out of the ordinary. I waited for the sound to go away, but it only grew louder.

Seconds later, I heard footsteps moving toward me on the grass. If I could have, I'd have ducked further into the hole – but it was so tight and shallow that I didn't even have room to squirm. I saw the beam of a flashlight bounce across the grate just over my head and before my brain even had a chance to react, there he was, standing right on top of me. The heel of his boot was so close I could have reached through the grate and touched it. All he had to do was glance down and he would have seen me.

The guard was probably only there for a few seconds, but it felt like forever. I heard a scratching, then the sound of a match being struck. He stopped whistling and lit a cigarette. When he dropped the match, it fell straight through the grate and landed on my wrist. Then he was gone, whistling that familiar melody I still can't place.

I held my breath until I was sure he was gone. My whole body was drenched in sweat. When it was finally quiet again, I let out a breath. That was a close enough call for me, but I knew it wouldn't be the last if I didn't move. He'd be back around again in less than half an hour, and I couldn't afford to be there if he decided to pass over the grate again. It was time to come out of the hole.

The fear of sitting there, readying myself to climb out, was like nothing I had ever experienced. It was paralyzing. The only thing that pushed me to action was the knowledge that if I didn't move now, I'd never get another chance.

I reached up, grabbed the grate with both hands, and pushed it up and out of the way. It made an ungodly scraping sound. I thought the whole world must be able to hear it. I tried to stand, but couldn't. My legs were completely useless, numb from hours of sitting with my knees bent up into my chest. So I did the only thing I could do – I stuck the pruning shears into my pants pocket, clamped the little improvised ladder between my teeth, and pulled myself out of the ground with my arms.

Once I was out, I rolled over onto my back and lay there waiting for my legs to wake up. I was completely vulnerable. Anyone looking in my direction could have seen me – especially the guard standing lookout in the new gun tower. I could see his silhouette from where I was, but for whatever reason, he didn't see me. My legs were taking too long to wake up, so I rolled over on my stomach and started crawling with my elbows.

From my position, I was finally able to confirm what I'd already suspected. If I lined myself up between the gun tower and the sally port pillar, I could get to the fence without being seen. I had to crawl about fifteen feet in plain sight before I could reach cover, but once I was out of the line of fire, I relaxed a little bit. Another thirty feet, and I was at the sally port. By then my legs had started coming back to life, so I pulled myself up and rested with my back against the pillar.

I peeked out from around the corner. I could see the gun tower guard clearly now. He was staring down at a glowing green console in front of him, totally unaware of my presence. All around, the perimeter was lit up like Christmas.

This is impossible, I kept telling myself. *He'll have to be blind not to see me.*

Then another voice inside my head chimed in, repeating the same words over and over like some kid's stupid playground mantra: *I am the invisible man... I am the invisible man...* It felt ridiculous, but it worked. It buffered my nerve. I reached into my pants pocket and pulled out the pruning shears.

There were two fences surrounding the prison. The inside fence was only eight feet tall, but the outside fence was easily twice that. Between them, in what everyone called the Kill Zone, were endless rows of razor wire. In order to get out, I would have had to climb both fences without being seen or heard and navigate straight through that minefield. But a major security lapse, caused by the intersection of the two fences at the sally port pillar, negated that.

All I had to do was cut my way to the top of the interior fence. Once I was up, I'd only have to clear a path through the razor wire coils on the connecting fence. From there, it was just a ten-foot drop into the open sally port exit. Simple enough... if I didn't get shot first.

The way to the top of the inside fence was blocked by two barbed wire extension arms. Each arm had six strands of wire. I was going to have to cut through all of that to get to the top of the fence, but that wasn't my only problem.

Just four inches under the lowest strand was the perimeter snitch wire. Even the slightest touch would set off alarms everywhere. It sat there like a viper waiting to strike. I was going to have to somehow swing my body over it as I climbed. I prayed all that bar work in the prison gym would pay off.

Again, those silly words: *I am the invisible man... I am the invisible man...*

My legs were shaking so bad that my knees were knocking. I knew I was going to have to be exposed to the security lights for at least two minutes, maybe longer. My only hope was that I could move fast enough to get out without being seen.

I reached out from behind the pillar and cut the lowest barbed wire strand. It twanged like a broken guitar string. I went for the second wire and drove the shears through that. Up to now, it was only my arm that had been exposed to the light, but I had to come out of the shadows to reach the third.

I leaned the ladder against the pillar and stepped up to reach the next strand, but my knees were shaking so uncontrollably that I fell over. I picked myself up and tried again. Thankfully, this time my legs cooperated and I got through the rest of the strands in a matter of seconds.

Now the hard part.

Just as I'd practiced it a thousand times in my head, I grabbed the fence post with both hands and threw my legs up and over the snitch wire. Both feet landed perfectly on top of the inside fence, but the impact was so loud I was positive I'd just given myself away.

I looked back up to the tower, expecting to see the barrel of a rifle pointing down at me. Nothing. The guard was still up there, but it was obvious he hadn't seen or heard a thing. I was just readying myself for the next step when I saw the lights of the perimeter patrol truck coming my direction.

All I could do was backtrack down the way I'd climbed. Pushing myself clear of the snitch wire, I jumped backwards and ducked behind the sally port pillar just as the truck pulled to a stop on the other side of the fence. I heard the doors open and saw two flashlight beams bobbing over the fence I'd just been standing on, then across the cut barbed wire strands that were now hanging loose. Two voices were talking over the hum of the pickup's engine, but I couldn't understand a word they said.

Had they seen me? If they had, every alarm in the prison would be screaming by now. Had someone tipped them off to my escape? If that was the case, they wouldn't have waited for me to make it this far before stopping me. Billy would never have breathed a word of it to anyone, and I knew I could trust Calvin with my life. Then I remembered the last conversation that I'd had with Daulton. Could he have done this to me?

Before I had a chance to finish the thought, the doors of the pickup truck slammed closed and it drove away. I watched it round the corner and disappear from sight. I didn't hesitate. I got to my feet and came back out of the shadows. I set the ladder back in place, boosted myself up, grabbed ahold of the post like I'd done before, and swung my legs over the snitch wire. My second try was sloppier, but I made it well enough to pull myself back up on top of the fence.

Now I could see there was still one more hurdle to overcome – a barrier of razor wire coils strung vertically along the intersection where the inside and outside fences met. Using the tips of my fingers, I gently took hold of the first lethal-sharp coil and hooked it onto the one above it. It held. It was painstaking work. More than that, it was costing me valuable time in the security lights. But there was no other way. Slowly but surely, I opened a path upward.

My fingertips were bleeding from the razor cuts. The blood concentrated my mind. The more I focused on it, the less I thought about the guard in the tower. There was nothing I could do about him, anyway. If he saw me, he saw me. If he didn't, he didn't. After about a minute, I had spread a path just wide enough to fit through. I inched my way through the opening and climbed to the top of the second fence, balancing myself like some insane tightrope walker.

This was it. I stood straight up and looked at the guard in the gun tower. He didn't see me.

I am the invisible man!

With that last thought, I jumped from the fence to the concrete below.

It wasn't an easy landing. The drop was only ten feet, but somehow my left shoe got snagged in the razor wire as I went down. It was the prison's last attempt to hang onto me, and it almost worked. I landed awkwardly and twisted my ankle, but I wasn't about to stick around to doctor my wound. I got up and hobbled to where the sally port driveway met the service road.

I turned right, away from the gun tower, and broke into a dash. The pain in my ankle felt like the stab of a knife, but I ignored it. I ran east, kicking up dirt between the outside perimeter fence and prison pump-house. I ran with everything I had in me, expecting a bullet to smash into the back of my head any second to end it all.

If I die now, I remember thinking, *at least I'll die on the free side of this damn fence.*

I cleared the east corner of the pump-house and hooked north, racing back into the bright lights, moving faster than I'd ever run before, knees and elbows all the way. Now I was running straight at the second gun tower, the one off to the northeast. I passed so close that I could have bounced a rock off its roof. Out of the corner of my eye, I saw the guard inside staring down at his glowing instrument panel. If he looked up, it was over.

My mind was screaming now...

Don't look up, you asshole, don't you do it!

...and just as my eyes focused on the tree line of the surrounding woods, I saw the guard reach for something...

Fuck me, he's going for his gun! It's over...

...but it was his thermos he was reaching for, not his rifle. The bastard never took his eyes off whatever it was that he was focusing on so intently, and that stroke of luck was what saved my life.

Suddenly I was out of the light – swallowed by darkness, shooting across the last two hundred yards into the safety of the tree line, lungs burning, sides aching, ankle throbbing, hands bleeding. But alive. And finally, free.

THE FOUR-SIDED TRIANGLE

Cait
(August 22, 1981)

Some days, life takes a cold, hard look at you and says, "Check it out! You're gonna love this." And off you go down some random side-street you never thought you'd travel. That's what happened on the morning of August 22, 1981 – the day I learned that Christopher Boyce had been recaptured.

It was a Saturday. One of the first in several weeks I was home and not waking up to the dubious morning comforts of the Lompoc Motel, eating Chinese nightly and spending every possible minute of the impossibly brief visiting hours interviewing Daulton.

Instead of hoisting myself up at the crack of too-early a.m., I let myself sleep in. This weekend, it would be me and only me. Part one of that was making a cup of the strongest brew in history. Part two was the daily paper, which lay waiting for me outside.

By the time I put my French press through the paces, it was already half past nine. Normally by that time on a day off I'd have taken my board to the beach and been ass deep in the surf, but this morning I was suffering the ill effects of another semi-all-nighter spent poring over the voluminous reams of Daulton's pre-sentencing report.

The pre-sentencing report (sometimes called a PSI, which is short for pre-sentencing investigation) is the document that a judge refers to before pronouncing sentence. Made up of in-depth interviews with the prisoner, their family members and other people in the community, it's considered the most confidential of all court documents and isn't even included in the court file or shared with the prisoner. The only people with access to it are the trial judge, the defense attorney and – further on down the line, sometimes decades or maybe never – the parole board. The purpose of the pre-sentencing report is to give a judge a comprehensive picture of the personality of the convicted. Their psychological health, their criminal history, the likelihood they'll commit more crimes in the future, everything.

Daulton's pre-sentencing report had painted him a dangerous sociopath. But the differences between it and his later evaluations were stark. By that, I mean like night and day. In contrast to his PSI, every single psychological and behavioral report he had received in the preceding four years described a model prisoner who kept his nose clean and did as he was told. The fact that there'd been such a dramatic change in such a short period of time was encouraging to say the least. I figured it would bode extremely well for him if he ever got an opportunity to sit down in front of the parole commission.

Of course, that was a mighty big "if."

I threw on a pair of shorts and a t-shirt and headed out the front door of my tiny, five-hundred-square-foot Hillcrest bungalow with coffee in hand to get the newspaper. Outside, the Santa Ana winds had arrived early. Hot dry gusts swept through the valley, rushing from the mountains to the coast to stoke the waves on the shore into a perfect frenzy. Days like today were the kind that every die-hard surfer looked forward to, and I promised myself I'd get to the beach to take advantage before too long. But the newspaper headline that stared up at me from the cracked cement sidewalk changed my plans.

FUGITIVE SPY CAPTURED ON WEST COAST.

I bent over and picked up the newspaper with my free hand, holding it before me like some curious discovery. To someone walking past, I probably would have looked like an illiterate trying to comprehend the meaning of the big black printed symbols. Fortunately, my neighbors already knew I was a bit crazy.

In smaller print just below the bold headline were these words: BOYCE LED MARSHALS ON 19-MONTH MANHUNT.

The sound of the porcelain mug shattering hit my ears before I even realized I'd dropped it. A full second later came the blinding sting of hot coffee scalding my flesh. I opened my mouth to scream but found my awareness yanked violently back to the headline. I might have stood there all day like that, wavering between physical agony and astonishment, if the phone inside my house hadn't started to ring.

I knew who it was before I even picked up the receiver.

"Did you hear?" Daulton's voice was urgent. It was laced with a bizarre mixture of horror, outrage, and a pinch of what I can only describe as spiteful joy. I could tell by the way he held the phone away from his mouth that he was struggling to restrain his voice. "My co-defendant's been apprehended."

I was still too dumbfounded to say anything, so I didn't. Instead, I unrolled the paper and laid it face up on my kitchen counter. There was a gritty black-and-white shot of Christopher Boyce in handcuffs underneath the headline, but with the story less than twelve hours old and no updated photos, the newspaper had re-run the now-familiar AP stock image taken in 1977 during the espionage trial.

"Cait?"

I grunted, my eyes still glued to the headline and the photo.

"They found him up in Washington. Caught him munching on a burger and hauled his ass to Seattle."

I cradled the phone between my shoulder and chin and leaned into the kitchen sink, running my wounded arm under a flow of cool water. "I know," I said, absently.

There was a silence on the other end of the line. Suddenly he blurted out, "You knew and you didn't think to tell me?"

"Daulton, relax. I just found out."

This time it was his turn to grunt, but that single vocal expression spoke far more than any words could have. He didn't believe me. That was no surprise. Daulton didn't come by trust easy these days, if he ever had at all. Who could blame him?

"This is good news," I said.

"Oh really? How do you figure that? Now thanks to this, my name will probably be plastered alongside his in every damn newspaper in the world. A lot of good that'll do me."

"At least now he'll be able to tell them you had nothing to do with the escape."

"Unless he decides to implicate me somehow. Which I wouldn't put it past him to do. If he does that, I'm screwed."

Daulton had an answer for everything.

"He wouldn't do that," I said. "I can talk to him."

More silence.

"Daulton?"

"I'm sure you'd love that. Maybe you can get his autograph while you're at it."

He hung up. I sighed, then set the phone down and read the article all the way through. I read it again, then a third time. Two days later, I was on a plane to Seattle.

***

Looking back on it now, it's hard to say exactly why I felt compelled to buy that plane ticket. It was even harder to justify it to myself at the time, but I think I was driven by the belief that getting as close to the story as possible would reveal something – anything – that might help me with Daulton's case.

It turned out to be a fortuitous journey. Not only because I was able to land a one-of-a-kind designer purse at killer cost, but because while I was up there, I met Denny Behrend.

Denny had been the arresting marshal on the case, the same guy who would go on to be credited for shouting the infamous words, "Drop the hamburger! You're under arrest." Later, Denny would tell me the truth behind that hugely exaggerated utterance and who had actually said it. But to be honest, I didn't give a damn.

What I really wanted to know was if at any time over the last year and a half the U.S. Marshals or the FBI had tracked Christopher Boyce's movements to southern California. Or any other tidbit of privileged information that would help me clear up the insane notion that had developed in my head, the one that kept telling me the mysterious Guy Blake was somehow connected to Boyce.

If it turned out to be true, I was in way over my head. The fact that Blake had reached out to me to try to communicate with Daulton might have meant that all three were involved in something I wanted no part of.

Asking Daulton point blank was out of the question. First, I couldn't let him know that I had doubts about his honesty. Second, if I was wrong and he had no knowledge of Boyce's whereabouts during his escape, my asking would destroy every bit of trust I'd managed to gain with him. I knew that if I let that happen, Daulton would spend the rest of his life behind bars. People weren't exactly lining up to help him out, if you know what I mean.

As soon as I had packed my overnight bag, I dug up the phone number of an old college friend who I knew worked at the federal courthouse in Seattle. I hadn't talked to Paula in close to three years and I felt terrible reconnecting just to ask her for a favor. Thankfully, she apparently didn't realize it had been that long.

I knew Paula wouldn't have enough pull to get me an audience with Boyce, so I told her I'd be willing to talk to anyone in the know who I could pump for information. As it turned out, she knew the one and only Denny Behrend. No lie – it's a small world, after all.

Denny had learned more about Boyce's whereabouts in the first few days following the recapture than in the whole nineteen months the marshals had been pursuing him. Apparently, Boyce liked to talk a lot. Although he wasn't as forthcoming with answers to the growing questions about his possible involvement in a string of bank robberies, he was known for regaling his captors with other tales of his escapades.

Ever the professional, Denny didn't tell me anything I couldn't have learned by reading the paper. I had to hand it to him. I tried hard, but he resisted harder. And through it all, he never once lost the easy-going charm that made him a natural leader among the tight-knit brotherhood that was the U.S. Marshals.

He was also one of the straightest shooters I'd ever met. Literally thirty seconds after Paula did the introductions – the three of us huddled in a closet-sized conference room somewhere in the back of the courthouse on the eve of Boyce's first court appearance – Denny asked me outright: "So what's your interest in Christopher Boyce that made you come all the way up here from San Diego?"

"Purely anthropological," I tried, but he wasn't buying it. I decided to come clean. "Actually, I'm representing Andrew Daulton Lee for parole."

Paula's eyebrows lifted so high they nearly ascended from her forehead. "Wow," she said. "You didn't tell me that." Apparently, in my rush to secure an "in," I had left out some major details.

I gave them the short version of the long story, which took about three minutes. When I was done, Paula was looking at me like I'd just revealed my plans to scale Everest by hand. Denny's reaction, on the other hand, wasn't quite what I had been expecting. Instead of exhibiting surprise, or immediate suspicion, he simply said, "Wow."

"And that's why I'm here," I said. "If there's any information that my client's co-defendant can offer up, I'm glad to make use of it." Daulton would have been so very proud of me for not saying the Boyce name aloud.

"What kind of information?"

"Well for one, a lot of people still think that Daulton had something to do with Boyce's escape. Some of the people who share that belief also sit on parole board commissions."

Denny nodded his head slowly. Finally he said, "Well I'm sorry. I'm not privy to any information that involves Mr. Lee in Mr. Boyce's escape plan. I'm also not privy to any information that proves he *wasn't* involved, either."

Strike one. Luckily, I still had two swings left. I had his attention, so I had to ask.

"Is there any way that you can get me in to talk to Boyce?"

Denny shook his head regrettably. "I'm sorry. That, I can't do."

Strike two. I decided to save my last at-bat for some other time. Paula shot me a quick *I'm sorry* glance that I shrugged off with a smile. "Nothing ventured, nothing gained."

"Good luck in your efforts," Denny said. "I'm sure you're great at what you do, but if you ask me, it'll be one cold day in hell when either of those two go free."

"We'll see about that."

My blind confidence must have been either remarkably admirable or astoundingly humorous, because Denny gave me his number to keep in touch. Naturally, I took it.

***

Outside the Seattle federal courthouse, news crews and photographers lined a cordoned-off path that led from the building's front door to an awaiting sedan surrounded by police cars.

The courthouse door flew open once. The waiting crowd tensed in anticipation, then relaxed as the door drifted slowly closed again. It looked like an accident, or maybe a false exit designed to alert the marshals to the presence of any snipers who fancied the idea of offing a "traitor." But after having spent just a few minutes in Denny's presence, I'd learned enough to know that the marshals sometimes enjoyed toying with their captive audience. Enough that maybe one of the junior recruits had shoved the door open just to get a rise from the waiting reporters. It might even have been Denny himself.

A full two minutes crawled past. This time, when the door finally did open again, an entourage of marshals spilled out, each of them casting watchful eyes for any irregular activity in the gathered crowd. They looked like Secret Service agents, only not quite so squarely dressed. All wore coats and ties and gave the appearance of a group of high-power executives heading out from the mother of all board meetings. It was only their stoic expressions and rapid movements that gave any indication they were anything more than that.

After a few seconds I saw Denny, ever the Dapper Dan, sporting a three-piece suit complete with a form-fitting vest that accentuated his athletic build. Moving along beside him, guarded by the circle of walking polyester suits, was Christopher Boyce.

His wrists and feet were shackled, and he had on a blue short-sleeved jumpsuit with the collar popped defiantly up. The top buttons of the jumpsuit were undone, revealing a bare chest underneath. The way he wore his hair made him look like a cross between Elvis Presley and James Dean.

I didn't exactly swoon. In fact, I almost laughed. But the moment Christopher Boyce fixed his stare on the small crowd of onlookers that had assembled where I stood, I was mesmerized.

My mother taught me a lot of things. One of them was to choose the men I fell for wisely. At that moment, just about everything she ever taught me flew straight out the window. Here was a man who looked like he was going to be busy for the next hundred or so years doing hard time for his crimes. And there I was, spellbound. *Oy vey.*

***

I'd have to be either lying or stupid to say that I had no clue how Daulton felt about me during those years. I was a single female and he was a desperately lonely man. What's worse, he was completely incapable of doing anything about his loneliness.

In many ways, I knew his attachment had less to do with me and more to do with what I represented. Not only had I become one of his few lifelines to the outside world, I had also come to symbolize something he wanted more than anything else in life – his freedom.

I never told him about my trip to Seattle. I figured there were some efforts I could undertake on his behalf he didn't need to know about. I certainly never breathed a word to him about my friendship with Denny Behrend, or the fact that I continued to stay in touch with Denny once his responsibilities to the Boyce case had finished.

Nor did I ever discover any connection at all between Christopher Boyce and the mysterious Guy Blake. As Boyce's trial proceeded and more details began to emerge about where he had gone after escaping, the more ridiculous it all started to sound. Gradually, I reached the point where I'd flush with hot shame any time I was reminded that I had entertained such a crazy idea to begin with. I finally forgave myself for my stupidity, but it was a forgiveness that was long in coming.

Back home, I kicked the work on Daulton's parole brief into high gear. I was convinced now more than ever he stood a good chance of at least being seen by the parole commission, thanks to none other than Boyce himself. I knew I could easily make the case that Daulton was a man who had assimilated into prison life peaceably and was considered a "model prisoner," but it was what would not be said that had the potential to make the greatest impact.

Even to someone with only a passing knowledge of the case, Daulton's prior association with Boyce would serve as a natural counterpoint. Here was a man who *didn't* do the kinds of things his former partner in crime did. Like escape from prison. Or rob banks. Or waste millions of taxpayer dollars making complete asses of the FBI, the U.S. Marshals, and Interpol. It was a long shot, but a shot nonetheless.

I could see the framework beginning to take shape. Yet I still felt contacting Boyce directly was the best way of covering all bases. Naturally, Daulton was vehemently opposed when I finally pressed the subject.

"You don't want to go there," he would say. "He'll drag you into his personal hell just the way he dragged me into his. Just look at the mess he got me into."

Even back then, I was under no illusions. I believed Daulton was just as guilty as Boyce and that both deserved equal blame for what had happened to them. But I knew arguing that point with him would serve no purpose other than to send him into another of his tiresome, brooding funks. So I decided to maintain the peace, and that required me to keep the news of my communications with Christopher Boyce entirely to myself.

Truth be told, I liked that idea far better anyway. And although I didn't fully realize it at the time, deep in the back of my mind I had already begun to chip away at the strategy that would someday result in Christopher Boyce's release from prison.

If I had known then how long it would take, or if I'd have been given a glimpse of all that would have to happen to get to that place, I might have run the other way. But I was young and headstrong and full to the brim with optimistic pride. And as everyone knows, youthful vigor always wins out over reason.

THE ROAD TO HELL

Chris
(March 26, 1982)

The first thing that went through Chris's mind as he was led into the graveyard-silent cell block of the Boise County Jail was that the crime rate in that part of the country must have been incredibly low. Aside from himself and his two escorts – Idaho's Supervisory Deputy U.S. Marshal and the Boise County Sheriff, both wearing cowboy boots and ten-gallon hats – there wasn't another soul in sight. Every one of the two dozen jail cells stood empty.

They walked him halfway down the length of the long corridor and stopped in front of a cell that sat directly below an enormous ventilation shaft in the ceiling.

"Freshest air on the block," the marshal announced as the sheriff plucked a key from a hoop ring attached to his belt and unlocked the cell door. Chris stepped inside and his handcuffs were removed.

The sound of the cell door being dragged closed again created an ominous growl that echoed from one end of the empty building to the other. It was punctuated by the deafening clang of steel against steel and the distinct click of the locking mechanism. The surreal scenario of having an entire cell block to himself seemed to jerk

Chris out of the dark, depressed silence that always descended on him when faced with the physical reality of confinement behind bars.

"You guys didn't have to clear the whole place out on account of little old me."

The sheriff, a rotund fifty-something man who'd greeted him with a handshake and heartfelt words of welcome, answered him from behind an enormous white mustache that concealed the lower half of his face. To Chris, the guy looked like an extra straight out of an old *Gunsmoke* episode. "Uncle Sam's orders, Mr. Boyce."

Chris bristled. It seemed that everywhere he went these days, people insisted on calling him that. Although he figured it was merely a show of respect or (more likely) a detached expression of formality, he found it acutely embarrassing to be referred to by a name he'd always associated with his father. "Is it normally this... barren?" he asked.

"Two days ago, this block was at ninety percent capacity," the sheriff said. "Today, and for the rest of your stay, it's all yours."

Chris looked at them both incredulously, and then turned his head to survey the rows upon rows of empty jail cells. "You're kidding."

"No joke," the marshal answered. "You're getting the VIP treatment from the great state of Idaho. At least until the trial's over and we deliver you back to the Bureau of Prisons."

The mere mention of the BOP was enough to cause Chris's stomach to double over onto itself, and despite his desire to be left alone to his thoughts, he suddenly wished for nothing less than a cell block overflowing with all manner of fellow internees and misanthropes – petty crooks, wife beaters, drunk drivers, belligerent assholes intent on sharing their misery with all those around them. At least the noise of their arguments and conversations might have been enough to keep the fear at bay, to temporarily still that intensifying gnawing in the pit of his stomach that had been with him since his recapture six months earlier.

In the intervening time, daily life had become a never-ending circuit of courtroom proceedings, visits with his attorney Bill

Dougherty, and what the marshals referred to as "perp walks" – carefully staged photo ops where a select group of reporters and photographers, usually those with the most recognizable names or the highest visibility, were given a heads-up anytime Chris was to enter or exit a building.

Instead of surreptitious entrances through back doors, the marshals – proud of having caught their man and all eager to have their names and faces displayed prominently in print – always insisted on bringing Chris through the front door, in plain sight of God and country, under the light of blinding flashbulbs and amid the incessant queries of reporters who shoved cameras and microphones into his face.

Chris! Did the KGB break you out of prison?

Is it true you robbed banks to finance an escape to the Soviet Union?

Are you planning to escape again?

He often found he had to bite his lip to prevent from spitting out the quips that came to mind following that particularly stupid question: *Haven't you heard? I'm escaping tonight at ten. News at eleven, asshole.*

And then, of course, there were always the go-for-the-jugular inquiries that seemed specifically framed to elicit an emotional response. These were always the worst for Chris, whose personal shame at having been caught was overshadowed only by the humiliation he knew his family was experiencing all over again.

Has your father forgiven you yet?

Are you on speaking terms with your family?

Despite these dizzying distractions, it was impossible for him to lose sight of what lay at the end of it all – a quick trip down the long, deep slide to hell itself. Even his sleep was tortured by that great awaiting fate, and if he didn't take conscious action to push his mind to other things, the weight of it all would become so overwhelming that he would become physically ill. As a consequence, he quickly lost some of the weight he'd managed to put on during his time as a free man in Bonners Ferry.

On February 23, 1982, U.S. District Judge Lawrence Lydick sentenced Chris to three years for escaping from Lompoc. With the case against him in Los Angeles wrapped up, it was time for Chris to be tried for the bank robberies he stood accused of committing during his time on the run. Boise, the capital city of the state in which he'd spent most of his time after his escape, would serve as center stage.

Charges had also been filed against two of Chris's closest friends, Calvin Robinson and Gloria White, for their alleged involvement in helping him plan the robberies. Since Gloria owned the cabin in Bonners Ferry where he had lived on and off before being recaptured, she was also charged with harboring a fugitive.

Chris was more worried about Gloria's fate than his own. Calvin was a friend who had put everything on the line to help him, but they both knew he was capable of fending for himself. Gloria, on the other hand, was a single mother with three underage children still at home. The idea that she might be taken down with Chris for having given him a warm place to sleep and some home-cooked meals was almost too appalling for him to consider.

"Can we get you anything?" the sheriff asked him. Chris was pacing the length of his cell, investigating his new surroundings. There was a bunk in the corner, one steel toilet, and a tiny sink – no mirror. "Some food, coffee, cigarettes... newspaper?"

He declined, but it wasn't long before he took his new jailers up on their hospitality. Every half hour, a different pair of sheriff's deputies would enter the cell block to check in on him and to ask him if he needed anything. It was a bit like having a constantly rotating staff of butlers. Only these servants had holstered guns and would likely not be agreeable to taking the night off if he asked them to.

The truth was, he enjoyed the company. Chris frequently went out of his way to talk with those eager to steal a word with the "infamous spy" or "daring escape artist" or "fearless bank robber" the press had built him up to be. He entertained their questions and sometimes even embellished his exploits for entertainment value and for the satisfaction of their rapt attention. But he came to form the strongest bond with a handful of marshals who'd been his constant attendants since his recapture in Port Angeles.

It was not a friendship, but a relationship based on mutual need. He needed the human interaction and the distraction that their company brought, and the marshals needed Chris on his best behavior. Each served the other well up to a certain point. Despite everything, the frequent conversations he had with the marshals always left him feeling desperately depressed. Most of the marshals he came into contact with were near his age, and they often caused him to think of the life he might have had now if he'd chosen a different path.

If any of the marshals close to him ever sensed this, they never said so in words, even if their actions indicated otherwise. Few ever spoke to Chris about their personal lives for more than a few minutes. It was as if they inherently knew that to share any more would have been like eating a five-course meal in front of a starving man.

"Go ahead and get comfortable," the marshal said. "The next ticket out isn't until tomorrow morning at eight. Then we'll head over to the courthouse and make all the formal introductions."

"Can't wait," Chris replied dryly, and the marshal and sheriff both chuckled. It was always easier to appreciate humor when you were standing on the other side of the bars.

In truth, he was looking forward to the start of the trial. Although he was no more eager to see the inside of another courtroom than he was a hellhole like Lompoc, the reality was even the stuffiest courtroom in the country was far better than the most luxurious prison cell the federal government could ever offer.

The idea of spending entire days among other free men and women, even at the price of having his hands and legs bound, was appealing, and Chris latched onto the possibility of a protracted trial. During that time, he'd at least have the opportunity to breathe free air. In prison, even the outdoor yards stank of captivity.

"We've also got a spacious shower facility reserved in your name," the sheriff said in a tone as cordial as a five-star hotel clerk. He motioned to the end of the corridor of vacant cells, where a tiled entry gave way to a long wall of showerheads. "You need a soak, just holler."

Chris thanked the sheriff; he thanked them both. It was an absurd act that made about as much sense as asking for another punch when you've just been beat to the ground, but these men were not responsible for his plight. When they left, he lay down on the bunk and closed his eyes.

***

A half hour later, the single steel door that barred exit from the cell block rattled open again and two pairs of footsteps echoed their way down the corridor toward him.

Chris looked up to see a female sheriff's deputy standing at the cell door, her golden hair pinned back in a regulation bun that took little from her appearance. She was holding a book in one hand and a pen in the other. Towering beside her was a muscular deputy with a Burt Reynolds mustache, carrying a food tray.

He had only enough time to wonder if mustaches were a prerequisite to men getting a spot on the local PD before the female deputy spoke up, her musical voice landing like a splash of color on a grey canvas.

"Would you care to trade your autograph for some coffee and éclairs?" she asked. He did not refuse.

Ten minutes later, the sheriff's deputies exited the cell block with an autographed paperback and an empty tray. It wasn't the first time Chris had been asked to sign the jacket of a book he hadn't written and it wouldn't be the last. He was polite about it, but the act felt vulgar. He didn't need any further reminders of the mistake that had landed him here.

As soon as the deputies were gone, he rose from his bunk and approached the cell door. It had only been opened once the entire time, to pass him a carafe of coffee and a tin mug, but for the remainder of the visit it had remained ajar. To the two deputies, the well-spoken prisoner had an air about him that seemed to betray everything they'd heard of his crimes until now – crimes that included not only selling classified secrets to the Soviet Union, but escaping from federal prison and embarking on a spree of bank robberies. Each had expected to meet a cold, calculating criminal. The person they met was instead intelligent, thoughtful, and had an understated wit that only made him all the more charming.

It was when the deputies rolled the jail cell door closed behind them that Chris noticed something strange. Different. The characteristic clang that had echoed throughout the building upon his first arrival sounded unusual. Lighter, as if it were missing some vital layer or component of sound.

He moved closer to the cell door, looking at it like some newly discovered curiosity. With one final glance around to ensure he was alone, he placed both hands on the bars. He took a deep breath and gave the cell door a gentle tug. It rolled open.

***

It's impossible to say whether or not Chris would have made it past the staff of the county jail even if he had been able to find a secondary unlocked passage out. Aside from the glaring oversight that had made escape possible in the first place, he had at least one thing in his favor: the clothes he wore were not prison regulation. Nor were they county jail attire. Rather than being forced to wear a standard issue orange jumpsuit, Chris was allowed to dress in a suit and tie for the duration of his stay in Boise.

It was a concession he'd insisted on and that his lawyer, Bill, had successfully lobbied for. And with the fateful twist of luck now before him, it was also the one thing that could have assured his chances of slipping unnoticed through the front door of the Boise County Jail.

But on that day, he never got the chance. He had spent the entire time since the departure of the sheriff's deputies tiptoeing around the immense, deserted cell block looking for any way out. He found nothing.

Once, he approached the cell block door but decided even if it had been unlocked, it would have been too risky. Twice, he re-entered his cell and peered out the rectangular barred window that looked down onto a fenced-in parking lot within view of the interstate, but saw nothing from that vantage point that could be of any help. He even stared up at the narrow vents in the overhead ventilation shaft but decided even if he could reach it, he'd never be able to fit inside. Eventually, he ventured down past the last of the cells into the shower room, finding just what he expected to find. A dead end.

At the very moment it occurred to him to get back to his cell before he was discovered, the main door to the cell block clanged open and the sheriff walked in, followed closely by Denny Behrend. When they saw Chris emerging from the shower room at the end of the corridor, the two men flew into a near panic.

"What the hell are you doing?" Denny shouted, and when he did, the alarm in his voice caused it to crack and pitch upward in pre-pubescent imitation. He raced forward, the color draining from his face at the realization that he'd come within a hair's breadth of losing the man he'd spent almost two years hunting down.

Chris motioned coolly over his shoulder to the shower room. "Where do you guys keep the soap?" This time, there were no appreciative chuckles for his dark comedic stylings.

"Get the hell back into your cell!" Denny ordered, sounding more like an irritated parent than an officer of the law. He then turned his outrage to the sheriff. "What the hell kind of place are you running? Aren't these cell doors locked?"

Equally shocked, the sheriff let a few choice expletives slip from his previously genial tongue that might have been funny under other circumstances. Feeling like a grade school child caught ditching school, Chris walked obediently into his cell and sat down on the bunk with a deflated sigh.

As the barred cell door rolled closed and the same thunderous crash resounded through the building, he became suddenly aware the luck that had smiled on him in Lompoc in 1980 – whatever once-in-a-lifetime alignment of perfect circumstances had secured his escape back then – would not happen in Boise, if ever again.

The following day after his initial appearance before the Boise Superior Court, Chris was flown to southern California in a private jet surrounded by a group of vigilant marshals who vowed never to let him out of their sight again. For the duration of the trial, he was kept in a maximum security cell at San Diego MCC and flown to Boise and back every day.

***

"The federal prisons that I've seen are far from cheerful places," U.S. District Court Judge Hal Ryan was saying, but Chris seemed barely to hear. The man behind the gavel halted his words as if to give him the opportunity to catch up. It was his life in the balance, after all.

He raised his bowed head to see the judge beckoning for his full attention with an expression that read more concern than indignation or agitation. The two made eye contact, and the judge went on. But all Chris could think about was the weight of the sentence he'd just been given.

"Yesterday," Judge Ryan continued, "I returned from touring a handful of correctional facilities where you'll likely be sent. I thought it only fair to see these places with my own two eyes prior to your official sentencing."

The room was spinning. Chris reached forward and placed a steadying hand on the table but found he didn't need it after all. His feet were firmly planted on the ground, his legs immobile as rocks. But upstairs, his perceptions had been given a mule kick and his mind was tumbling end over end at the realization that this slide was just about ready to deposit him at rock bottom. He looked at Bill Dougherty, who stood staring ahead with a dour yet unsurprised expression, then back at the judge again.

"They are very grim places," Ryan said. "But they are places you can survive in."

The tone of the judge's statement was unconvincing. Chris tried to ignore it. His mind rushed to do the math. Another twenty-five years on top of the roughly thirty-six he still had left of his original sentence (plus the additional three years for escape) would make him eligible for parole in about sixty-four years. 2046. Just in time for his ninety-third birthday.

That Judge Ryan had decided in his apparent compassion to run the sentences concurrently instead of consecutively – a total of twenty-one felony counts for bank robbery, conspiracy, and breaking federal gun laws – was no comfort to Chris. As far as he was concerned, he would never live to see that day anyway.

There was not a delusional thought in his mind, nor had there been in the months leading up to this day. He had always accepted that his recapture would leave him buried in an avalanche of charges far deeper than any he'd received before. Still, it was one thing to anticipate a sentence. It was another thing entirely to hear it pronounced aloud. In his mind, he likened it to waiting for a firecracker to pop. You could light the match with cautious hands, watch the fuse wind down, and plug your ears against the sound – but when it finally blows, everybody jumps.

"With the right attitude," Ryan continued, "you can work yourself to a better place. You can do good time or you can do hard time. It's up to you."

Chris felt his lips moving, but heard no sound. He stopped and tried to swallow, but his mouth was dry as sand. Clearing his throat before he spoke, he finally pushed the words out. "I never meant to harm anyone. And I never did."

"But you have," Ryan retorted immediately. "You've harmed all of the people you threatened. Every single person you held a gun to during those bank robberies walked away from the experience changed, and not for the better."

Chris could think of nothing more to say. He knew what Ryan had said was right. In the past seven years since he'd stepped willingly into this nightmare world of his own creation, pointing a gun at perfect strangers had been the only crime he had committed he genuinely regretted, the only transgression that hadn't come from any other place but callous disregard. Everything else could be rationalized, dissected, psychoanalyzed. That could not.

"You've also caused harm to the people you associated with after your escape," Ryan added. His use of the word *people* was not lost on Chris. It was obvious that Ryan was talking specifically about Gloria, who stood to do some serious jail time for her alleged participation in two of the bank robberies despite Chris's vehement denial that she'd had nothing to do with them.

She's guilty of being my friend, Chris had written in a note to Judge Ryan. *I invite you to throw the book at me. I am guilty and I deserve to be punished. Gloria White did nothing more than give me food and shelter. If that's a crime, let her be judged. But she had absolutely nothing to do with the bank robberies.*

Having realized there was little he could do to save himself from spending the rest of his life in prison, he pled guilty to all charges in the hopes that doing so would exonerate his friends. Calvin had been lucky; all charges against him were dropped for lack of evidence. Gloria's fate was more severe. In the weeks following, she would be found guilty on all charges and sentenced to five years in prison.

Back up on the bench, Judge Ryan seemed to be searching for an answer that had baffled most everyone, even Chris. "You're an obviously intelligent, educated man. Sentencing you for these additional crimes isn't a task that I or any other judge cares to do. You did a very dumb thing a number of years ago. You got yourself into it and you couldn't get out, and I can understand and even empathize with your desire to want to escape from federal prison."

It was the first time since his recapture that Chris had heard anyone other than himself or his attorney voice that sentiment aloud. It wasn't going to get him off the hook or make things any easier, but the words made him respect Ryan all the more for having spoken them.

"However," Ryan continued, "it's difficult to understand why a person of your background would turn to pure street crimes, and dangerous ones. You will have plenty of time to think about it. I hope you reflect on all of this, and reflect positively."

Ryan shifted in his seat, looking like a man torn between great sympathy and his duty. He leaned forward and looked at Chris with imploring eyes and said, "I do wish you the best of luck."

"Thank you," Chris replied. He knew he was going to need it.

***

Outside the courthouse, flashbulbs burst and an uproar of murmuring voices melted into static as a trio of marshals led Chris in handcuffs to a waiting car. There would be one final flight from Boise to southern California. From there, he would be shipped out to whatever federal prison the cards held in store.

The blockade of reporters and photographers parted. Chris passed through their midst in total silence, transfixed by the sight of a small group of locals who had gathered by the curb outside the cordoned-off perimeter. Two of them were holding up a large handwritten sign adorned with a crude drawing of a falcon. The words beneath read GOOD LUCK, CHRIS! COME BACK TO IDAHO ANYTIME. When they saw him look their way, each lifted a hand and waved. But there was no enthusiasm in the motion, only a heaviness that seemed to match their solemn expressions.

He tried to force a smile, found he couldn't without it looking like a grimace, and simply nodded his head in their direction. As the car pulled away from the Boise Superior Court building for the last time, he continued to gaze at the small group until they were finally out of sight. Then he turned and stared forward. In the harsh afternoon light, Chris could have sworn he saw flames licking at the edges of the road ahead.

DESCENT

Chris
(May 1982)

The prisoner's scream echoed through the cavernous hulk of cold, grey cement. Its shrill pitch traveled the full length of the cell block, then ended abruptly.

Chris dropped the book he was reading and jumped to his feet. He crept forward and positioned himself inches from the threshold of his open cell door, hands balled into fists, his body like a tension wire with extremities.

At first he could hear nothing above the crashing of his own heart in his ears. Then slowly the rhythmic pounding receded and was replaced by an urgent thrashing sound on the tier outside his cell. Just beyond his field of vision something was moving rapidly, throwing violent shadows against the concrete floor in the pale afternoon light.

He considered sticking his head through the open doorway to see what was happening. All it would take was another step forward, but he found himself incapable of motion. All he wanted now was to retreat to his bunk, bury his head in his pillow, pretend nothing was happening – none of it, this hellish place, the killings and the savagery, the monsters that roamed the alleys by day and slept in dark corners by night, the pointed rifle scopes, the steel-barred windows, the razor wire barriers, all of it a horrifying nightmare

He thought if he tried hard enough, he could somehow will himself away, force the calendar backwards, and wake to find himself back in his tiny Redondo Beach apartment before any of this. He would rise and dance, and scream and sing. He would burst out the door into the warm night among the free, racing down sidewalks, darting across traffic-crowded streets. He would build a life for himself – a real life – where such wretched places existed only as rumor and where regret was just a concept formed from unspoken words and unrealized dreams. He closed his eyes and prayed for this with all his might. But the muted gurgling sounds coming from outside his cell called him back to reality.

Chris retrieved the blunt lead pipe from underneath his pillow. It had been bequeathed to him by a fellow inmate and had become a vital component of his contingency plan for survival. With the pipe in hand, he shuffled one step closer to the open door. He braced himself against the wall and leaned forward, poking the tip of his head through the threshold just far enough for one eye to clear the thick jamb where the cell door's locking mechanism lived.

Out on the elevated tier that ran the length of the prison cell block, there was a man lying on his back in the center of a rapidly growing pool of blood. His arms and legs were flailing wildly and he looked absurdly like a turtle struggling to right itself. There was a second man seated on top of him, one hand planted firmly over the bleeding man's mouth, the other hand twisting a shank into his neck.

Chris's stomach somersaulted. He swallowed the urge to cry out. In this place, any outward expression of fear would mark him for the others. Instead, he gritted his teeth and wrapped both hands around the pipe. On the floor, the dying man must have felt the end draw near because he began to buck and strain even harder.

The killer, cradling his victim's head like a lethal vise, leaned forward and placed his lips against the dying man's ear. He whispered a single word in Spanish.

"*Aceptalo.*"

The gentle, cooing manner with which he spoke betrayed the vicious twisting motion of his hand as he plunged the weapon deeper.

"*Aceptalo*," he said again, and it was not the way the dying man's chest heaved as he fought for life or how his limbs began to slow that would haunt Chris for the rest of his life, but the soothing voice of his murderer urging him to "accept it" in a tone that sounded almost compassionate.

"*Aceptalo... aceptalo...*"

There was another fierce moment of struggle, then something disappeared behind the victim's eyes and he was still. A dark stain spread out across the murdered man's crotch as his bowels let go. In an instant, the stench of excrement filled the air.

Chris felt a sudden sensation of falling backward, but at the moment his head would have gone crashing through the edge of his bunk, he continued moving, his body now tumbling end over end into a black void. He started awake suddenly, unaware of where he was. The surface below his body was yielding, soft. He knew only that there was comfort here.

He stared into the darkness, eyes slowly focusing on two pinpricks of growing light in the distance. He didn't know where he was, but he knew where he wasn't. Gone was the heavy, claustrophobic presence of the prison walls. In its place, a cool and quiet place.

His mind flashed back to the man with the shank in his neck. Was the body still there? He reached back groggily for a memory and then remembered. They had taken the body but left the blood. It had stayed there for hours, days, coagulating into a grisly black mass that could have been mistaken for crude oil if not for the coppery scent that lingered. Eventually it had simply eroded, trampled under a thousand feet until all that was left was a sticky residue – and finally, a stain.

The stain had still been there on the night of his escape. He wondered now if enough time had passed to erode the evidence of its existence. How long had it been since he had last been back there? Months? Years? Maybe both, he thought, then realized none of that mattered anymore. He was free. He closed his eyes again and drifted.

Now he heard someone saying his name. Calling out to him. Over and over, as if to rouse him gently from his sleep.

"Chris. We're here."

A man's voice. Dad? No, too young. But familiar. Plus, it was usually Mom who did the waking at the end of long road trips, while Dad piloted the Cadillac to a rolling stop.

He opened his eyes and stared out the window of the car. He let his eyes focus on the great, sprawling stone structure that ran in a straight line from east to west, as far as the eye could see. At its center, a lighted dome top rimmed with circular windows extended above the rest of the edifice like an enormous battle helmet. There were pillars two stories high flanking the building's front entrance, which lay at the end of a steep run of cement steps.

His wrists were bound; he felt this and remembered everything now, even before he saw the razor wire or the words UNITED STATES PENITENTIARY carved onto the face of the building above the pillars.

The voice spoke again. This time he recognized it. "End of the line," the marshal said. "Welcome to Leavenworth, Chris."

***

Give a man enough time to contemplate his decisions and mistakes – allow him to do nothing else but examine the paths he's chosen and consider the injury that he's caused to himself and others – and he'll do one of two things: become enlightened or grow bitter.

In the months that led up to his return to federal prison, Chris had run the emotional rollercoaster through dips, drops, hairpin turns and nauseating loops. He wept in his cell the night he was sentenced to an additional three years for escape, but slept a dreamless sleep after getting an additional twenty-five for the bank robberies. There was seldom any rhyme or reason. Only action and reaction.

The arraignments and the trials, even the dreaded perp walks that always made him feel like a shackled King Kong on display, lasted months and delayed the inevitable. Chris was ping-ponged back and forth from one part of the country to another as the machinations of justice ran their course. Now that it was all over and life had devolved again into the excruciating, moment-by-moment observance of time with no measurable end in sight, the black cloud that had followed him every day since his recapture descended like a shroud.

From his cell in the isolation wing of Leavenworth Federal Penitentiary, Chris planned his own death. He let his eyes trace every inch of the small enclosure. There were three walls, one ceiling, no windows. A single barred door looked out onto a narrow walkway and a solid wall. There was a bunk in the corner and a steel toilet situated only feet from it. Between them was a water faucet. All were attached to the wall, immovable. He spat and missed the toilet.

Solitary confinement was protocol for new arrivals everywhere and Leavenworth was no different. The prison staff had to keep him separate until they could determine if he would be a threat to other prisoners. They also had to be sure he'd be no threat to himself. Which was probably why the walls and ceiling were perfectly smooth. Without grip points, it would be impossible for him to fashion a noose from his pants and attach it to anything. The bastards wanted him alive as long as possible so that they could feed him to the sharks in their own time.

He wished for a razor so he could beat them to the punch. The darkness inside was like a tumor that had grown, leaving no room for anything else. It had even begun to change him physically. Long before his arrival at Leavenworth, he could see it himself, each time he looked into one of the reflective stainless steel mirrors that were the trademark of every holding facility and correctional institution from San Diego to Boise – a change so dramatic that it would have deeply troubled him if he gave a damn anymore.

His face still looked young. He was only twenty-nine, after all, and neither Mother Nature or Father Time had seen fit to leave their marks on him yet. But his eyes had gone through a transformation: somehow, they had turned a shade darker. As if every horrible thing he'd seen over the last five years had driven something from them, leaving a residue of filth where the light of existence once shone.

He recognized the change like a detached observer. For a while he wondered if it wasn't only in his head, then realized it didn't matter. He had become little more than an observer in his own skin, conscious of the transformations taking place inside and out, yet too defeated to do anything but watch them take their course.

He picked up the thin bunk mattress and looked at the frame underneath. Its edges were rounded, ensuring it would be virtually impossible for him to slice through his own flesh into an artery. He dropped to one knee and began to feel around underneath the frame. He flinched, then a dark smile spread across his face. There was something sharp underneath there.

He thought about Dave Jackson, his old friend. The two had known each other since the first grade and had played ball together on the Palos Verdes Little League team. After the Jacksons moved away in 1966, the boys did their best to keep in touch – but in the end, both had succumbed to that great killer of all childhood friendships, the lack of immediate proximity.

By the time their paths crossed again in 1981, the world had become a much smaller place. Distance no longer an impeded communication. Their lives had also changed dramatically. Dave was a writer and had worked his way to a position of prominence as a journalist for *Time Magazine*; Chris had just come off a nineteen-month run as the number one most wanted man on the U.S. Marshals' list of fugitives. The two old friends had plenty of stories to swap and a lot of catching up to do.

Dave visited when he could, but wrote more often. The sense of isolation and signs of depression in Chris's letters always troubled Dave, but there was little he could do aside from offering his constant support.

Anything I can do to help, he wrote to Chris not long after his recapture, *you can count on me. It's easy for someone without access and freedom to see others and to feel cut off and to feel he's without friends, but I don't think you should succumb to that. There are many of us eager to be helpful, to lend a hand in whatever way we can. It's important for you to know we are not far away. There are those who may try to intimidate you, for whatever reasons, and make you feel you will be forgotten, or no one cares. It's not true; don't believe them.*

He knew Dave meant well. But words were insufficient armaments against walls and fences and spotlighted perimeters. Like letters received from family, messages from Dave were always treasured. But they were also cruel reminders of everything Chris had destroyed.

Dropping to his belly, he peered underneath his cell bunk and found what he had been looking for. A single screw jutted out of the wall where the edge of the bunk met the cement. It was no razor, but there was no doubt in his mind that far more motivated individuals had met their ends working with much duller implements.

Acting like a man against a stopwatch, he bent the wrist of his right hand backward and drew the edge of the screw against his flesh. There was a moment of sharp pain. He rolled over onto his back and held his arm up, examining the raised red line that looked more like a cat scratch than a failed suicide attempt.

A tiny trickle of blood worked its way down his elbow. He lay there and studied it and wondered if the sun was out today. He thought of his parents. He hoped they had found a way to move beyond the grief he'd given them. He thought of his brothers and sisters and school chums and hawking buddies, all going about their lives.

He could feel them now as sure as he could feel the breath rushing in and out of his lungs. On the outside, life was being lived. On the inside, there was no such thing. Here, everything existed in a state of suspended animation. There were no good experiences in prison; no passions to pursue, no beautiful discoveries to be made, no loves to be gained or lost. Only the bitter awareness of what he had been too terrified to face: life wasn't simply passing him by – it was speeding away and kicking up a trail of dust in its wake. What purpose was there to going on?

Chris stared at the blood on his elbow until it dried.

***

Smith was trying to talk the prisoner out of it, but he was getting nowhere.

"You really don't want to do this," he insisted. Smith was the prison captain, chief of all guards. He wasn't used to having to convince inmates to yield to his will, but Christopher Boyce was a son of a bitch.

Ever since his arrival at Leavenworth, things had grown complicated. Boyce was a high profile figure, about as high profile as they came. There had even been a book. Smith figured the initial notoriety would have faded and been forgotten by now, but the young bastard had broken out of Lompoc, hurling himself back into the public eye. And now there was even talk of a movie.

Bringing Boyce to Leavenworth had been a coup for the warden and the prison administration. Of that, there was no doubt. Prison wardens were known for collecting notorious figures and flaunting them like trophies. It was a status thing, strange as it was. Adding Boyce to the roster was like carving another notch in the wall of fame. But the media spotlight that came with Boyce's arrival was nothing Smith wanted any part of. He saw him as more of a liability than anything else.

"I think I do," Boyce answered. "I do want to do this." The expression on his face was boyishly innocent. But underneath it, Smith could sense the venom in his words.

"You better think long and hard about it," Smith said, starting over. He folded his hands on his lap and leaned back in his office chair. It was a cue that said he was getting comfortable. He figured Boyce might be a tough nut to crack, and he was preparing himself for a lengthy discourse. "You just got here. You haven't even been moved into the general population yet. There could be repercussions."

Boyce was sitting on the uncomfortable wooden inmate's chair opposite the captain's desk. The cushion-backed seat, the good one, had been drawn aside in preparation for his visit as it always was when inmates were brought to the office for a one-on-one. It was important not to let the prisoners get too comfortable. But now Smith found himself wishing that he'd left the finery out. Boyce was obviously one of those types much more easily smoothed over when he was relaxed.

Smith made a mental note of this and went on. "You bring that reporter and all those film cameras into a place like this, it could stoke resentments among other inmates. And to top it off, they're not even American. As you might imagine, foreigners don't go over well in places like this."

"They're Australian," Boyce replied. "Not American, no, but... I don't know that you can categorize them as foreigners. Not in the way you mean, anyway."

"What way do you think I mean?"

"Not white."

"Boyce," Smith said, sounding agitated, "don't give me that bullshit. I don't give a good goddamn if that TV crew's full of homegrown crackers or the kind that spring up down under. Bottom line is I don't want a news crew in my prison."

Smith shifted in his seat uncomfortably, regaining his composure. "But the fact is, I can't stop it. All I can do is convince you that it's a bad idea and remind you really bad things could come as a result."

Boyce seemed to think it over for a second. He pursed his lips together and cocked his head sideways, but Smith could tell that he was only imitating someone giving something serious consideration. Mocking him. Smith was livid.

"You know what, captain?" Boyce snapped his head forward and gave Smith a look that said if he could spare the spit without earning a severe beating for it, he'd lay one on the desk that separated them. "I'm gonna do that interview. You can block it in advance, if you want, but I'm going to do it – and if that crew isn't allowed inside on the day, I imagine they'll have something to share with their viewers about that."

Smith glared at the insolent prick in front of him for a full ten seconds before speaking again. The Boyce kid dropped his gaze and stared at his shoe with an expression on his face that read *I'm not sure I should have said it like that. Not to the head of the most powerful gang in the prison, the ones with billy clubs and rifles.* But it was too late to call it back now.

"That's fine," Smith finally said. His voice took on an oddly congenial tone, one that didn't sound right coming from his mouth. It was more frightening than his stern, you-better-do-what-I-say voice. "You do what you think is in your best interest."

The charge in the air that followed hung there like an undetonated explosive.

"We're done," Smith said. "You can go back now."

Boyce stood and the guard standing at relaxed attention at the office door led him back to his cell in the solitary confinement wing.

***

Three hours after the film crew departed Leavenworth with the interview footage in tow, the door to Chris's cell in the solitary confinement wing was unlocked and opened.

"Your time at the Hilton's up," one of his uniformed escorts intoned in a monotone voice. "Rotation into general population, effective immediately."

As scared as he was of being put out among the other prisoners, Chris was also relieved. Solitary cells were tomblike enclosures that had a way of making you long for the sight of other human beings, regardless of who they were or what horrible crime they'd perpetrated to send them to a place like this. There was a reason they called it The Hole: as soon as you went in, you felt like you were never getting out. He was glad to be leaving it behind. But that relief was also tempered with nervous suspicion.

"So soon?" He tried to sound conversational. It was easier to get straight information from a hack if you didn't come off too inquisitive or concerned.

"Orders from up top. You've been accepted into the club. Lifetime membership starts today."

Back at Lompoc, a prisoner's time in solitary confinement prior to being transferred to the general population could last a month or more – long enough to assess the inmate's attitude and suitability for assignment to a specific cell block. The same had been true about San Diego MCC and Terminal Island before that. But only two weeks had elapsed since his arrival at Leavenworth.

"The sooner it starts the sooner it ends," Chris said, mostly to himself. The solitary cell had proven to be suicide proof. He thought he might have better luck in a standard cell, one that was a little less institutional. Moving briskly, he gathered up the few belongings he had been allowed: a carton of cigarettes, a two-month-old newspaper, and a book. Churchill's *A History of the English-Speaking Peoples*.

It was early afternoon and the cell block was open to the yard for another few hours. He was eager to get outside under the sun. Too much time surrounded by four walls without a window to gaze out of played hell on the body and mind. As soon as he was led to his new cell, he stuck his possessions inside the locker at the foot of his bunk and walked out into the yard.

The sun was riding high above the flat earth of northeastern Kansas. He basked in it. He moved past the tennis and basketball courts onto the running track that encircled the inmate's baseball diamond, exploring the layout. All appeared battered by time, although Chris hardly believed that. The constructions looked like they'd been designed to appear drab and old from day one.

He kept his eyes open and his guard up as he walked, looking directly at no one, yet fully alert to everything within a twenty-foot radius. He'd picked up a few things from Calvin and Billy and others on the inside over the years. It was a skill he hadn't used in a long time and one he hadn't ever hoped to need again, but he was glad now he hadn't forgotten it.

Just because he was flirting with suicide didn't mean he wanted any of the savages in here to do it for him. Besides, offering yourself up as a victim didn't always guarantee a clean and easy death.

Sometimes, survival was the truly horrible fate. And God knew there were things far worse than murder that could happen to someone in here.

He completed a full circuit of the track and tried to blend in as best he could, but everywhere he moved there were eyes on him. Assessing glances, watchful looks, penetrating stares. It was always the same the first time in the yard for any new arrival. He might as well have been holding up a sign.

He didn't notice the four men follow him when he came in off the yard. After he entered his cell, he lit a cigarette with his back to the open doorway – his first mistake – and turned around into a hurling fist.

The first blow struck him like a two-by-four between the eyes, blinding him. There was a flash of outrage as he quickly understood what was happening, but then the pummeling began and chased all rational thought from his brain.

Rock solid punches began to land on his face and head in rapid succession. He tried lifting his arms to shield himself from the rain of knuckle and bone, but doing so only seemed to piss off his attackers even more. On the tenth consecutive punch, Chris dropped – but not before a firmly planted knee missed his groin and connected with his ribs.

While two of the men remained on point outside his cell, the other two – he never got a good look at them, but determined by their strength and ferocity that they were sizable creatures – took full advantage of his vulnerable position. With deliberate accuracy, they took turns polishing their steel-toed work boots on the top and sides of his head.

At a certain point, the pain began to subside. His body was going into shock. Every kick now felt like it was coming from a thousand miles away, which was even more alarming than if he'd been able to feel the extent of damage each one was inflicting. Outnumbered, he could do nothing to defend himself. He curled himself into a ball and waited for what he knew would come – the knife edge that would pierce his ribs and leave him bleeding to death on the floor of his prison cell. He was terrified, yet at the same time he welcomed what he knew would be sweet relief.

The knife never came. A final kick caught him square in the ear, drowning out all sound. At last, Chris drifted into blissful unconsciousness.

***

May 29, 1982
Dear Dave,
Greetings from grim city. Don't hold it against me for not writing, really haven't written anyone. In the main I've just been hibernating. No, never received your postcard from Italy. And wouldn't be at all surprised if you didn't get this one.

I've had a little fun here in the last three weeks. Anthony McClellan, producer for the Australian 60 Minutes, showed up here. Nice guy. He finally convinced me to be interviewed in front of their cameras by Ray Martin. McClellan said that there are an awful lot of Aussies who would like to get their government back. I figured what the hell? (And don't hold this against me, nothing personal old sod, but since they weren't American journalists, I decided to go for it.)

Mainly, we talked around the destabilization of Prime Minister Whitlam's government in '75 and its collapse. Before the interview, the administration hinted to me that in all probability if I gave the interview that certain inmates would take offense to it. Forewarned, so to speak.

I was cut loose from the hole when the filming was completed and three hours after the Aussies took off, four members of a gang not to be named here (although I'm pretty positive you and I previously discussed the neo-Nazi freaks) paid me a visit. I had come off the yard, went into my cell, lit a smoke and turned around into a sucker punch uppercut right between the eyes. Two stayed on point outside and two came on in. After about ten blows to the head I went down and then proceeded to get kicked in the head with steel-toed boots until I was seeing nothing but stars. No knives, thank God. My face and the back of my head was a bloody mess, nonetheless. Broke a rib. Lots of fun.

To make a long story short I rallied a few friends, kept my back to the wall under the gun towers and two days later the staff threw me back into the hole. But before I was locked up I sent lines out everywhere to find out just what had been on those jerks' minds. The story that kept coming back to me was that a staff member had told certain individuals that I had been talking about their organization during the TV interview. A bit underhanded, eh what? These simple ignorant convicts are so easily manipulated.

I'm running out of paper. What this letter is, Dave, is a call for assistance. It bugs the hell out of me when an attempt is made to intimidate me. I mean, after all, how am I ever going to run this country if I'm perforated before I'm thirty!

Regards,
Chris
P.S. I want to drink buckets of vodka and roll in the snow!

MESSAGE IN A BOTTLE

Cait
(June 1982)

June 17, 1982
    Dear Mr. Boyce:
My name is Cait Mills and I am representing your co-defendant, Andrew Daulton Lee, in his bid for parole. As I am sure you are aware, you and Mr. Lee were sentenced under 18 USC 4205(b)(2). While I am sure your lawyers have explained this to you, the long and short of this is: any federal prisoner sentenced under this statute may be released on parole at any time at the discretion of the U.S. Parole Commission.

You and Mr. Lee will be afforded a parole hearing every twenty-four months in front of an examiner from the U.S. Parole Commission and you will be allowed a representative to be able to present a case for parole. Mr. Lee has asked me to be his representative at his next hearing. In that regard, there are several questions I have that will better equip me to help him. I would appreciate it if you could answer these questions for me so that I may represent Mr. Lee to the best of my ability.

While I know that I am asking for a lot, I believe that he has a fairly decent shot at being paroled. I also would like you to know that this is my idea and not Mr. Lee's, as he is opposed to my contacting you. While I am not allowed to offer any pay for your answers, I would be happy to send you a book of your choice. I understand that you enjoy books on history and I have access to some pretty obscure selections.

My questions:

1. Lee claims that you received a check from the CIA as payment. Can you verify this? Did you ever tell him that you were an agent with the CIA?

2. Lee claims that he was never at TRW at any time but his fingerprint was found inside a safe. Is this a true statement?

3. Lee claims that you told him he was doing a service for the U.S. government. Though this was disproved at trial, did it happen? Did he have a reason to believe that what he was doing was sanctioned?

4. You testified that Lee threatened you into continuing the espionage. As part of your defense, you also told the jury about other people that Lee had threatened in his drug business. Can you tell me if this was true or just a part of the defense that your attorneys presented?

5. Can you estimate "how guilty" Lee was? In other words, the parole commission will look at culpability and attempt to determine who had more – you or Lee. Given that you have been sentenced to more time, I am asking if you can shed some light on how much time Lee really should serve.

6. Can you tell me about Mr. Lee in general, family closeness, community support, etc.?

Importantly, if you have any other information that I should be aware of, please let me know. I appreciate any help you can give to me and I look forward to hearing from you at your convenience.

Best regards,
Cait Mills

***

Christopher Boyce was buried. Before his escape, he'd been the better off of the two. Forty years beats a life sentence every time, hands down – you don't have to be a math whiz or a legal expert to know that. But now that he was caught, it was all over.

If he hadn't busted out of Lompoc and gone on that bank robbery spree, Boyce would probably have been paroled by around 1987. Not exactly the day after tomorrow, but not a lifetime away either. His recapture, and the additional twenty-eight years that came as a result (three for the actual escape and twenty-five for having made a bunch of unauthorized bank withdrawals by pistol) pretty much sealed his fate.

I knew there was nothing I or anyone else could do to help his cause. There was only one way Christopher Boyce was ever getting out of prison again, and unless he lived to be about ninety-five, the front door was completely out of the question. But I had an itching sensation in the back of my brain telling me he might be able to offer some help in my case for Daulton.

As with most issues having to do with his "co-defendant," I chose not to breathe a word to Daulton about my letter to Boyce. I had intended to write him as early as September of 1981, about a week after his recapture, but decided to hold off. Mainly because I wasn't sure he'd be in the best frame of mind to want to give his old pal a hand. There was also the fact that he was being moved around so much I couldn't be sure when he'd get my letter, if ever.

I thought about passing an envelope off to Denny Behrend for about three seconds, then decided against it. Not that I didn't trust him. Despite his questionable line of work, he was a trustworthy man and he treated his charges with kindness and respect. I was sure he'd have delivered my message. I just didn't feel right entrusting such an integral piece of my strategy for Daulton's parole to the guy who'd just nailed his partner in crime. The thought of it played hell on my sense of order and balance.

Instead, I continued to carve away at the misshapen ball of clay that was Daulton's only chance at release before qualifying for an AARP card. I went about the task with blinders on, keenly aware that no attorney worth their salt would have taken on a case as hot as his. And so I chose not to acknowledge this. As I've always said, a little denial can sometimes help you pull off the impossible.

I finally sent the letter off in June of '82. By then, Boyce's escape and bank robbery trials had all concluded and I knew where he could be found for the next sixty or seventy years – Leavenworth Federal Penitentiary. The letter wrote itself; I had written the thing so many times in my head over the last ten months I didn't even have to think about it. When I was done, I slapped a single stamp on the outside of the envelope, dropped it off at the post office, and waited.

A month and a half passed. By that point, I was visiting with Daulton one weekend per month and spending the other three holed up in my Hillcrest bungalow, working on his parole brief on my kitchen table where I was constantly within arm's reach of a steady coffee supply.

During the week, I worked as a paralegal for a small defense law office in San Diego. Not exactly the most scintillating job in the world – most of the time I was immersed in the minutiae of researching precedents and laws, organizing data, prepping and proofing court documents – but it paid the bills and put my education to use. It was also a perfect training ground for the kind of work I would do for the next twenty years while I worked to get Daulton his parole date.

My trips to the beach became fewer and further between. Surfing buddies eyed me suspiciously, probably wondering if I'd been trading my weekend shore visits for the pew. Beach acquaintances took a lot more time to remember my name. Close friends asked me if I'd become obsessed. I shrugged it all off; that's what you do when you're committed to a singular purpose. You keep your nose to the grindstone and you squeeze in everything else when you can.

Another month crawled by. Summer's end loomed. I was starting to think I'd never hear back from Boyce when his letter arrived. It showed up on a deliriously hot Saturday afternoon, just in time to save me from lapsing into a work-induced blackout. The kitchen table was littered with papers – mostly Daulton's behavioral reports and statements from his friends and family – and I was staring down onto a short checklist of to-dos when the mail slot on the front door suddenly spat forth its daily harvest. I saw it at once, a dog-eared envelope lying face up with the handwritten name *Chris Boyce* above a return address in Leavenworth, Kansas. I opened it immediately.

July 31, 1982
Dear Cait,
Thanks for writing me. I'm being housed in a cell deep in the bowels of the solitary confinement unit here at Leavenworth, so apologies for the delay in responding to your message.
Apparently, they had a run on ink and papyrus in my neck of the woods and it took them a dog's age to get me the necessary tools to write back. I'd have sent message by smoke signal, but lately they've been discouraging inmates from lighting fires in their cells. This has been the first opportunity I've had to respond.
It was nice to learn that Daulton is attempting parole. I doubt whether I will attend my hearings because I really have no hope that I will ever be paroled.
I'm glad to answer any of your questions to help with Daulton's parole, although I'm not sure if they'll be of any use to you. Hopefully, they are. I take no comfort in knowing that somewhere on the other side of the country (is he still at Lompoc?) Daulton is suffering right along with me for the mess we got into. If anything, I'd love to see your efforts succeed. No sense in both of us rotting away.
Please tell D that I recently got my ass kicked by a group of extremely tall ruffians who would make him look like one of Tolkien's Hobbits. I'm sure he'll get a kick out of hearing that news, if it hasn't already worked its way back down the grapevine. Speaking of grapes: how's that sweet southern California wine? Last time I had a taste there was a Democrat in office and people still questioned if blind patriotism was a good thing. What's the world coming to?
I've answered all of your questions below. Don't hesitate to write me back if I can be of any further help or if any of my answers

need clarification or don't make any sense. If that's the case, I humbly beg your pardon. I'm a little out of practice communicating with other living beings. Too long in the dungeon does a brain bad.

No, I never received a check from the CIA and I never told Daulton that I worked for the CIA. I know that was part of his defense, but it was never true.

I really don't have any idea if the fingerprint story was true. I also don't think Daulton was ever at TRW. It could be something that was made up because I don't think it was ever proven.

No, I never told Daulton we were doing anything that was a service to the government. Daulton and I discussed taking the documents to the Russians from the very beginning.

Daulton has a long history in the drug trade and he had some clients who were seriously unhappy with him. I really wouldn't be comfortable saying a lot more about it.

I doubt that anything that I could ever say would help Daulton get parole. I doubt that Daulton and I will ever be paroled. Daulton and I are doomed. Me probably more than him. As for who is more guilty, I don't even know how to answer that. I can say that Daulton knew as well as I did how much risk and trouble this would cause. He had a serious drug problem and didn't care. I guess I didn't, either.

I'm not much help.

So you're from San Diego? I was in San Diego at the MCC for a brief stint. Are the peregrines still there? What kind of bookstores do you frequent? Do they have books that are out of print? I'd love to know more about it. Can you keep me updated on your work with Daulton? I'd also like to know how that works. I wish I could be more helpful but this place isn't the best place to brainstorm ideas.

Keep in touch!
Sincerely,
Chris Boyce
Political Prisoner, Ph.D.

***

When Daulton called the next day, I told him about the letter. I had to. It was one of the most significant moves forward I'd made in weeks. Regardless of the fact that Daulton never wanted to hear *that name* ever again, I knew getting information from Boyce was vital.

"I thought I told you not to do that," was Daulton's response.

"I'm a big girl. I do what I want. You should be happy to know the information he gave might help us out."

Maybe that was a bit of an exaggeration, but I said it anyway. I decided to stay mum on the ass-kicking Boyce had mentioned in his letter. I didn't want to give Daulton any more ammunition, or – heaven forbid – a perverse thrill.

"Yeah? Well it wouldn't surprise me if it was full of a bunch of half-truths and outright fabrications."

"Daulton, your vindictiveness is going to give you an ulcer."

"And your curiosity is going to kill your cat."

"I don't have a cat."

"See? It's already too late."

I rolled my eyes. "Not your best knee-slapper ever."

"You'll be falling down laughing in about ten minutes."

Daulton was trying to lighten up, but it wasn't working. His words were coming through now with a briskness that made me second guess having told him anything. We'd been here before. But this time, that familiar lick of venom was muted by a subtle sense of... I don't know what. Defeat? Resignation, maybe.

We struggled through another five minutes of small talk before he abruptly said he had to go.

"I'll see you soon?" I asked.

"You know where to find me."

"I need to get back on the waves next weekend, but I was thinking I can drive down the weekend after that."

Daulton seemed to think it over. "Probably not. My brother's coming to visit me one of those two days. Sunday, I think."

"Great," I said. "I'd love to meet him."

Daulton's reply was practically inaudible. "Of course."

"What do you mean by that?"

"Nothing. You should come by. I'll let him know to wear his Sunday best. See you then." And he hung up.

I made myself another cup of coffee.

***

I wrote Boyce back the following week, after I'd had a chance to go over every line of his response twice to make sure I didn't need any additional clarification. Two weeks to the day after I fired off my response, the letter was sent back unopened. RETURN TO SENDER was stamped across the front like a curt insult. The trademark illustration of the mail carrier's pointing finger didn't do anything to lessen that impression.

I stared at the outside of the envelope and wondered what the hell had happened. My first thoughts were that Boyce had either refused the letter, had slipped his captors yet again, or had been buried so deep and far they'd forgotten about his existence. But none of those explanations made any sense.

The only one that did was that Boyce had been moved again, this time to an undisclosed location. Maybe for his safety, or maybe as a way to make him pay. I had seen and heard enough by now in my career to know this was a distinct possibility, and one well within the capability of the Bureau of Prisons. It was another three months before I learned exactly what they'd done with him. He was buried, alright.

INTERNAL EXILE

Chris
(August 1982 – April 1985)

The concrete womb enveloped him. No matter which direction he turned, its walls were there. Even when he closed his eyes, he could sense its presence. Staring down on him from above. Gazing up to him from below. Closing in on him from either side. Folding him into its snug, smothering embrace.

If he lay here long enough, the womb would eventually absorb him. If he tried to remove himself before it was ready to let him go, it would pulverize his bones to sandy grains. He was trapped. All he could do now was sleep and dream of birth.

***

In the beginning, there was hope. But as the days melted into weeks and the weeks into months, the flame began to dim.

What started out as an attempt by Judge Hal Ryan to save Chris from being murdered in prison had somehow snowballed out of control. After hearing about the Leavenworth assault, Ryan contacted the Bureau of Prisons and insisted that Chris be transferred someplace safer. The Bureau of Prisons director agreed

– much to the delight of the Leavenworth staff, who had by now all come to the conclusion that Christopher Boyce was bad news.

After eighty-one days in solitary confinement at Leavenworth, he was transferred to USP Marion, a federal prison in Illinois. K-Unit, the secure housing section where inmates were kept in isolation around the clock, was to be his new temporary home.

One year later, he was still there.

Despite Judge Ryan's explicit recommendation that the transfer should only be a temporary solution, the Bureau of Prisons decided otherwise and numerous requests to transfer him out of solitary were rejected.

Chris thought it was roundabout payback for having escaped Lompoc. The way he looked at it, prison wardens were all part of a proud brotherhood of graduated disciplinarians, and the wardens of federal penitentiaries were among the elite. Would he put it past them to inflict retribution against an inmate who had made one of their number look bad? Not for a moment.

His lawyer Bill Dougherty wasn't as convinced. He blamed it on a combination of institutional incompetence and cold indifference. To his mind, that was an even more frightening scenario than the idea of a star chamber of sadists doling out psychological punishment to those who crossed them. There was one thing, however, that both men did agree on: whatever it was, it stank to high hell.

USP Marion was known as "the New Alcatraz." The only Level 6 federal prison in the country, it was home to 350 of the most violent and unruly offenders in the system. But if Marion was the Bureau of Prison's answer to Alcatraz, then K-Unit was a modern day interpretation of the sensory deprivation cells of French Guiana a half century earlier. The only things missing, Chris thought grimly, were the spiders and the centipedes.

In K-Unit, he was confined to isolation in a windowless cell for twenty-three hours a day. During that time, his only interaction with other human beings came through a food slot that was opened three times a day for meals. Above that, a 12"x18" pane of shatterproof glass in the solid steel door looked out onto an empty corridor.

The guards who delivered meals through the food slot seldom spoke. When they did, their words were few and their tones curt. Even the prison PA, a rotund man who looked more like a medical school dropout than a physician's assistant, was loath to make conversation. His job was to perform a daily health check of all K-Unit inmates, but it was a checkup that consisted of little more than visual confirmation the prisoner was still alive.

This was accomplished through the observation pane, with no hands-on contact. Chris discovered early on that if he didn't lift his head from his bunk when the PA arrived, the petulant bastard would stand there and kick at the door until he did. In time, he came to ignore the man's presence altogether.

Every few hours, guards would perform headcounts by peering into the inmate's cell through the observation pane. Prisoners were required to stand to be counted, but he had no complaint there. It was a rule that had been implemented across all federal prisons as a result of his own escape from Lompoc years before.

For one hour a day, he was handcuffed and taken to a larger room intended for recreation. Once there, the cuffs were removed and he was left alone. On rare occasions, he would be taken to a roofless concrete cubicle where the only view was straight up. Its position, built into the wall of K-Unit, kept the small enclosure out of direct sunlight for most of the day. Soon his skin took on a sickly pallor. He called it his prison tan.

Not even the small black-and-white TV that played closed-circuit religious and educational programs offered any diversion from the intense isolation. If anything, it only made it worse. Many times, he caught himself talking back to the television. Soon he stopped turning it on altogether.

With phone calls restricted to two per month and a strict time limit of ten minutes imposed on each, written correspondence became his only reliable means of communication. He spent hours writing longhand letters, mostly to his family and Dave Jackson, but he was also beginning to write with growing frequency to Cait. Somehow, she had managed to track him down after he'd been whisked away to Marion. Her resourcefulness impressed him. He began to wonder if maybe Daulton would have a shot at parole, after all.

Letters from perfect strangers were also frequent, and Chris juggled them all with the dexterity of an air traffic controller. The activity kept his mind alive. For a while, it almost convinced him that he wasn't alone. But every illusion eventually gives itself up for what it is. In time, the words began to slow and he found himself writing more and more often to a single recipient: himself. At least the postage was cheap.

I'm beginning to feel like a mute, he scrawled in long, looping letters on one of the note pads Dave had sent him. *My voice has taken on the scratchy tone of pencil against paper. The voices of my family and friends have become the sounds of papers rustling. Sometimes days pass without my uttering a sound. Times like these, the occasional cough or sneeze become startling events. Symphonies that break the stillness with the force of a hammer against breakaway glass. If I could carry a tune, I'd sing. But for some reason the thought of bringing music into this environment feels like sacrilege. Places like these should be silent. Sterile. Clinical. Attempting to believe otherwise is an effort to lie in the face of truth. And I won't do that. I've told enough lies to last a lifetime.*

He set the notebook down and lowered himself onto his bed. He closed his eyes and thought of faraway places he would never see again.

***

It was fall, 1968. Chris didn't have his driver's license yet and so Daulton was forced to do the driving. Neither minded; Daulton was a born rambler, and being passenger meant Chris could keep a better eye on Primo, his Harris' hawk. Primo was a bunny-chasing bundle of pandemonium that weighed only twenty-three ounces but could haul down jackrabbits three times his weight. For now, Primo calmly sat hooded on his perch on the back seat.

When they arrived at their usual campsite in the wooded hills outside Lompoc, Daulton called up the first order of business. He popped the cover off the steering wheel of his Mustang and pulled a small baggie of joints from the column. Chris laughed. Daulton's secret stash was considered "cop proof" by all of his admiring friends. It was that sneaky resourcefulness that always caused him to look at Daulton in awe.

It was still early morning, but the boys had been awake for hours. Music spilled from the car speakers and Jim Morrison sang about a place called Love Street. They climbed out of the car and stood shoulder to shoulder, passing a joint between them and gauging the wind. It was a perfect day for hawking.

When they finished the joint, they retrieved Primo from the back seat. Being a leftie, Chris slipped his right hand into his falconer's gauntlet. He stepped Primo backwards onto his fist by pressing gently on the back of the hawk's legs. Daulton gathered up a knapsack and threw on his flannel jacket. As an afterthought, he grabbed a tattered ranger hat from the trunk where they'd stowed the camping gear and set it down crookedly on Chris's head.

"That'll keep you from getting sunburned," Daulton said. "It's gonna be bright out today."

Chris righted the hat with his free hand. "Thanks, pilgrim."

"It's more for me than you. If you go home looking like a piece of jerky, your folks'll blame it on me."

They left the Mustang and set out hiking into the rolling bunny fields. The sign of jackrabbits and cottontails was everywhere. After a short hike, they stopped at the crest of a hill overlooking a flat stretch of land and removed Primo's leash. The wind was just right. It was behind them and not too strong. They were after a downwind slip. Most days, hawking was a crapshoot. On this day, the trio had hit a jackpot of perfect weather conditions.

Using his teeth and free hand, Chris opened the two braces on Primo's hood and then gingerly popped it off the bird's head. Primo roused his feathers, wagged his tail, and turned his head upside down to watch rising skylarks.

Primo knew this game well. He took off in a burst of feathers and few into an oak tree, his eyes searching for movement in the bushes and brambles below. Soon, he was bobbing his head intently.

Daulton spoke softly, his voice coming like a whisper. "He sees something."

"Let's flush it," Chris said.

They worked their way in the direction of Primo's stare, kicking at bushes as they went. Every rabbit in the field below him the hawk would have noted his landing above them, frozen in place, not even daring to blink for fear of being spotted. They wouldn't run, not until the boys were upon them. Daulton and Chris worked the bushes like medieval beaters. Visible only for a blink, a cottontail scooted between them, shifting only several feet from brush pile to bushes.

Daulton saw the rabbit before Chris did and pointed. "There, there. Right there, see that?"

"I saw it."

They looked back up toward Primo in his oak tree, craning his neck for a flush, and then whooped and hollered as they advanced toward the bunny's bush. When the rabbit could no longer stand their boisterous approach, it broke cover and raced out across the open, running for safety toward the brambles bordering the opposite side of the field.

Chris looked over his shoulder and saw Primo come flying out of the tree, so fast that it was only a blur. The rabbit was now up to full speed, jigging and jagging for all he was worth – but his warren was a long way off. The hawk was closing the distance fast. In another second, Primo was on him. He planted one talon on the bunny's behind and nailed him in the back of the head with the other. They rolled together from the impact, the doomed rabbit curling into a ball. And then it was over.

Chris and Daulton slapped hands in the way that only teenage boys sharing a mutual passion can do. It was a Saturday morning in the dawn of their lives. Monday was still an eternity away. In that fleeting moment, no two luckier people existed. They raced across the open field, out to where Primo sat huddled over his kill, squeezing the lifeless cottontail in his talons. The hawk ate his reward and the hunt continued.

They flew him through the rest of the day, sometimes allowing him to take the lead from the tree tops, other times flying him from the gauntlet at rabbits flushed out of the brush at their feet. When the hawk had grown tired and the day late, they fed him up on his fifth rabbit and then returned to the campsite.

At dusk, the boys pitched a tent and set Primo on his perch inside the canopy. He pulled up one foot and dozed. The boys drank beer and laughed while they barbecued cottontail rabbits on sharpened spits over an open fire. The meat sizzled as they listened to owls hooting and coyotes singing. The night was unusually warm for this late in the season, so they pulled their sleeping bags out onto the cool earth to sleep under a brilliant blanket of stars. They smoked and talked and smoked some more, until sleep finally overcame them. In the stillness of the early autumn night, they dreamed of birds of prey and exotic women, of riches beyond measure and glorious escapades.

Neither boy dreamed of the concrete beast that even now lay patiently in wait for them less than a mile away.

***

The voice coming from the other side of the food slot had a detached quality about it. If he wasn't absolutely certain, he might not have known it was addressing him at all. But Chris had been here long enough now to know the drill.

"Have you experienced any loss of appetite?"

He thought about it. "Not exactly. I always clean my tray, but I think I'm losing weight. I'm not sure that's normal."

The man on the other side of the food slot was Hill, the prison psychologist – a stuffy, aloof creature who showed up once every quarter, planted himself on a small stool outside the closed cell door, threw open the food slot and rattled off a mouthful of questions from a clipboard on his lap. When he was done, he would disappear for another three months to whatever office desk he spent his days behind.

"Are you having problems sleeping?"

"No. Not really. In fact, I think I do too much of it."

"What about self-destructive tendencies? Thoughts of suicide? Depression?"

Chris hesitated. "I... I don't think so. I mean, I used to think not. I guess I'm starting to feel detached."

There was a momentary silence. Hill scribbled some notes into the margin of the questionnaire and continued.

"Any physical ailments? Headaches? Stomach aches?"

Chris sighed. It was always the same. He might as well have been talking to a robot.

"No sir. Picture of health."

He answered the rest of the questions as quickly as he could so that Hill would disappear again. Sometimes, isolation was the preferable alternative.

***

Chris gazed at the typewriter.

Mine, all mine.

He had requested it six months ago. Its arrival was proof positive that with enough constant pressure, any wall could be made to crumble.

Now if I could just figure out where to apply pressure to make that cell door open on its own, I'll be out of here like a jackrabbit.

They had even included a complementary box of typing paper. Mighty nice of them – and smart. He hadn't thought of it himself. Somebody out there in the no-man's land beyond his sealed cell door had both brains and sympathy. Imagine that.

I'll write Dave first. No, Cait. Maybe Mom. But Dave would appreciate it more, I think. The typewriter is one of the tools of his trade, after all. And how long has it been since I wrote him? Poor old sod probably thinks I've lost my mind and can't put two sentences together. In that case, he'd only be half right.

He sat down at his desk and leaned forward so he could admire the typewriter at extremely close quarters. It was boxy and compact and its finish was a gorgeous olive green that needed polishing, but otherwise it was a thing of beauty.

He thought again about writing Cait. It had been far too long since they'd corresponded. One of the last letters he'd sent her, written in painstaking longhand, had been more a message of condolence than anything else. Daulton's bid for parole had been denied and it would be another two years before he could try again. Chris had done his best to congratulate Cait on her efforts, but he wasn't surprised by the results.

They'll free Charles Manson before they turn either one of us loose.

He picked up the typewriter to get a look at its undercarriage and nearly dropped it when he read the manufacturer's plate: MADE IN EAST GERMANY.

What the hell is an East German typewriter doing in a federal prison? Maybe it's bugged! In that case, I better give them something real good to talk about.

He licked the tip of his forefinger and picked up a single sheet of paper. He was laughing so hard that it took him three tries to feed the sheet into the roller straight.

***

November 7, 1983
FEDERAL BUREAU OF PRISONS REQUEST FOR ADMINISTRATIVE REMEDY
TO: Warden of Institution
FROM: Boyce, Christopher J.
I have been shut up in K-Unit for over a year and it is my impression that the Bureau of Prisons intends to continue housing me here indefinitely. This is a comparatively new unit designed to totally separate inmates from one another. I never requested such housing from the BOP. After I was assaulted at Leavenworth, I expressed the opinion that the BOP was legally accountable for my future safety. I never asked to be brought to Marion or K-Unit. My housing in K-Unit is a direct result of the BOP's inability to prevent armed gangs from terrorizing its own facilities. I did not cause this problem.

If I saw any end to my housing in K-Unit I would not write this letter. Housing in K-Unit consists mainly of being locked in a room and although the room is larger than a regular cell and has a television in it, there is no escaping the fact that I remain confined in a room. Once a day I am cuffed and taken for an hour or two to a larger room or, on an irregular basis, put in a small, roofless, concrete cubicle built into the side of K-Unit. This latter viewless cavity is considered a reasonable permanent substitute for the regular outside facilities available to inmates not held in disciplinary units. Any comparison between the two is ludicrous.

***

November 30, 1983
RESPONSE: This is in response to your request for administrative remedy in which you request to be moved to a different penitentiary with more freedom of movement and where you will not be attacked by other inmates.

The units you are living in were designed for longer term cases where a threat to safety existed in a regular prison setting. Your current placement is not for punitive purposes. Careful consideration of your needs has led to the determination that K-Unit is the most appropriate placement currently available. You will have the opportunity to discuss your concerns with the executive review panel at their next scheduled meeting.

Your request is denied.

If you are not satisfied with this response, you may appeal to the Regional Director, North Central Regional Office, 10920 Ambassador Drive, Suite 200, Kansas City, MO 64153, on a form BP-DIR-10, within twenty calendar days of the date of this response.

***

Chris sat on the edge of his bunk and thought of Steve McQueen. He was tired of thinking about Timothy Hutton. He was a nice enough guy, Hutton, but Chris felt he was much too tall to accurately portray him on film. Of course that fact would only make the Penn guy look shorter than he really was, which made perfect sense. He figured it would all work out in the end.

If it didn't, his conscience was clear. He had done everything that Hutton had asked him to. The handful of occasions they'd met face to face in the unit visiting room had left Chris feeling like a bug in a jar. But he knew that it was necessary.

When Hutton mailed him an early version of the screenplay, Chris wound up taking a pen to it and making the kinds of bold suggestions and sweeping changes he never would have dreamed of making had he been a free man. That was the peculiar thing about being completely cut off from the outside world. It insulated and emboldened you. It made you immune to the kind of mundane embarrassments to which most free people surrender their full control. Now that his work was done and Hutton had returned to the land of the living, it was time to focus his thoughts elsewhere.

And so he thought of Steve McQueen. The quintessential rebel that no walls could ever hold. Surely, a guy like him would have found a way to blow this joint by now.

**

He dreamed himself at the foot of an enormous altar. Dark red smudges marred its ivory finish. A trail of bloody footprints led in a circle around its base.

He looked down at his hands. They were caked with blood. Holding his arms out before him, he saw he was dressed in the black cassock and white cotta of the altar boy. He wanted to pull it off, but he was too terrified to touch the garment with his bloody hands.

A voice spoke to him from somewhere above and just beyond his field of vision. "YOU ARE NO MORE WORTHY TO WEAR THE FLESH OF YOUR BONES," it boomed, and Chris immediately knew the proclamation to be truth.

He nodded his head. His lips began to move, at first slowly, then with increased urgency as his voice grew from a whisper to a cracked croak and finally, to a terrifying scream.

Ashamed.
I am so ashamed.
Forgive me, father. I'm so ashamed.

***

He stared at the wall. The wall stared back. He tried to hold its stare, straining not to blink, but always gave out first in the end. In all of their staring contests, the wall won every time.

Chris rubbed his eyes vigorously and stood. He walked the length of his cell – three full paces – to the small desk that held his papers. He opened a pocket-sized notepad to the first page. Its spine was worn from use and he had filled nearly every page with scribblings. Most of them were half-written letters home, early drafts of later versions he would agonize over before typing up and sending. When you have all the time in the world, it can take forever to write a single sentence.

He flipped the notepad open to the calendar on the first page, then picked up a pencil and drew a meticulous X through a tiny square. February 16, 1984. Today. His thirty-first birthday.

Somehow, it was more shocking to contemplate than thirty had been. Turning thirty had been like taking his first tentative steps into unknown territory. If he lingered long enough on it, it could almost sound exciting. Thirty-one, on the other hand, had a ring of finality to it. Confirmation that the clock had begun to tick just a little bit faster. Proof positive for the disbeliever that the calendar wasn't going to turn back. At thirty-one, you were committed. Full steam ahead to whatever hell the future had in store.

He thumbed through weeks and months of mad scribblings and oddball doodles to the first blank page he could find. He touched the tip of the pencil to the paper and wrote the words: *If thirty-one is any indication of what thirty-two will be like, I can't wait to double down. Sixty-four should be a real riot.*

He stared at his own words and let his jaw go slack. Sixty-four. Surely he would have croaked long before then. As it was, he was shocked to still be sucking oxygen at thirty-one. By all rights, someone should have put a knife into him ages ago.

He thought of his father, now barely fifty-nine and still the picture of health. With his luck, Chris would hit his sixties in fine condition. Just fit enough in body to consider another three decades before drawing close to release age. Genetics be damned. Chris fumbled for a cigarette and lit it, intent on making sure when forty came calling he'd be nowhere above ground for it.

***

"Have you experienced any loss of appetite?"

Hill, again. Armed with the same old questions. Emanating that unmistakable who-gives-a-shit attitude.

"Yes. Everything tastes like cardboard."

"Are you having problems sleeping?"

"I don't sleep anymore. I fade in and out."

Chris leaned forward from his squatting position and peered through the food slot, determined this time to make eye contact. Seated on his stool on the other side of the door, Hill kept his eyes resolutely trained on the checklist before him as he always did.

"What about self-destructive tendencies? Thoughts of suicide? Depression?"

Chris didn't know anymore what was more outrageous – the absurdity of the questions, or the man's ability to recite them time and again with a straight face.

"God damn you. Of course I'm depressed."

Hill bristled. Chris enjoyed the reaction. He decided to make this a Q&A the son of a bitch would remember.

"Is that a real question, doctor? I've been locked in this room for more than two years. In that time I haven't been under the sun once. I'm two thousand miles away from my family and I get twenty minutes of phone time every month. Tell me. How is that not supposed to drive someone to serious depression?"

For the first time, Hill pulled his eyes from his clipboard and looked through the food slot at Chris. As he spoke, his eyes darted back and forth nervously like synchronized pendulums and his voice maintained the same lifeless, monotone drone. "Mr. Boyce, those facts have no real bearing on your mental health."

"I don't agree."

"It's true."

"How do you figure that?"

"The fact is that you are, by definition, a psychopath."

"A psychopath," Chris said. He turned the word over in his head and wondered what the good doctor would label him if he were to suddenly reach through the slot and grab him by the collar. "Is that your professional opinion, or just the label you people stick to anyone you have to talk to through a door?"

Hill folded his eyes back down to the clipboard again. "Being able to visit with your family or sit in the sun for a few hours a day – none of these things would have any benefit on your psychological well-being. Not for someone with your... condition." He tapped the clipboard with his ballpoint. "I just have a few more questions and then we'll be done."

"We're done now," Chris said, then stood and walked to the other side of his cell. If he could have, he'd have slammed the food slot closed himself. Since he didn't have that option, he merely turned his back and folded his arms.

On the other side of the solid steel door, Hill stood and dragged his chair to the next cell down the line. Chris tried to think of the word for the psychological affliction that caused human beings not to give a fuck about others. At one point he almost had it. Then it was gone.

***

He was beginning to think he was losing his mind. Certainly the first sign of that was entertaining the kinds of ideas that had come to him lately. He had spent so much time and expended so much energy firing one missive after another to the warden and the Bureau of Prisons regional director, only to wind up back at square one. But now the answer was occurring to him. If he couldn't force any movement with his own efforts – if he could not make them liberate him from this hell of isolation – he'd simply have to let someone else do the work for him.

Dougherty was out. Anyway, in the end he was just as powerless as Chris was, and not nearly as motivated. That didn't mean he didn't honestly care. He did. It only meant that he could take a break from it, which was a luxury that Chris didn't have. The man could only do so much.

It was an oddly liberating thought to realize that things hadn't changed at all since Lompoc. He knew that if he was going to get out of this at all, he would have to gather his resources. But as hard as the Bureau of Prisons was pushing to keep him locked down in solitary for the rest of his life, he would need a giant on his side.

That was when the idea came to him. It arrived in a flash, like the lost remnant of a life lived long ago suddenly pushed up out of the ground. What did the denizens of Tokyo always do when a big bad menace was on the loose? They woke up Godzilla, that's what they did. And then they got the hell out of the way.

Now all Chris had to do was find Godzilla.

Yes, he thought. *I am definitely losing my mind.*

***

It took Godzilla another year to come calling, but it eventually happened. In that time, Chris had done all he could and exhausted every resource at his disposal to stave off the pull of outright lunacy.

He had come to discover that sanity was relative. And that there were varying degrees of it, just as he was sure now there were varying degrees of mental illness. It wasn't always a life of rational thought that preceded the sudden death-plunge into madness. Sometimes it came in waves that you could steel yourself against. If one was good enough at it and could hold the reins tightly enough, it was even possible to glide into moments of insanity only to pull yourself back to reality at will.

Surely the flights of fancy on which he had embarked didn't necessarily qualify as madness? Depending on who you were, where your trip took you, and what methods you employed to anchor yourself to reality, you might even be called an astral traveler in some circles. But since Chris's physical existence was limited to a constant company of one, he had no circles to inform him if his daylong mental adventures were the product of a sick mind or an incredibly imaginative one.

As much as he preferred the latter explanation, there were days when Chris would *emerge* from flight to find himself standing at attention in the center of his cell for the mid-day headcount, unaware of how he'd gotten there. On one occasion, the bemused expression from a guard on the other side of the observation pane made him wonder if he could have been standing in that position all day – but he quickly discarded this as too frightening to consider. Besides, freaking out unnecessarily fucked up his ability to focus.

The afternoon he received the news of Godzilla's discovery, Chris was just coming down from a five-hour walkabout in the Australian outback. It was a place he'd never been. But he had seen it and smelled it and felt it just as powerfully as he had anything in his life before. He couldn't wait to get back. As soon as he was done roaming, he wanted to explore the bush. Then finally, Sydney for a spell. He might even decide to pick up that beautiful accent while he was there. But first, he had a call to place.

Word had arrived from Bill Dougherty in the form of a short letter. It was actually more like a telegram. All it said was: MUST TALK ASAP, CALL MY OFFICE WHEN YOU GET THIS.

Bill must have sent it off in a hurry before the postman arrived. It wasn't the most private way to get a message through – all mail was read before he received it and after it left his hands – but it was still the most efficient method. Inmates couldn't receive calls, only make them. He hoped whatever Bill had to tell him was worth the call; it was only the tenth and he'd already used half of his allotted time for the month on a quick call home to make sure everybody was still alive.

He hailed a guard and asked to have his name added to the schedule for phone time. The exchange was, as always, unpleasant. But today he didn't give a damn. His curiosity had gotten the better of him and his mind was calculating the possibilities. He spent the next fourteen hours dreaming up all sorts of fantastic scenarios.

They made a mistake on your sentencing! Bill would shout in triumph. *You were supposed to be out last month! Pack your things, my boy!* Or: *Mother Russia called. They want to trade you for an American spy.* He chuckled at that one. Little did anyone know or suspect, but he would rather be a chained man in America than a free man in the USSR.

The next day, his door slot opened at the appointed time and a telephone receiver was handed in. The guard then dialed Dougherty's number in California.

When Bill came on the line, there was an unusual excitement in his voice that Chris had never heard before. It got his attention right away.

"Chris! Good to hear your voice. How are you?"

"I've been better. Not much has changed. You sound sprightly. What's this message of yours all about?"

"I was just about to lay it on you. How would you like to take a field trip to Washington, DC?"

Chris thought for a moment. "There's no federal prison there."

"I said field trip, not transfer. You won't believe who called me."

"Ronnie Reagan."

"You're warm, but wrong party. Senator Sam Nunn's minority counsel. Looks like Nunn and his Republican buddy William Cohen are interested in having you testify at a hearing. In person."

"What kind of hearing?"

"Senate Subcommittee on Investigations."

"You mean like those old mafia hearings?"

"Even better. They want to get your take on the whole top security clearance issue for government workers. Maybe give them some helpful advice. They want to send somebody down soon to talk it over with you. What do you say?"

Chris held the phone to his ear in silence, taking in Bill's words and trying to wrap his mind around them. *They want to ask the monster how to stop other monsters from being born,* he mused.

"Chris?"

"I'm here, Bill."

"I don't think I have to tell you, this could be a great opportunity. Not every person in your position gets a chance to talk in front of the Senate. It'll be one damn fine thing to add to your resume."

And not a bad publicity move on your part, Chris remarked to himself, then banished the thought. Bill Dougherty was a good man. He had accepted no money from the Boyce family throughout this long ordeal. So what if he wanted a little face time in front of the most powerful men in the country? He deserved that much. Besides, he was right. It was an opportunity that no amount of money could ever buy.

Chris chuckled. "All this time I thought Godzilla was just science fiction."

"What?"

"Nothing," he said, realizing he'd thought aloud. Like a fog burning off under the light of day, his mind was beginning to clear. "I just have one question."

"What's that?"

"Can we visit the Lincoln Memorial while we're there?"

Bill laughed heartily.

The wheel was in motion.

***

He couldn't go back to Australia. Not yet, anyway. As much as he wanted to return, and as strong as the pull was to simply lie back on his bunk, close his eyes and fly, he had to stay focused. Otherwise, he ran the risk of coming off like a blithering idiot in front of all those men in suits and the cameras that would likely get it all down for posterity. He had to get his tongue and brain back into synch.

Chris rifled through the stack of books piled at the foot of his bunk. There were close to seventy now, if he didn't count the duplicates. They'd been sent to him from all over the world. Most of them from strangers. The book on medieval falconry had come from a girl in the Midwest. The one on Winston Churchill, from a guy in Perth. Another, a beaten and battered Louis L'Amour, from a housewife in Mississippi. One by one, he set the books aside until he found what he was looking for.

Resting with his back against the concrete bed frame, he set the book on his lap and cracked it open. It was a leather-bound collection of poems by Alfred Lord Tennyson that Dad had sent him. He flipped ahead past the table of contents, scanning over chunks of italicized text and flashing past familiar titles. There were poems in here that he'd known by heart once, but that was long ago.

He found what he wanted a hundred pages deep and read the first line, certain it would all come rushing back to him. When it didn't, he frowned. Maybe it had been even longer than he thought. He shrugged nonchalantly, cleared his throat, and started from the beginning. This time he read the words aloud.

"Half a league, half a league, half a league onward, all in the valley of Death rode the six hundred."

THE BODY, PART 3

Cait
(August 2005)

Chris was right. There were cops everywhere. I don't know what the hell I expected to find. Your husband calls you up out of the blue and announces there are police cars swarming the property, what else should you expect to find when you get there? Still, I was shocked. It looked like 1977 all over again. Or '81. No wonder he sounded so freaked out on the phone.

There were about a dozen sheriff's cruisers parked up and down the length of the driveway leading in from the main road. At the end of the line, I could see a coroner's wagon with its rear door hanging open. Beside it was another vehicle, a dark van with the letters CSI stamped on the driver's side door below the local cop shop insignia.

"What the *fuck*?"

A uniformed deputy approached as I came up the driveway. He held his hand up for me to stop. I did, just long enough to roll down my window and stick my face out into the hot air.

"This is my house!"

The guy looked at me like he wasn't sure he should believe me, but after a second or two of consideration he nodded his head and waved me past.

I parked behind the CSI van and the coroner's wagon and ran into the house, ignoring the stares of the handful of deputies who were standing nearby. The rest of the party was taking place out back – I could hear men's voices and crackling hand-held radios in the distance – but these guys looked like they were stationed here to make sure nobody left without permission. It sent an ice cold chill through me.

Chris was inside. He had his back to the door and was peeking out from behind the blinds into the backyard. It sounded as if the whole sheriff's department had set up shop there. The dogs were going crazy, barking their heads off in the other room. He whirled around suddenly when I shut the door. Everything about him, from his body language to the look in his eyes, told me he was terrified.

"What the hell did they find out there?" I asked.

He sighed heavily as he fought for control of his nerves. "I don't know any more than what I told you on the phone."

"Did you see it?"

"Yes."

"What did it look like?"

He shook his head. His upper lip curled down over his lower one like he was fighting the urge to retch. "Like a rotten body in a bag."

"Well, was there a skull?"

"Maybe. I didn't get that long a look."

I walked around the couch to the window and pushed the blinds aside. There was nothing to be seen beyond the crowd of uniforms that blocked my line of sight to the property line where the center of the action was.

"Did they say anything else?"

"Just enough to make it clear they think I put it there," he replied.

"That's ridiculous. How long does it look like it's been there?"

He was standing in the center of the room now, staring down at his shoes. Contemplating. "I don't know."

"You're sure it's not one of your falcons?"

"Positive. I haven't lost a falcon since we've been here, anyway. And those weren't bird bones. They were big. They looked human."

My mind was racing. The people who had owned the house before us had been an older couple. To the best of my memory, they'd been in the house at least ten years. He was a war vet with a limp and she, about 350 pounds. Not exactly the usual suspects for such a thing.

I thought of our neighbors, Gary and Jeri, the ones putting up the fence on the property line. After about a nanosecond, I crossed them off that list. Even if I believed for a moment either one of them could be capable of doing something as heinous as burying a corpse on the property line – and I didn't – it wouldn't make any sense for them to allow a fencing crew to come in and start digging around. It had to be something else.

"Okay," I said. "We'll let the police do their thing and hopefully they'll be out of here soon. But we're not answering any questions. Especially if they're laying on accusations."

Chris gave me *that* look. The one that let me know he'd done something stupid. "Too late."

"What do you mean?"

"The sheriff was just in here before you came up."

"You invited him inside?" I wrung my hands together to prevent from reaching out and wringing his neck. "How many times have I told you…?"

"I know," he snapped, now sounding as if he were reaching his own critical level of exasperation. "What was I supposed to do, slam the door in his face? It's not like we have anything to hide."

"Even so, did it ever occur to you that it could have been put there by some nut eager to see you back in prison?"

Chris looked at me and I could see the muscles of his jaw tensing and releasing. "Who would do something like that?"

I sighed. "What part of *some nut* didn't you get?"

The even more frightening scenario was the one I didn't dare speak. Because fitting someone's motives into the loony category is comforting. It allows you to breathe easier. The fact is, society isn't as teeming with sick minds as some would have you believe. People with dark agendas, however? Individuals willing to bend the law – or in some cases, break it – in order to ensure that someone who sold secrets to the Russians thirty years ago isn't allowed to continue to walk among the free? Those people are everywhere. I have encountered them, I have talked to them and I have had my life threatened by them. These are the people that truly frighten me.

Outside, the sound of slamming car doors. We hustled up to the bay window that looked out onto the front lawn just as the coroner's wagon was backing up the long and crowded driveway.

Standing beside Chris now, I could see his salt-and-pepper hairline was damp with perspiration. It was hot outside. But not that hot.

"Are you okay?" I asked, even though I already knew the answer to the question.

He continued to stare through the window as the wagon reached the end of the driveway and disappeared with its gory find. "This is just stirring up some bad ghosts."

I couldn't begin to imagine. In all our time together, I had never seen him this afraid. Life since prison had been hard for him, a lot harder than even I could have anticipated. You don't just snap your fingers and go from twenty-five years of complete confinement to absolute freedom without experiencing something profound.

For Chris, that transition had been so difficult that he had lived his first few years as a free man in a constant state of alert. Like waiting for the dream to end and the nightmare to begin again. It was only in the last year that I had seen him finally begin to relax into his new life. Into our life together. He was finally able to walk fifty paces in public without stopping to make sure nobody was following him. The nights when he woke up in a start, not knowing where he was, were coming with less frequency. Now this.

He turned to me and put his hand on mine. That's when I noticed it was trembling. He opened his mouth to speak when a knock came at the front door. In the other room, the dogs started going crazy again.

"Go quiet the dogs down," I told him. "I'll take care of this."

I waited until he was gone before I opened the door. One of the sheriff's deputies was standing on the other side. The moment his eyes met mine, he immediately started looking past my shoulder for Chris.

I intercepted his eyes with my own. "Yes?"

"Are you..." he began, but I cut him off: "I live here with my husband."

The deputy went on, unruffled. "We're just about finished for today. But we'll be leaving the caution tape in place for a few more days until the investigation is complete."

"Are you considering it a crime scene?"

"Until we can determine the origin of the bones, yes."

I asked no more questions and the deputy yielded no more information. When he was gone, I closed the door. Chris was standing at the threshold of the living room with his arms crossed tightly in front of him.

"There's nothing to worry about," I said.

His body language told me that he wasn't buying it. To be honest, neither was I.

MR. BOYCE GOES TO WASHINGTON

Chris
(April 18, 1985)

A spectator standing in the shadow of the Capitol dome on the morning of April 18, 1985, might have thought the Queen of England had just rolled into town. Or that maybe the President himself had decided to swing by to check on his fellow statesmen to make sure they weren't all sleeping on the job. Certainly nobody could have guessed that at the center of all the commotion sat a bewildered thirty-two-year-old California boy with handcuffs on his wrists and leg irons around his ankles.

Outside the U.S. Capitol building, a fleet of unmarked sedans pulled to a halt. Buffering the front and rear of the convoy was a battery of state police cruisers, flashers ablaze. Leading the way were two police motorcycles, their sirens now winding down to silence. A police helicopter circled several hundred feet overhead.

Car doors flew open. In seconds, a cluster of bodies converged around the limousine parked at the epicenter of the motorcade. The rear passenger door was opened and a slender man in a light blue sweater and tie stepped out into the sunlight. Only the subtle lurch in his walk and the unnatural way he held his wrists together in front of him gave any indication that he was wearing restraints.

Nearby, a crowd of onlookers murmured and pointed their cameras. Some took note of the dozen or so news vans parked north of the Senate building and began putting the pieces together.

The circus had officially come to town.

***

Chris thought his first visit to the nation's capital could have been a little less conspicuous, but by now he had stumbled beyond the point of criticism and well into the territory of disbelief.

The trip to DC had begun a day earlier and eight hundred miles east, in Illinois. Waiting for him at the front steps of USP Marion had been a small army of escorts – almost two dozen men, including Bureau of Prisons guards, state police officers and U.S. Marshals. All of them had looks on their faces that said they'd rather be anyplace else, but in truth every man present had volunteered for the opportunity to play a part in what would likely be one of the most high profile Capitol Hill testimonies since the Valachi hearings of '63.

Standing in sunlight for the first time in almost three years, Chris lifted his chin and closed his eyes. The tingling of the sun's rays against his pale skin felt like a kiss from an old friend. When he raised his eyelids, he scanned the sea of faces that had turned their attention toward him.

He couldn't remember the last time he had seen so many people at one time. It was probably in Leavenworth general population, just before they'd thrown him into isolation. Now that he was no longer alone, the reality of all those staring eyes became overwhelming. He took a deep breath and closed his eyes and concentrated on the feel of the sun against his face.

They walked him to an awaiting car and sandwiched him in the back seat between two marshals. As soon as the door was closed, everyone filed into their mix-and-match battalion of police cruisers and undercover sedans. In moments, the cavalcade was on the road.

Far ahead of the procession, motorcycled police blocked off intersections en route to the local airport, their tinny sirens blaring. It wasn't until they were halfway there that Chris noticed the whirlybird shadowing their moves from far above.

If he didn't know better, he would have thought it was all a joke.

The invitation to Washington had come weeks earlier, straight from the office of Senator William Cohen. Chris was asked to testify before the Senate Permanent Subcommittee on Investigations, which would be holding hearings on the issue of security clearance for government employees.

He didn't have to wonder why he'd been chosen. Since his arrest in 1977, he had become a poster boy among government agencies and their contractors for the need to implement stricter screening procedures for employees. The subcommittee needed a star witness. With a Hollywood movie about him playing in theaters, Chris was the obvious candidate.

Cohen assured him his testimony would be invaluable. Chris had his doubts, but after having spent years in an isolated cell where sometimes all he did for hours was stare into space, he was willing to do just about anything to get the hell out.

He agreed, on one condition. "You have to get me outside," he told Nunn's minority counsel when she flew to visit him at Marion to iron out the details. "I need to be able to see the sun again. And not just for the duration of the trip to DC. I mean afterwards. Even if just an hour a day."

The reply – "I'm sure the senator will do everything he can" – was better than he had expected, but he wasn't holding out hope. A request like that wouldn't be easily accommodated. Marion didn't have a segregated outdoor yard for the inmates in isolation and it would probably be a chilly day in Hades before the prison administration would change that on their own. Still, it was a shot worth taking. And if it didn't work out, at least he'd get a change of scenery for a few days.

The caravan approached the airport. Before reaching the terminal entrance, it made a detour and passed through a guarded gate that led directly onto the tarmac. A Coast Guard jet sat gleaming in the brilliant morning light, waiting to shuttle Chris and his entourage to Quantico Marine Corps Base in Virginia.

Two hours later, the jet touched down and Chris was taken to a single-bed cell in an isolated wing of the brig. It was Boise all over again, only this time his jailers were Marines instead of local deputies. The U.S. Marshals, terrified of losing their trophy catch, refused to let him out of their sight. With Chris locked down tightly for the night, they formed a perimeter around the exterior of the building and took turns sleeping in shifts.

He slept fitfully that night, dreaming of falcons in leg irons and cavalries on horseback that never arrived.

***

In the morning, he was taken to a small room with two long clothing racks on either side and told to change out of his orange jumpsuit. The racks were stuffed with an assortment of shirts and pants of all styles and sizes, looking like an excruciatingly organized lost and found.

The change of clothes had been Chris's idea. His rationale was unimpeachable: with the hearing to be televised, his testimony would be far less impactful if delivered by someone dressed like the Son of Sam's cellmate. His true motive was far simpler. His family had been through enough. He just didn't want them seeing him that way if he could help it.

He picked through the gently worn wardrobe and chose a white collared shirt and a striped tie. After a bit more rummaging, he found a thin blue sweater and matching slacks and took them back to his cell. It wasn't dapper, but it would do.

He was still fumbling with his tie when the sergeant in charge of the brig arrived to oversee his transfer back to the marshals. A barrel-chested man in his late forties with graying temples and a baritone voice, the sergeant immediately pointed to the tie.

"That looks terrible."

Chris looked down at his chest and back up at the sergeant. "It doesn't match?"

"Who taught you how to tie a tie?"

"My father," Chris replied. "But it's been so long that I'm a little out of practice."

"That has to be right," the sergeant snapped as he stepped around Chris and moved in behind him. He reached his arms over Chris's shoulders and undid the knot. Then, with hands that moved at lightning speed, he refastened it.

"There."

"Thanks. Tell the senators I'm ready for my close-up."

***

The trip from Quantico to DC was the shortest leg of the journey, but no expense was spared to transport Chris to Capitol Hill in overdone fashion. This time he was flown by a U.S. Marines chopper to a small airfield in DC, where a diplomatic limousine sat in wait amid yet another armada of squad cars, unmarked sedans and police motorcycles. The police helicopter was also back.

As the motorcade made its final approach up Pennsylvania Avenue and the Capitol building came into view, one of the two marshals seated next to Chris turned to him and fixed him with a stony glare.

"Just so you know," he said. "If anybody tries to break you out of this caravan, the first thing I'm going to do is shoot you right between the eyes."

Chris was too flabbergasted to respond. Three years earlier, his transfer from Leavenworth to Marion had been performed by a couple of over-the-hill BOP guards wielding sidearms and a single pair of handcuffs. The U.S. Marshals, on the other hand, apparently had him pegged for some sort of magician.

Just as well, he said to himself. *Let them think that. I'm not the one giving myself a heart attack.*

Up ahead, a crowd of tourists saw the motorcade coming and took their places on the sidewalk for a better view. As the limousine drove past them, he raised one shackled wrist and waved at the onlookers. They waved back.

"Knock that shit off," the marshal growled.

Chris rode the rest of the way with his hands folded obediently in his lap.

***

Flashbulbs popped and camera lenses shuttered as he entered the Senate hearing room. The shackles had been removed just moments before his entry, as agreed. In one hand, he held a stack of typewritten pages that contained the statement he'd worked on for days; the other hand was trembling. Bill Dougherty followed closely behind as both men were led to an oblong desk facing a raised podium where the senators sat.

There was a voice coming from the PA system somewhere near the back of the large room. Suddenly Chris became aware that it was addressing him. "Mr. Boyce," the voice said, "before you're seated, would you raise your right hand?"

He turned his attention to the podium and saw the face of Senator Cohen. Standing at full attention, Chris held his right hand up.

"Do you swear to tell the truth, the whole truth, and nothing but the truth, so help you God?" Cohen asked.

"I do."

"You may be seated."

***

"Mr. Chairman," Chris began, "several weeks ago I spoke to the minority counsels of this subcommittee about my recollections and personal feelings concerning espionage and the government's personnel security programs. All of my adult life I have seen government as a steamroller headed in my direction, a thing to be opposed at all costs. The minority counsels surprised me. During those conversations, I felt for the first time that persons from authority were speaking to me as one human being to another. As long as I can remember, I have tried to tear down that which I could not accept instead of trying to build something better. It is my hope here today that I am performing a constructive act by relating my memories. I have come here in good faith to assist this subcommittee if I can, but perhaps I need to say these things even more than you need to hear them.

"In early 1975 at the age of twenty-one, I took my first stumbling steps toward the KGB. I was a totally naïve amateur. I lacked even the most rudimentary skills this subcommittee would associate with espionage. But even today I am still astounded at how easy the thing was to begin and, given the security system, how near impossible it was to prevent.

"On April 28, 1977, at the age of twenty-four, I was convicted on eight counts of violating the espionage statutes and given a sentence of forty years. My boyhood friend and co-defendant, Andrew Daulton Lee, was convicted in a separate trial on twelve counts of espionage and sentenced to life imprisonment.

"In mid-1979 I was finally sent to Lompoc Prison, where I was put in the incorrigible unit with the hardcore convicts. One day, I was reading a book on my bunk and one of the gangs entered the cell next to me en masse and stabbed my neighbor to death. I remember watching his blood puddle out on the walkway. And not long after that, they did the same thing in exactly the same way to the man in the cell behind me. I heard it all, the screams, the death gurgle. I was the son and nephew of former FBI agents. I did not expect to live long at Lompoc and I decided that being shot off the prison fence was a better death than the knives. But I wasn't shot; I got away one night in January 1980.

"For eighteen months I remained a fugitive, despite a manhunt as far away as Costa Rica, South Africa and Australia. I spent my days in Idaho and Washington State. It is a frightening life believing that every law officer in the country would be proud to put a bullet in you. I was desperate; I thought returning to prison meant my death. To live on the run, I began holding up federally insured banks. I learned about that from all the idle talk in prison. It was terribly wrong, but I never intended to harm anyone, and I didn't. All during this time, I did not hide my true identity and past from dozens of new friends in the Northwest – they were fully aware of what had gone on between the Russians and myself and they knew I was a fugitive.

"Finally, I was turned in by a friend wanting to collect the reward, and I was arrested on August 21, 1981, in Port Angeles, Washington. I pled guilty to everything and now have sixty-eight years instead of forty. The government now keeps me locked in an isolation cell in Marion, Illinois, where I have a lot of time to think about all this in peace.

"I have been told that the facts underlying the original charges against myself and Daulton are generally known by the members of the subcommittee. I don't think I need to recount a long narrative of what we did. Suffice it to say that from March 1975 through December 1976, I removed or photographed a sizeable number of classified documents from the highly secret 'Black Vault' of TRW, a CIA contractor in Redondo Beach, California, and sent them on with Daulton to the KGB in Mexico City. I was able to obtain those documents through my position as a specially cleared TRW employee, working in the Black Vault, located in building M4. On more than a dozen occasions I removed documents from TRW and photographed them. On approximately six occasions, probably more, I personally photographed documents while within the vault itself. Daulton, in turn, delivered and sold the documents to KGB agents working out of the embassy in Mexico City. The documents pertained in part to the existence and operation of then highly secret intelligence satellites.

"As an employee of TRW, I not only received Confidential, Secret and Top Secret clearances, and access to Special Projects, but I also was supposedly restricted by the prescribed physical security measures for classified documents. Obviously, neither the government's clearance procedures nor the company's security procedures worked very well. In fact, the company's security procedures were a great help to me in compromising a CIA project to the Russians.

"I started at TRW as a general clerk making approximately $140 per week. I was immediately given what is known as a 'Confidential' clearance. Almost immediately, my supervisors submitted my name for receipt of Secret, then Top Secret clearance, then access to two Special Projects, and finally, access to NSA codes. By December, all those clearances had been approved and I was assigned to the Black Vault, which I subsequently learned to be one of the most secret and classified areas of work at TRW. It was only then that I learned that I would be working on a Special Project involving the CIA.

"I was assigned, with my immediate supervisor, to monitor and process secret communications traffic between the CIA, TRW, and other CIA contacts around the world. My work included daily contact with the intelligence satellite program.

"In looking back, I remember being surprised that I was given such relatively free access so very quickly to these supposedly highly guarded materials. I used to sit for hours and stare into the satellite guts. It was all science fiction to me.

"I've been told that in other espionage cases, there were some obvious 'red flags' of potential security violators which went unnoticed in background investigations and by co-workers: heavy financial indebtedness, sudden affluence, alcoholism, disgruntlement.

"What was my red flag? Using those indicators, probably none. I was the oldest son in a well-respected, stable, upper middle class, Catholic family. My father had a fine reputation in professional positions of trust. I had performed moderately well in school. While my background investigations were underway, I heard that friends of my parents had been contacted as references. Speaking as adults, they told the investigators that I was the courteous, bright, responsible son of a good family, exactly as they were expected to say. This was the extent of the investigation, as best as I can tell.

"What the investigators never sought was the Christopher Boyce who moved in circles beyond the realm of parents, teachers, and other adult authority figures. To my knowledge, they never interviewed a single friend, a single peer, during the entire background investigations.

"Had they done so, the investigators would have interviewed a room full of disillusioned longhairs, counter-culture falconers, druggie surfers, several wounded paranoid vets, pot-smoking, anti-establishment types, bearded malcontents generally, many of whom were in trouble. In 1974, I believe that the majority of young people of my generation could not be considered politically reliable by CIA standards. I am sure you remember. Had the investigators asked any of those friends what I thought of the U.S. government, and in particular the CIA, I would never have gotten the job. Had they asked, they would have learned that I had first begun smoking pot at sixteen and that I had experimented with a variety of other drugs along with everyone else I knew in my age group. Had they asked, they would have learned that one of my closest friends and later partner in espionage was Daulton Lee, whose record on drug charges and probation violations was, by age twenty-two, quite extraordinary.

"On the question of physical security at TRW's Black Vault, I can answer it simply and quickly: there was none. In my view, and I believe in the eyes of my fellow workers there, security was a joke, certainly nothing to be taken seriously.

"I suppose most people view security regulations as something that should be held in awe by employees. That was clearly not the case at TRW. A number of employees made phony security badges as pranks. My immediate supervisor once made a security badge with a monkey's face on it and, to everyone's amusement, used it to come in and out of the building.

"Aside from badges, there was almost no supervision over access to the building and the vault. Although my comings and goings at building M4 were logged by security guards, there was nothing to stop me from entering at any time during the day or night. On occasion I returned to the vault late at night without being questioned or even raising suspicion. There was simply no questioning after-hours access as long as one mentioned any plausible excuse in passing, such as, 'I forgot my tennis racket.' And once inside there was no monitoring of my after-hour activities in the vault. None of the security guards who would log my entrance or inspect the premises had authorized access to the Black Vault.

During some of these after-hour visits, I photographed and removed documents.

"Within the TRW vault, management had effectively 'compartmentalized' security away. By making the vault such a highly secret area, those of us inside had been given, in effect, total autonomy. We worked under our own set of rules, or more accurately, lack of rules. We brought in an un-cleared company locksmith and altered the numbers on the vault tumblers by half clicks to prevent unauthorized access by our supervisors. We did not want them trespassing on our private preserve. We regularly partied and boozed it up during working hours within the vault. Bacardi 151 was usually stored behind our crypto machines. Under security regulations we were required to destroy the code cards for the machines daily in a destruction blender. We chose instead to throw the code cards toward, but not necessarily in, canvas bags in the corner. We used the code destruction blender for making banana daiquiris and mai-tais. Although only about eight people had authorized clearances to the vault, often many non-cleared members of our 'club,' so to speak, would be in the vault for libations. On occasion the Project Security Manager would join us for a drink on the house.

"Part of our informal duties included frequent runs to the liquor store with 'orders' from various employees throughout the building. We used the satchel for classified material as a cover to bring in their peppermint schnapps, rum, Harvey Wallbanger mix, what have you, along with our stout malt, back into M4. In doing so I sometimes used the satchel to take classified documents out. To return the documents, I used packages, potted plants, and camera cases. Packages and briefcases were never searched by the guards.

"On one occasion I needed to return a rather large ream of documents that I had taken out earlier in the satchel on a Rhyolite beer run. I went to a floral shop and bought two large clay pots about two feet tall. I put the ream of documents in one after wrapping them in plastic, covered it with dirt and then stuck bushy plants in both pots. I brought one of the plants into the building myself and asked the security guard to carry the plant holding the documents back into the building. He obliged.

"A more severe security breach regularly entered our vault over the encrypted teletype link from Langley. Routinely, we would receive from the CIA communications operators misdirected TWXs on other contractors' projects. We were not cleared for these projects and there was no accountability for the misdirected TWXs we received other than a lackadaisical request to 'destroy' typed from the Langley communications operators.

"I distinctly remember one of the two government inspections. The code cards for the crypto machines came in checkbook-style binders sealed in clear plastic envelopes. The envelopes were to be unsealed and the binders removed only at the beginning of the month they were to be used. At the time of the inspection, I had been unsealing some of these 'future' codes, removing them, and photographing them. I would re-seal the plastic with the heat from an iron or with glue and then replace them in the vault. They were all packaged in an official established manner. The inspector came across one code binder that I had replaced upside down and face down, and then resealed. Once tampered with, the plastic envelopes never looked quite the same, despite my botched effort at resealing them. He noticed it, looked puzzled, but instead complained about some other relatively insignificant missing item – one that no one could remember. He had looked closely at the displaced code card binder, but chose to pass over the broken seal.

"My experiences at TRW have caused me to come to certain conclusions about personnel security. I know that a number of changes have been made in the way the government conducts background investigations that supposedly alert the investigators to potential security risks. I have been told that there is now greater emphasis on peers in background investigations. This was a basic reform if it has stuck. Friends of my parents could simply not give a true insight into what made Christopher Boyce tick. As I said before, if this had been done, I believe that I would never have gotten this job in the first place.

"I should have been interviewed in great detail regarding my lifestyle and attitudes. I was never questioned about these points which seem to me to be important indicators for future security breaches. Had I been interviewed in this manner, I also believe that I would have never been assigned to that sensitive position. I know that if I had been polygraphed solely on attitudes toward the government and the CIA or even marijuana use, I probably never would have been considered for the job, but then neither would most of the friends that I grew up with.

"All of this brings me to another point I would like to raise. I am convinced from my own experiences that what I say now is by far the most useful contribution I can make to this subcommittee's study of personnel security. While I think these security regulations you review are important to maintain the integrity of the government, I believe they are next to worthless if each of the four million Americans with security clearances do not have a grasp of how espionage would affect them personally.

"No matter what security procedures are devised, if a man built it, another man can circumvent it and usually in the most simple way. At best, physical security can only make things tougher. The increase of espionage that you are experiencing will not be a passing phase unless popular myths about espionage are debunked for the fraud they are.

"I think, even in these reasonable times, that if not carefully monitored, the intelligence community of any Western nation can be potentially, a threat to an open society. But there is nothing 'potential' about the KGB. That state apparatus not only threatens every open society, but it crushes open societies. That is the distinction I could not see at a rebellious twenty-one. It is a distinction which Americans must see.

"When I was at TRW, I and several hundred other relatively fresh employees were given a group talk on the perils of espionage. A clean-cut, all-American type addressed us from the podium. Here I sat with the KGB monkey already on my back, surrounded by all these young people who were being fed totally inaccurate and inappropriate descriptions of espionage. They were given the impression that espionage was some exotic, glamorous escapade. Handsome Slav spies would seduce young American secretaries on their vacations in Brussels and bend them into secret agents for the KGB. That type of approach to preventing espionage was and is disastrous. That was just what all these bored, young secretaries around me were dying to hear.

"It was surreal. A government spokesman, automatically accepted by everyone as competent, stood there entertaining all those naïve, impressionable youngsters around me with tales of secret adventure, intrigue, huge payoffs, exotic weaponry, seduction, poisons, hair-raising risks, deadly gadgetry. It was a whole potpourri of James Bond lunacy, when in fact almost everything he said was totally foreign to what was actually happening to me.

"Where was the despair? Where were the sweaty palms and shaky hands? This man said nothing about having to wake up in the morning with gut-gripping fear before steeling yourself once again for the ordeal of going back into that vault. How could these ordinary young people not think that here was a panacea that could lift them out of the monotony of their everyday lives, even if it was only in their fantasies?

"None of them knew, as I did, that there was no excitement, there was no thrill. There was only depression and a hopeless enslavement to an inhuman, uncaring foreign bureaucracy. I hadn't made myself count for something. I had made my freedom count for nothing."

For the first time, Chris's voice trembled. He pursed his lips together in a grimace, struggling to contain the emotion that had flooded so unexpectedly to the surface. Everyone had been listening intently to his words, but now an even deeper silence filled the chamber as all eyes regarded the evidence of his pain. Chris reached across the table and took hold of the glass of water that had been set out for him. He drank, cleared his throat, and continued.

"As we sit here, a half dozen, perhaps a dozen, perhaps more Americans are operatives of the KGB. Perhaps some of them have been in place for years. I tell you that none of them are happy men or women.

"And I would suspect that there are hundreds of other Americans out of the four million with security clearances who have given serious thought to espionage. Those are the people that you must seek out and reach with the truth. It is infinitely better for you to make the extra effort to ensure that your personnel understand beyond a shadow of a doubt how espionage wounds a man than for more and more of them to find out for themselves. No American who has gone to the KGB has not come to regret it.

"For whatever reason a person begins his involvement, a week after the folly begins, the original intent and purpose becomes lost in the ignominy of the ongoing nightmare. Be it to give your life meaning or to make a political statement. Be it to seek adventure or to pay your delinquent alimony. Be it for whatever reason, see a lawyer or a psychiatrist or a priest or even a reporter, but don't see a KGB agent. That is a solution to nothing.

"I only wish, Senators, that before more Americans take that irreversible step, they could know what I now know. That they are bringing down upon themselves heartache more heavy than a mountain."

***

When Chris finished, you could have heard a pin drop.

LA CAGE AUX FALCON

Chris
(1985 – 1988)

The guards called it Boyce's Playpen. Chris called it a damn fine improvement. Six months after his testimony before the Senate, the Bureau of Prisons yielded to the repeated requests of a few powerful politicians – Sam Nunn and William Cohen included – and gave orders for an outdoor enclosure to be built specifically for Chris.

Security at Marion in 1985 was the tightest it had ever been. Two years earlier, the prison had been put into permanent lockdown following the murder of two guards in separate incidents only hours apart. For the construction of an outdoor activity pen to be built for a single inmate during this time was an accomplishment on the scale of a grand miracle.

He would be able to breathe fresh air and feel the sunlight on his skin on a regular basis for the first time in three and a half years. He wished he could have offered more to the senators by way of thanks. If he hadn't forfeited the privilege and could have pulled it off without committing voter fraud, he'd have voted for them both. Even Cohen, the Republican.

The enclosure was a vast improvement over the conditions of isolation he had endured since his transfer to Marion. Although twenty-three-hour-a-day confinement was still enforced, his new outdoor area was a far cry from K-Unit's dehumanizing, dog-run-like cubicle. In comparison to the claustrophobic spaces he had almost grown accustomed to inhabiting, its dimensions were enormous.

Situated in an unused corner of the activity yard, Boyce's Playpen was forty-five feet wide and one hundred feet long. Inside of it there were pull-up bars for exercise and a large grassy patch adorned with shrubs and flowers. The whole enclosure was surrounded by a twenty-five-foot fence. Steel girders held up a heavy wire covering, which was presumably there to prevent him from flying away – either of his own powers or through the help of some rogue helicopter pilot. He didn't let this bother him; as long as he could feel the sun through the wire and stretch his arms without touching a wall, he could close his eyes and pretend to be anywhere he wanted.

Often, he brought his letters outside with him to read. The light inside his cell cast a dismal hue over everything and he longed to be free of it. He found that reading his letters by natural light somehow imbued them with a greater vibrancy. Sometimes he would wait for days to read letters from home, saving them until he could take them outside. Doing this gave him one small thing to look forward to. In an existence where such things were scarcely found, he took what he could get and held it close.

Life continued in this manner for years. He began to track the passage of time not by digits on a calendar, but by milestones. Each formed its unique mark on the framework of his reality, leaving notches and splotches as the measurements of minor eternities. Here, his sister Kathy wrote to tell him she was having another baby. There, separated by a gulf of untouched space, the snapshot that arrived in the mail to boast the evidence of her labor. In another space, the image of Dave and his new wife staring out over an ocean of sand with the Pyramids of Giza at their backs to commemorate his assignment to Cairo. Where the assignment ended, a simple curved line marked their journey back home. All Chris had to do was concentrate and it would all appear before him, like pushpins on a mental map that made his own timeless existence almost bearable.

Sometimes when he slept, his dreams were haunted by the specter of a giant hourglass, the pyramid pile inching slowly toward the sieve as he watched powerless. On these nights he would awaken with a homesickness and a longing so powerful he could feel it feasting on his insides like a cancer.

In August of 1987, he received a letter from Cait telling him she was moving on. He didn't blame her. He knew she was committed to fighting for Daulton's parole and that her plate was full. She also had her career to think about. Cait told him she was leaving San Diego behind and heading north to San Francisco, where she intended to open her own consultancy. *Good for her*, he thought. There was plenty of life out there to be lived. Better she take advantage of everything she could.

There's nothing more I can do for you that you aren't already doing for yourself, she wrote. *When we're at our absolute best, we make what we can of what we're given. This is what you've done.*

Off in the distance, a bird cried. He threw his head back and searched the sky for the source of the sound. His eye landed on a lone magpie just as it darted deftly out of sight behind one of the nearby cell blocks. He kept reading.

Let's be perfectly honest, Chris. Even the best team of lawyers in the world couldn't have pulled you out of that dungeon you were thrown into. You pulled yourself out. You had the courage to stand up in front of the whole world and pour your heart out. You took your turn at bat and you knocked that son of a bitch out of the park. As hard as the BOP worked to make you invisible, you forced yourself to be seen and your voice to be heard. Yes, those senators reached out to you first. But most men in your position would have cowered and declined. You didn't. And that's what has made all the difference.

He smiled. There were few things in this infinitesimal speck of dirt between heaven and hell that had the power to make a man swell with pride more than the praise of a beautiful woman. Forget public accolades. Never mind the approving glow of prideful parents. This was where it was at. He felt a moment of embarrassing stupidity for his indulgence. Then he promptly sent that dogmatic little angel on his shoulder straight to hell. He put the letter to his nose, convinced he could smell her.

I admire the hell out of you for standing up and I want you to remember that. In the end, it will be that resolve which sets you free. Chris, your lasting escape won't come through stealth or brute force, but through the concentrated removal of one brick at a time. You are well on your way there. I wish you only the best.

He read the letter again, then folded it up and placed it in his pocket. He wanted to write her back. He wanted to call her. He wanted to tell her that until their first conversation, he had never allowed himself to believe in the possibility of a life outside the nightmare. That it had been her sheer audacity and her bullheaded resolve to champion for Daulton's parole amid the derision of just about everyone in the world – and despite the serious misgivings of Daulton himself – that had inspired him to hope in the first place. But he didn't. Instead, he only smiled and wished her well.

***

In June of 1988, bowing to years of pressure from a loyal network of letter-writing supporters and a few key players in the Senate, the Bureau of Prisons transferred Chris out of solitary confinement and into the general population of the Minnesota Correctional Facility at Oak Park Heights.

He had spent a total of six years in isolation.

Godzilla – bless his colossal green ass – had finally come through.

MATCH POINT

Cait
(1982 – 1995)

A lot of people have asked me how I succeeded in getting Daulton out of prison. I always wink and smile and say something like "I've got friends in high places" or, if I'm in a particularly feisty mood, something stupid: "Ancient Irish secret." The truth is, I've never met anybody with enough influence to spring a couple of convicted spies. The only secret was one people searching for an easy shortcut often overlook: hard work.

I also knew the law.

Back in 1977 when Daulton and Boyce were convicted, there was no requirement in place compelling judges to impose minimum sentences on convicted criminals. The Sentencing Reform Act of 1984 changed all that, which is why nowadays federal judges attach mandatory minimum sentences to federal crimes. They don't do it to be pricks. Not always, anyway. They're just following guidelines.

Since Daulton and Boyce were considered "old law prisoners" with no minimum requirements attached to their sentences, they were both technically eligible to apply for parole every twenty-four months. That didn't mean there were any guarantees. Whether or not their parole would even be considered was a whole different story, but that's where I came in. It was my job to see that the parole commission had enough information in front of them to at least mull it over.

Daulton had been sentenced to life. What most people don't understand about "life" is that it doesn't necessarily equate to being locked up until you draw your dying breath. At the federal level, a life sentence is defined as no greater than thirty years. This was the basis on which I began putting together a case for Daulton Lee's parole.

My first step was getting my hands on the behavioral reviews and psychological profiles he'd undergone since sentencing – all of which showed that Daulton had assimilated well to prison life and was living by the rules. The good news was I had easy access to these reports. The bad news was this would never be enough. Even a rookie prison guard can tell you the same. Just because someone's terrified into behaving like a civilized human being in prison doesn't mean they've actually been reformed.

The next step was reaching out to people who knew Daulton – family members, friends, prison counselors and community leaders who were sympathetic to his situation – and asking them to write letters of recommendation for parole on his behalf. This actually turned out to be easier than I anticipated. While Daulton had previously associated with a lot of people in the drug underworld, this didn't mean there was any shortage of "honorable citizens" willing to speak up for him. I even got Joel Levine and Richard Stilz, the guys who prosecuted the 1977 trial, to provide written statements recommending he be paroled. Both had gone on to establish successful private defense practices, which made them significantly more agreeable to the idea.

In the six months leading up to each of Daulton's twenty-four-month parole hearings, I would begin the process of putting together my brief. This was essentially an in-depth summary that highlighted what the backing documentation supported. Meanwhile, Daulton would write long statements attempting to make amends for his behavior. When I was convinced we had everything we needed, I would package it all together and submit the packet to the parole commission for review. After it was received, the commission would assign Daulton a date to appear.

When the day came, I would drive to the prison, pace the halls until they called my name, then take my place beside Daulton at a conference table facing two or three of the most dour and intimidating-looking people you'd ever want to lay eyes on. It was worse for Daulton. From the moment he was led inside until the moment that exit door closed behind him, he was like a bug under a microscope. At least I had the luxury of having him there to deflect the feeling of being onstage, which made it easier for me to do my thing.

Hitting them with my best Perry Mason (minus the baritone voice and hopefully not quite so butch), I stood and gave the parole commission everything I had. I would make my argument, referring frequently to my brief and to various case laws. I talked about how much time Daulton had already served, emphasizing the fact that he had been forced to spend long stretches of that time in solitary confinement because of concerns for his safety. Then I'd present Daulton's written statement, along with the letters of endorsement from others. After that, I would call him to testify and bring forth a handful of witnesses to speak on his behalf. Most of the time, the witnesses I called were prison counselors who had worked with Daulton and who had only good things to say about him.

Early on, it occurred to me that the biggest hurdle before us was the need to somehow divorce Daulton from Christopher Boyce – to create a line of distinction between the two so clear that even the black-and-white thinkers on the parole commission couldn't miss it. This meant doing a hell of a lot more than presenting a bunch of letters of recommendation and asking for forgiveness. It meant painting him as the anti-Boyce.

In order for that to work, I did everything I could to characterize Boyce as the offender who bore the majority of the culpability. I reminded the parole commission that he, not Daulton, had been the mastermind of the plot to sell top secret documents to the KGB. It was pretty much the "blame it on someone else while taking a modicum of responsibility for our own actions" defense. I didn't reinvent that wheel. I simply reshaped it to fit.

Conveniently enough, Boyce's escape from prison and subsequent bank robberies served as the ideal counterpoint to Daulton's obedient conduct. But his prior drug record effectively rendered that angle a wash, and in our first go-round before the parole commission in '82, we were swatted down like a couple of amateurs.

The same thing happened in '84.

And then again in '86.

Each time, we would be sent into the hallway to await the commission's decision. While Daulton sat calmly with his hands folded in his lap, I resumed my pacing routine. We never had to wait any longer than fifteen or twenty minutes. Invariably, the commissioner elected to speak would say the same thing: "After long and careful thought, weighing all of the good and the bad, we've decided to keep Andrew Daulton Lee's ass in a sling for another two years." I'm paraphrasing, of course. The language was a lot more flowery than that, even if it all amounted to the same sentiment.

It was a rubber-stamp job, all the way. The commission had no intention of ever releasing him, and as much as I knew that, it was always a kick in the teeth. It broke my heart to see the tears welling up in Daulton's eyes every time that judgment was pronounced. For him, it was like reliving the moment of his conviction all over again. For me, it was the realization that not enough time had passed.

By the time 1987 rolled around, our appearances before the parole commission had become perfunctory – too perfunctory to really be effective anymore. I decided it was time to change things up. I didn't want to present a carbon copy of the same unsuccessful argument just to have it slapped down again. We needed more, and there was still one approach we had never tried.

"You need a better act of contrition," I told Daulton.

The Lompoc visitor's room was stuffed to the gills. There were screaming babies and dozens of people talking at once. We were seated in the middle of the racket, hunched forward in a huddle, the picture of concentration in the center of a raging storm.

"What do you mean?"

"You were an altar boy," I reminded him. "Surely you have some ideas."

"Don't give me that. I'm not the only one who used to spend Sundays trying to convince my folks I was an angel." He pointed a finger at me as if to drive home the point. I couldn't argue. Somewhere, in a well-thumbed photo album tracing my evolution from cutesy toddler to hell-raising teen, existed the evidence of my own Catholic school indoctrination.

"You don't have to turn water into wine. I'm thinking something a little more... human."

"If you're suggesting I get down on my knees and beg, you're fired."

I shot him a condescending smirk. "I'm talking about your letter to the parole commission. We need you to lighten up on the victim angle and go straight for the mercy plea. Ask for forgiveness. Admit your wrongdoing. Load up on the remorse. They eat that shit up."

He looked offended. "I'm not taking responsibility for what someone else got me into."

I was amazed – still am – at how much he was willing to give up in exchange for his pride.

"Okay," I said, exasperated. "What do you suggest?"

That's when he said something under his breath. For the all the noise around us, I could hardly make it out. I understood only one word. *Helicopter.*

"What did you say?"

He shook his head dismissively. "Nothing."

But it wasn't nothing. I could tell by the expression on his face. I tried to recall where it was I'd first heard the connection between Daulton and helicopters. It played on the tip of my brain like a forgotten word or a misplaced association.

"You said something about helicopters. What was it?"

He laughed. "I did?"

"Yes. You did."

He folded his arms and shrugged. "I don't remember what I said. It's so loud in here I can't think."

It tortured me for the rest of the day, bouncing around in my head for the duration of my drive back to San Diego. Then, just as I walked through the door of my bungalow and kicked my heels off, it came to me.

Has Daulton ever talked to you about helicopters?

Blaine? Black? No, Blake. Guy Blake! That was his name. The nut in the beach parking lot all those years ago. Telling me he had important information that could help Daulton. Something to do with helicopters.

Had he been planning an escape? Did Blake have something to do with it? I knew I couldn't ask Daulton point blank. He'd already demonstrated an unwillingness to clarify his verbal slip-up. So I opted for a sneakier route. The next time he called, I waited for a lull in conversation. Then I asked, "Do you know anyone by the name of Guy Blake?"

"Is that someone you're representing?"

Either he genuinely had no idea what I was talking about, or he was far better at lying than I'd ever given him credit for.

"No," I said. "Just a name I heard somewhere. Does it mean anything to you?"

He seemed to think about it. "Sounds like an alias."

"Why do you say that?"

"Well, do you know who Guy Fawkes was?"

I did, vaguely. Tried for treason sometime in the 1600s. Tortured and executed for his role in the failed attempt to blow up Parliament and assassinate King James. Or something like that.

"Blake was his mother's maiden name," he said. "Unless I'm mistaken."

"How do you know that?"

"Because I read. And because I knew someone once who was really into Fawkes. He even named one of his falcons after him."

"Who, Boyce?" I bit my lip, convinced I could see Daulton jerking his head away from the phone as if I'd blown a whistle into his ear.

There was a brief silence as he smoothed his ruffled feathers. "Yes. Him. Why? Is someone with an alias stalking you?"

Not anymore, I almost said, then stopped myself. Now it was my turn to be evasive. "No reason. I heard the name somewhere and couldn't place it."

We spoke for another few minutes, mostly small talk. He told me that his mother had gone to dinner recently with Sean Penn and Madonna. During dinner, Mrs. Lee – who had obviously never watched a single moment of MTV in her life – had turned to Madonna and asked, "What is it that you do, dear?"

As soon as we hung up, my head began to spin. I racked my brain to recall when it was that I'd received that first call from Blake but could find nothing that would help me place the timeframe. The fact was, I had spent so much time in Lompoc over the course of the last six years that it could have occurred at any time.

That night, my dreams were haunted by a faceless specter. Each time I tried to draw close, it only pulled further away. When it spoke, its voice came through like barely discernible babble from an out-of-tune radio. The rest was drowned out by the sound of pounding surf.

By morning, the fragments of the dream had dissipated to vague impressions. So had my paranoia. There was nothing there anymore. There couldn't be. I pushed it from my mind and checked the calendar. Time was racing; 1988 was right around the bend. I got busy working on Daulton's next parole brief.

***

Standing before the parole commission always made me feel like a member of a comedy duo still smoothing out the rough edges. For all of my hard work, I couldn't help thinking my requests always served as the parole commission's comic relief. But that never stopped me, or – to his credit – Daulton. Maybe that's why he and I got along so well. We were both a little crazy, and a lot audacious.

I moved to San Francisco in late 1987, leaving my hometown of San Diego behind forever. After that, it became impractical for me to visit Daulton so frequently in person but we made up for that by writing more often and continuing to talk on the phone every day. When another twenty-four months had come and gone and it was time to take another swing, I made the five-hour drive to Lompoc to represent him.

In January of 1992, Daulton reached a depressingly dismal milestone: the fifteen-year mark of his incarceration. As my eleventh year of representing Daulton for parole approached, I decided I was through playing games. It was time to draw out the big guns – even if it meant getting shot down. At least nobody could say I hadn't tried.

I began to double up on my research, reading everything I could about successful paroles. I dissected the cases, taking bits and pieces from each one and adding them to our game plan. I studied the commission's rules until I could recite them backwards and forward.

I also began conducting a series of interviews with noteworthy prosecutors as a way of feeling out precisely what the parole commission was looking for. There was no road map; every attempt was a shot in the dark, and what might work with a certain group of parole board members might not work the next time around with a set of fresh faces.

I asked broad, generalized questions and took copious notes until I got more adept with my shorthand than I ever had or would again. Afterward, I combed through my notes obsessively. I was looking for a single kernel that would pop a light on over my head.

Finally, it came when I met with a federal prosecutor in the Bay Area who had successfully prosecuted an espionage case. He told me precisely what it was I was missing: a recommendation for parole from the sentencing judge himself. Having that, he said, would be the equivalent of bringing an A-bomb to a fistfight.

Just the thought of it made me queasy. From my careful review of trial transcripts, I recalled Judge Kelleher stating on record that if he'd had it in his power to do so, he would have sentenced Daulton to death for his crime. Later, I read several interviews with Kelleher where he referred to him as "pond scum" who would never amount to anything. Not exactly a ringing endorsement. Certainly not any indication that the man would be willing to turn around and recommend Daulton for parole.

By the early nineties, Kelleher was the senior sitting judge on the U.S. District Court for the Central District of California. In other words, a pretty big deal. As terrified as I was to reach out to him, I became convinced that without his letter of recommendation, Daulton didn't stand a chance in hell of being paroled. I began to formulate my plan of attack.

The next time Daulton called, I discussed it with him. Actually, "discussed" is the wrong word. I told him what I wanted to do and he laughed his ass off.

"It's a great strategy," he finally said when he was done cackling. "Let it never be said that you don't have a huge set of balls. But it's impossible."

Alas, my least favorite word.

"Nothing ventured, nothing gained," I said. "We have to try."

He laughed again. It only strengthened my resolve to prove him wrong.

I knew asking Kelleher outright would go nowhere, so I started putting together a presentation of sorts – a packet that I believed would convince Kelleher to go to bat for Daulton. It consisted of:

✓ Letters of recommendation for Daulton's parole, including those written by prosecutors Levine and Stilz. I had also managed to get similar letters from the warden and several counselors from Lompoc.

✓ All prison reports regarding his conduct, groups he was involved with, and projects he had completed.

✓ Daulton's certificate from the National Board for Certification in Dental Laboratory Technology. This was crucial. He had become the first and only federal inmate to graduate and pass the certification test, which essentially made him the resident dentist wherever he was. Seeing that they could save thousands of dollars a year, the Bureau of Prisons assigned him as the main dental technician in several facilities.

✓ An accompanying cost analysis of how much money Daulton was saving the Bureau of Prisons by providing his dental services.

✓ Daulton's letter of contrition.

By this time, I had finally managed to convince Daulton I was right about his need to accept responsibility for his part in the crime – if not in his heart, then on paper. To his credit, his letter was impeccably written. He was contrite; he was humble. Most importantly, he asked for forgiveness for the damage he had done to his family and his country. Reading it almost convinced me he had actually decided to own up to his share of the responsibility. Almost. I knew him too well. If he was getting on board, it was because his desire to get out of prison was beginning to eclipse his pride.

It took me two months to put the Kelleher packet together. When I was finished, I set it aside and spent an entire weekend on my surfboard to clear my head. Looking at it again with fresh eyes, I knew it still wasn't complete. I needed to write a cover letter that would pique Kelleher's interest so he wouldn't toss the package aside without reading it.

I started doing a bit of digging into Kelleher's background. What I learned about his favorite pastime proved to be key. Kelleher was a rabid tennis supporter. When he was younger, he had been a championship player and was still heavily involved with the Southern California Tennis Association. The minute I read this, I knew I had my hook.

Daulton was also a tennis player. Since being locked up, he had developed a proficiency on the court that surprised everyone, especially him. Nobody expected a guy his size, who had to grip the racket with both hands when he swung just to get the ball over the net, to be such a skilled player – but more than once, he entertained me with stories about how he had repeatedly defeated inmates with far greater athletic prowess. Seizing on that common thread between Daulton and Kelleher, I got to work on my cover letter.

Two days and about four dozen rewrites later, I was done. It was a work of art. The letter was a concise summary of all the best bits from my previous parole briefs – *Andrew Daulton Lee's Greatest Hits*, if you will (and even if you won't). It spoke to the inner work he had done since his conviction; how he had accepted responsibility for his crime; the regret he felt for the damage he'd done. At the end of the letter, I included these words: *In his spare time, Mr. Lee is an award-winning tennis player.*

Then I stuck the cover letter in with the rest of the packet and mailed it to Kelleher's office in Los Angeles before I could lose my nerve.

Weeks passed. Nothing happened. I was glad I hadn't told Daulton I was going through with my strategy. The last thing he needed was to have his hopes crushed. When I still hadn't heard anything after three weeks, I gathered up my nerve and called Kelleher's office.

The clerk I spoke to could have put me off. She didn't. Instead, she put me on hold – long enough for me to have to endure a torturous muzak rendition of "Can't Smile Without You" and the opening strains of "Send in the Clowns" – and when she came back she informed me, "The Judge has received your correspondence, but he hasn't had time to read it yet."

I thanked her and hung up without getting any indication of how much longer I'd have to wait. Another two weeks went by and still, nothing. I called again. *What's the worst he can do?* I asked myself. *Ignore me? He's already doing that.*

This time, I got a slightly better response. "He's read your packet and says he will be in touch." Lovely. I settled in for another excruciating wait and tried to busy my mind with other things.

Three days later, my phone rang. It was Kelleher. I was blown away. I hadn't expected him to call me back, hadn't even expected that he would read the packet to begin with. Now here he was.

"What is it you want me to do?" he asked.

I experienced a flash of panic. Was it possible I had put that entire packet together and not mentioned why I was sending it to him? Right now, that didn't matter. I had Kelleher on the line. This was my moment.

"Could you see your way clear to either writing a letter to the parole commission recommending Mr. Lee for parole or, at the very least, writing a letter to tell them you don't oppose his release?"

I closed my eyes. I might even have crossed my fingers. All I remember clearly was the long silence that preceded Kelleher's next words.

"Let me give it some thought. I'll be in touch in a few days."

Those few days turned into a few weeks. I didn't dare call back. The last thing I needed was to piss off the one and only guy in the world whose words could sway the parole commission in Daulton's favor. A few weeks turned into a month. Still nothing.

Right about the time I was coming to the conclusion that my effort had failed, I got an envelope in the mail with a return address from the District Court in Los Angeles. I opened it. Inside was a copy of a letter Kelleher had written and sent to the U.S. Parole Commission. It was dated October 22, 1992.

I have been made acquainted with the pending application of Andrew Daulton Lee for release on parole. I have studied the file carefully and have otherwise informed myself concerning the status of the petitioner.

I am informed that the Assistant United States Attorneys who prosecuted Lee before me have written letters to you recommending the grant of parole. I am further informed from what appears in his file that he has acquired a license to practice as a dental technician.

Based largely on the fact that his prosecutors favor release on parole by the fact that Lee would apparently have an employment opportunity upon release and based further on the fact that few defendants under my sentence have ever shown significant progress on rehabilitation, I consider Lee to be a favorable candidate for release.

If it were my decision to make, which I realize it is not, I would grant parole on such conditions as the Commission might impose.

Very truly yours,
Robert J. Kelleher
United States District Judge

I stared at the letter for a very long time, trying to make sure I wasn't imagining words that weren't really there.

Holy shit...

Although it would probably be really cool and theatrical to tell a lie and say that I ran around my office with my arms in the air whooping and hollering, the reality is a lot more mundane. When I finished reading Kelleher's letter, I sat down at my computer and composed what still stands as the most heartfelt thank-you note I've ever written.

Daulton was dumbstruck when I talked to him that night.

"I *told* you so!" I chided. "Does this mean I can finally start getting paid for my legal services?"

"Not so fast there, counselor. A letter of endorsement from a federal judge does not a parole guarantee make. If this doesn't work, I'm going to bill *you* for all of the therapy sessions I'll need to recover."

"I have a good feeling about this," I said. "It's going to work."

It did.

It didn't happen overnight. It took months for the parole commission to even acknowledge Kelleher's letter, which pissed him off to the point of writing a handful of letters to the commission asking why they had chosen to ignore his recommendation. Lesson learned: federal judges don't like to be blown off. Eventually, the commission deferred – albeit grudgingly – to Kelleher's pressure.

In October of 1994, Daulton took a seat before the parole commission for what would be the final time. When the hearing was over, the commission's verdict was returned: PAROLE DATE RECOMMENDATION, JANUARY 18, 1998.

***

April 5, 1995
Dear Chris,
Long time, no talk. I bet you never thought you'd hear from me again. If you're wondering why I'm writing after all this time, it's

not because I missed your sense of humor. Okay, maybe that's one reason. But there's another, bigger reason. I have some news. Big news. Six months ago, Daulton's request for parole was approved.

Hey, it only took about fifteen years and I had to convince Judge Kelleher himself to give his endorsement (which is a long story in itself), but it worked. Daulton's release date has been officially set for January of '98, and if all goes as planned I will be able to have him released six months early to a halfway house. So we're looking at mid-'97 at earliest.

Now it's your turn, if you're interested. I guess I don't need to tell you that Daulton's release pretty much paves the way for yours. If you think your case is hopeless, you're wrong. I took the liberty of doing a little bit of digging into your bank robbery convictions and saw that Judge Hal Ryan not only sentenced them to run concurrently, but he also sentenced you to a (b)(2), which as you know means there's no minimum time required for you to serve before you can be considered for parole. I'm sure this isn't news to you, but it was to me – and it's given me something to work with.

Are you ready for a parole hearing? I've included my phone number below. Call me, there's lots to talk about.

Cait

THE UGLIEST WORD IN THE WORLD

Cait
(October 1996)

The boy in the pristine white *dobok* lifts his knee and sends the roundhouse kick flying. His leg cuts through the air like a horizontal catapult, creating a perfect arc as the instep of his foot crashes against the woman's exposed upper rib cage. There is a thump of muscle against flesh, then an infuriated cry as she hits the padded canvas floor.

"*Shit!*"

Her words ring out through the crowded *dojang*, turning heads.

"Omigod! Are you okay?"

It's the little bastard, no more than twelve, standing over her with his fingers touching his lips. The expression of regret is so sincere that she can almost forgive him.

"I didn't mean to kick that hard!"

Kids, she thinks. *They spend the first fifteen years of their lives never realizing their strength, then their last sixty forgetting they ever had it.*

Half the room is standing still now, watching the redhead on the canvas as she clutches her injured chest. The *Sabumnim* comes jogging over and kneels at her side, but not before striking the repentant child with a disapproving look.

"Are you okay, Cait?"

"I think so," she says. Her words sound more like a moan.

He helps her to her feet and motions for the rest of the class to resume their sparring exercises. The silence gives way to huffs and puffs and the sounds of Westerners mispronouncing *kiai*.

"I'm sorry," the boy says again. Cait sees tears brimming in the boy's eyes and extends her arm to pat his shoulder.

"I'm okay," she assures him, vowing never to spar without her chest protector again. "You kick like a mule, kiddo."

Beneath the thick cotton of her Taekwondo *dobok*, the flesh of her breast has already begun to bruise and swell. By mid-afternoon the next day, the discoloration has spread to a dark, ugly splotch.

I'm getting too old for this shit, she thinks.

***

"You should have kicked him in the balls."

Christopher Boyce was a boy once himself and he knows that sometimes, an injury returned is the best lesson of all.

"I could hardly stand up," she tells him, "let alone kick back."

"The next time you're in class, kick him in the balls." He seems to relish the idea a bit more than he should. "Pretend it was an accident, then buy him a lollipop and tell him you're sorry. That'll teach him."

"I'm not going to kick a twelve-year-old kid in the balls. I save that sort of thing for grown men. I don't want to sterilize the poor fucker."

"You'd probably be doing the world a favor."

"Stop it."

"He started it."

Boys.

It's been a year and a half since they first got back in touch. In the beginning she tried to divide her time evenly between Daulton and Chris, but now the juggling act has become almost impossible to keep up. She and Chris have grown much closer than either thought they would. His phone calls to her have grown more frequent. Lately, the language in Chris's letters has become more florid. Cait doesn't mind; it's been a long time since anyone made her feel this way.

She changes the subject. Chris's parole hearing is less than five months away and although she's been putting the pieces together for some time, there's still much to be done. Making a case for Daulton's parole ultimately proved easier since he had been a model prisoner. The Boyce escape and bank robberies would make his case an enormous pill for the parole commission to swallow.

"I need your letter to the commission," she reminds him. "ASAP. That is, if you're not too busy looking over your shoulder to avoid the next assassination attempt."

Three years earlier, Oak Park Heights inmate Earl Steven Karr had attacked Chris and tried to electrocute him with an improvised electric prod. Fortunately, Karr was as unlucky as he was insane. Chris got away with a few bruises and an eyeful of homemade jalapeño mace. Karr was committed after admitting the voices made him do it. Cait brings up the incident frequently to remind him to never let his guard down. It was stupid to turn his back on a convicted pipe bomber. She thinks if she mentions it enough, the warning will stick. Christopher Boyce is sometimes much too trusting for his own good.

"Alright," he agrees. "You'll have it soon."

He's not looking forward to writing the letter. Apologies have never been his strong suit.

She checks her wristwatch. "Now if you'll excuse me, I have an appointment in about six minutes to talk to your old partner in crime."

"How is Daulton?"

"Eager for July '97 to hurry up and get here, as you can imagine."

"Does he know about us?"

She laughs. "You make it sound so *sordid*."

"Are you kidding? This is the steamiest romance I've had since the seventies. I wouldn't go so far as to call it sordid. But that doesn't mean I don't have my share of bad thoughts."

"You're a sick man, Boyce."

She doth protest, but the smile on her face and the tone of her voice giveth her away.

***

Her conversations with Daulton have become strained. Something's changed. As much as she wants to believe it's him, challenging her in the way adolescents challenge their parents the closer they near their independence, she's beginning to realize it's she who longs for freedom.

"I called you earlier," he says.

"When?"

"Fifteen minutes ago."

"Oh. I was out."

"I got a busy signal."

"What is this, Daulton? Are you checking up on me?"

He doesn't answer.

She steers the conversation to legal matters.

"So, everything's looking good for your early release to the halfway house."

"Yeah."

He sounds disinterested, his freedom now a foregone conclusion. The awkwardness is almost too much for her to bear. This used to be fun. Now it's become a chore.

She wonders if she should tell him she's been talking to Chris. The thought has already crossed his mind. Neither are willing to broach the subject.

Dishonestly is the killer of trust.

***

In the shower, two weeks after the roundhouse kick to her left breast, she finds a lump. It's been four months since her last routine mammogram and three weeks since she last performed a self-examination. Neither turned up anything. The lump is the size of a grape. She exits the shower immediately and wraps herself in a towel.

What now?

She tries to remember everything she's ever been taught about what to do, but her mind is a blank slate.

Is this the onset of panic? Stop. Think. If I call and ask Mom, it'll just freak her out.

Out of the corner of her eye, the telephone beckons. She picks it up and auto-dials the number for her doctor. Within five minutes, the appointment is scheduled. Mammogram, MRI and needle biopsy.

She arrives at the clinic eighteen hours later. The doctor is a kindly looking man in a flamboyant purple shirt. She'll remember that shirt for the rest of her life, as she will the understanding smile that spreads across his face when she says, "Please don't tell me I have to come in to get the results. Just call me and tell me. Can you do that?"

"Absolutely."

Three days pass.

No news is good news.

She hasn't told a single soul. Not Chris, not Daulton, not even her mother and father.

There may be nothing to worry about. It happens all the time. I have that going for me. Plus, there's no history of breast cancer in the family. It's probably nothing.

Just after lunch, the phone in her office rings.

She picks it up hesitantly. "Don't keep me in suspense," she begs.

"The results of the needle biopsy came back positive."

For one brief, flickering instant her heart leaps. Then she realizes what she's just heard.

"It's cancer," the doctor says, confirming her worst fears.

She doesn't react the way she imagined she would. Few people do.

"I want to get you scheduled for a lumpectomy as soon as possible. I'm sending you to a surgeon for a consultation and to go over the details."

A numbness settles over her.

"Tell me when and where and I'll be there."

***

Her brother Tim goes with her to the surgeon's office. They told her to bring someone to act as a second set of ears. This sort of thing is routine for them, she realizes. The surgeon takes a seat behind his desk, but not before placing a box of tissues between him and his patient. Everything is cold, methodical.

There is a checklist of questions on her lap. Only one demands to be answered first.

"What are the chances the lumpectomy will take care of the problem?"

"There's a possibility the procedure may not get it all," the surgeon says. "We won't really know the extent of it until we go in. Even after that, you'll very likely have to undergo additional treatment and routine follow-up tests."

"What kind of treatment?"

"In a worst-case scenario, chemotherapy and radiation."

She turns to look at her brother. He looks shaken. The irony that she will be the one to comfort him causes a laugh to rise in her throat. The urge subsides when the weight of her predicament descends. Maybe nothing will ever be funny again.

Cait looks the surgeon square in the eye. "If you find out it's worse than you thought, please don't wake me up to tell me. Just do what has to be done. Can you do that?"

He doesn't say yes; he doesn't say no. He only bows his head in acknowledgement of her request.

Cait takes her brother's hand.

After the consultation, they sit together in the courtyard of the medical center. The espresso before her is bland, more tasteless than any vending machine slop she's ever suffered through before. Tim positions himself next to her and leans in close, trying in vain to shield her view of the bald women who enter and exit the doors of the cancer clinic across the street.

Each time her eyes wander that direction, he squeezes her hand and tries to tell her everything will be alright. She fakes a smile and tries to believe it.

***

When Daulton calls that night, she considers saying nothing. So far, nobody else knows – not her mother, not her father, not even Chris. Especially not Chris. Who knows how he'll take it? With Daulton, it's different. They've shared a lot in the last sixteen years and the moment she hears his voice, she finds herself telling him every detail.

He listens quietly, saying nothing at first. His response is cautious. Uncertain. Almost as if trying to determine if he's being lied to.

Finally, he responds. "Cait, that's terrible."

"It's not good, no. I think I'm in shock. In fact, I'm pretty sure I am."

More silence, enough to make her feel uncomfortable.

Maybe I shouldn't have said anything.

"And you're sure it's cancer?"

"Well, no. I'm not. But the doctor seems pretty convinced. I figure he knows a hell of a lot more about it than I do."

"Hm."

Did I expect him to break down in tears? No. Not Daulton. But did I expect this cold reaction? Never. I might as well have told a stranger on a bus.

"I'm sure it'll be okay," he says. "It's just a procedure. They do it all the time."

"I hope you're right."

"I always am."

His declaration doesn't make her feel any better.

***

"We're dropping this," Chris says.

"Dropping what?"

"My parole request. You need to take care of yourself now. We'll worry about me some other time."

"We're not dropping anything," she informs him calmly. "As soon as they're done cutting me open, I plan on getting back to work. We've still got a few months to get everything together."

"You talk about it like it's nothing."

"I'm not letting this stop me, Chris. It'll slow me down, but once I'm healed up, I'll be back at it."

"No!" His voice sounds desperate now, insistent. "You're going to have to go through treatment after. Chemo. You told me."

"I told you that's what they *recommend*."

"Don't be stupid, Cait. Just do what the doctors say." His voice is trembling.

She doesn't tell him that she's already decided not to go through with chemotherapy.

It works by bringing you to death's door and hoping the cancer exits before you do. If I were to put that strategy on paper anywhere else in the world, it would never pass. My body, my choice, my gamble. Fuck the chemo.

"I love you too much to see you put your treatment on hold."

This is the first time he has said the words out loud. She thinks for a moment, unsure of how to respond. Then the right answer comes to her.

"I love you too, Boyce."

He starts to speak, then chokes on his words. This is the first time she has ever heard him cry. His sobs are mournful, violent. They are the cries of a man willing to do anything, yet powerless to even try. When he's able to form words, he tells her that he loves her. Over and over and over again.

***

Cait arrives at the hospital at seven a.m. on the day of the procedure. She's home by five p.m.

Drive-through slice and dice. Can I get fries with that?

On the third day, she returns to the hospital with her bandages and drains, and a weight like an albatross around her neck. This time, her mother is with her. They wait together in the examination room and hold hands. When the surgeon enters, Cait sees the tired, drawn look on his face and suddenly wishes she was somewhere else.

"What's the good news?" Her words are hopeful, even though she already knows there's something wrong.

"Cait, I have no good news." His voice is lifeless; he sounds like a machine. "I have bad news. We found two large tumors down near your chest wall. I have you scheduled for surgery again tomorrow to remove them."

He hesitates before delivering the rest of the news. "We have to perform a mastectomy down past the muscle wall. Unfortunately, nothing of your left breast can be saved."

Cait listens as more horrible words spill from the doctor's mouth.

The tumors are massive. One is 2.5 centimeters. The other is 3.7 centimeters. Stage IIIB invasive lobular carcinoma. Only Stage IV is worse, and there is no such thing as Stage V. From the size of the tumors, he estimates they may have been there for seven or eight years, growing slowly. The grape-sized lump turned out to be no more than a raised bruise brought on by trauma. Had it not been for that wayward roundhouse kick, what lay beneath may never have been discovered. Not until it was too late.

"At this point," he tells her, "it may be a good idea for you to get your affairs in order." Then, from some even more distant place, she hears the words, "One in ten chance of survival."

Her mother, a woman much stronger than she, begins to cry. All Cait can think of is Chris.

"Do whatever you have to do," she says.

So that I can do what I have to do while I still have time.

***

The world is a deep, black sea. She floats through it weightless, dimly aware of her own existence. Then a dull, throbbing ache pulls her closer to the surface and she thinks she can remember where she is and how she got here.

Up above the surface of the water, a voice is calling her name. Its kind, welcoming tones draw her closer to waking. Now she can feel someone holding her hand, tapping it gently, rousing her to consciousness. Shadows begin to play against the backs of her eyelids. Her lips part to respond, but before she can utter a word she's hit with the greatest sensation of pain she has ever felt. It rakes viciously across her like a claw, from her left armpit to the center of her chest, taking her breath away.

Just as she thinks she can stand no more, the darkness begins to envelop her again. Somewhere far away, an anguished voice cries out. As she sinks back into that painless, welcoming sea, she realizes the voice is her own.

***

The recovery takes longer than she thought it would. A helpless sensation of time ticking away into eternity grips her. From her bed, she stares at the calendar on the wall and realizes there are less than two months before Chris's parole hearing.

"Fuck this," she grunts, wincing as she pulls herself into a seated position.

It takes her fifteen minutes to change the bandages. She averts her eyes the entire time. Once, a week ago, she dared look at her reflection in the mirror. What she saw made her cry out in alarm. This didn't look like the work of a surgeon. It looked like the work of a butcher.

When she finishes, she reaches into her medicine cabinet and takes out a bottle of Extra-Strength Tylenol. She stopped taking the

Percocet four days after the surgery. Chris doesn't need a drug addict putting together his parole brief. She swallows two caplets and makes her way down the hall toward the dining room.

The table has remained untouched since the eve of the surgery. Neat piles are spread out before her, covering every visible inch of table. They are the pieces of the jigsaw puzzle, the documents she hopes will be enough to set Chris free.

I may not be able to be there for the hearing. In fact, there's no way I'll make it. Not in this shape. But I'll be goddamned if I'm going to let him go before those bastards empty-handed.

Slowly, with great deliberation, she sits down and resumes her work.

***

On the morning of March 24, 1997, Christopher Boyce takes a seat in a small room in the administrative offices of Oak Park Heights prison. Seated across from him is U.S. Parole Commission Examiner Kenneth Walker.

Walker reviews the parole brief Cait has meticulously put together. When the time comes, he asks Chris if he has any words.

This will be your big moment of truth, Cait told him. *Don't blow it, Boyce. You may never get another chance.*

Cait's words echo in his head. He clears his throat and begins to read aloud from the statement he's written. Walker listens intently, knowing his decision today will determine the fate of the man addressing him.

Chris almost makes it to the end. But the moment his thoughts turn to Cait, it's all he can do to keep himself from falling apart. He wonders what his life will become if he loses her. How terrified must she be right now, not knowing if she'll live or die? He takes a deep breath and clears his throat again. An awkward silence fills the room. When he finally starts to speak, there is a noticeable tremolo in his voice.

He finishes his statement, folds his hands on the table before him, and sighs.

Ten minutes later, Walker renders his decision: "I am recommending immediate parole for the first time in my fifteen years with the Bureau of Prisons."

A suggested parole date is forwarded to the Eastern Regional Office of the United States Parole Commission in Chevy Chase, Maryland, for final approval: March 15, 2003. One month to the day after the hearing, the recommendation is rejected by the United States Parole Commission.

MINNESOTA NICE

Cait
(May 1997)

For as long as Chris and I had known each other – starting with that first letter in 1982 and culminating with my decision to represent him for parole – we never actually met face to face until May of 1997.

Nowadays, that sort of thing isn't so rare. With the invention of the Internet, it's not uncommon to form lifelong friendships with people you've never met. But back in the dark ages of the seventies and eighties, things were very different. People actually talked on phones instead of sending truncated text messages. We wrote letters and mailed them back and forth. Sometimes it took forever, but if you ask me, that's what made it all the sweeter. Alas, I'm probably aging myself. I better shut up and tell the story.

The notice of action Chris received from the U.S. Parole Commission rejecting Walker's recommendation left him devastated. It only strengthened my resolve. It gave me something more to fight for than my health. To be perfectly honest, I was tired of worrying about my physical body. Although the results of the follow-up tests I'd been subjected to were encouraging, each doctor's visit brought a renewed frenzy of anxiety. The challenge the parole denial presented was exactly what I needed.

"You did everything you could," Chris told me on the phone the day he got the letter. "Maybe it just wasn't meant to be."

A saner person might have agreed, but I've always been a little crazy. It wasn't over. In truth, we weren't even back to square one. Not yet, anyway. Not as long as I had an opportunity to appeal the commission's decision.

The fact that nobody had ever successfully appealed a parole commission decision should have scared the living hell out of me. It didn't. Blame the cancer. Or credit my refusal to accept that anything was over 'til the credits rolled. We had less than two months to file the appeal. There was no time to waste freaking out.

"I'm flying out to see you," I decided. "We have work to do."

"Can you do that?"

"Fly? Why wouldn't I be able to?"

"I'm thinking about your health. Should you be traveling?"

"Chris, I'm fine." That was a lie, but he didn't need to know any different. The mastectomy had thrown me for a loop, both physically and emotionally. Not only did I look like a hapless victim from a *Jaws* sequel, I was also getting little sleep. That's what happens when you're plagued with worry that there might still be some tiny cell in your body plotting your demise – one the doctors missed.

"Don't you think it's time we finally met in person?" I added.

His response wasn't quite what I anticipated. "I'd love to see you, Cait. I just don't think you should waste your time or energy. You need to concentrate on getting well."

That's when I exploded on him. I still swear I heard him flinch, even though I know damn well my ears aren't that good.

"God damn it!" I snapped. "I'll make the decisions about who and what to waste my time on, Boyce. And I'll be dipped in shit if I'm going to pass up our legally given right to an appeal just because you're ready to drop out. Guess what? *I'm* not ready to drop out. So you're just going to have to go along with me a bit longer before you can lie down."

The silence on the other end of the line was concerning. At first, I thought he'd hung up. Then Chris suddenly burst out laughing.

"What's so funny?"

"Nothing." His laughter diminished to an amused chuckle.

I took a second to compose myself. When I replied, my voice was level. "Then what are you laughing at?"

"You," Chris answered, but before his words had an opportunity to trip my defenses, he added: "If I'd had you in the courtroom in '77, I wouldn't be talking to you on a communal phone from the pits of hell."

"We wouldn't be talking at all. At least not long distance."

"Good point." He finally grew serious again, clearing his throat the way you do when you're trying to get down to business. "You want to appeal the decision, then I'm all for it. If you want to fly out to talk over a strategy, even better."

And that was that. Eight days, four hours and fifty-seven minutes later, I was touching down in Minneapolis. I rented a car for the half-hour drive to Stillwater, a small town of about fifteen thousand people that sat on the Minnesota side of the St. Croix River. From there, it was just a three-mile drive to Oak Park Heights.

I got into town about an hour before sundown, so I checked into my hotel room and unpacked my travel bag. Thanks to a three-hour nap on the flight out, I still had enough juice left to go exploring. Flashbacks to Lompoc and the first time I took up temporary residence in a hotel to visit someone else I was representing for parole became impossible to ignore. Only this time, everything was different.

First of all, it was spring – a beautiful, true spring, the kind that makes you disbelieve in the existence of melt-your-brain summers. There were no Pakistani-owned motels and the only Chinese place in town had been closed for years, but I became enamored of Stillwater just the same. There were cobblestone streets in its downtown area, and enough bookstores and coffee shops with quaint alcoves to keep this California girl far from homesick. The people were so friendly that it bordered on disturbing. There was a bridge on the east end of town that spanned the width of the St. Croix

River into Wisconsin, and everywhere I looked I was encountered with more greenery than I'd seen in ages. Most importantly, there was a guy named Christopher Boyce less than five minutes away.

I'd be lying if I said the thought didn't give me butterflies. Let's face it. I wasn't just there to see someone I was representing. If that was all there was between us, I could have saved a chunk of change on airfare and done my work from home. I was there to see someone I was in love with. As much as you can be in love with someone you've never actually met face to face, anyway.

Daulton would have laughed. He would have told me I was venturing into dangerous territory, and who's to say he wouldn't have been speaking the truth? But I guess that's the truly unpredictable thing about matters of the heart. You don't get to pick how you feel. I hadn't chosen to fall in love with Chris. I just had. And the thought of finally being with him in person was terrifying. Not because I was afraid those feelings wouldn't be there at the moment of truth, but because I was positive they would. And because there was still no guarantee he would ever be released from prison.

My appeal to the parole commission was a long shot, at best. If it didn't work, Chris wouldn't get another chance for at least two more years. At this point I couldn't be sure I'd still be around by then. And if I wasn't, who knew if Chris would even be interested in trying anymore?

That first night in Stillwater lasted an eternity. I knew I had to be up by dawn to make the most of my visit, but damned if I could sleep. The idea of being so near to Chris now was exhilarating. Sleep finally found me somewhere between two and three in the morning. In my dreams, I heard the sound of a train whistle in the distance.

Driving the short distance to Oak Park Heights, my stomach knotted. Prisons are decidedly unpleasant places, whether you're doing time or just visiting. They leave the same impression on everyone who's ever ventured past their guarded entry gates: *Don't ever come back here. Not if you can help it.* I could have helped it, but here I was anyway. Willingly offering myself to the search and interrogation I would have to endure just to gain entry to the visitor's area.

By the time I pulled into the visitor's parking lot, my face had transformed into a full-blown scowl. I saw it for myself when I pulled the rearview mirror down to check my makeup. I looked like someone who'd just had a handful of lemons shoved into her kisser. I considered taking a few minutes to try to meditate the vitriol away and figured it would be a waste of time. I still had to deal with security.

Just then, I caught sight of a uniformed guard walking toward me. He stopped about a dozen feet from where I'd parked and waited. "And it begins," I growled. "Let's get this over with."

I climbed out of my rental and fixed the guard with a steely glare. He returned a warm smile. This guy was good.

"Miss Mills?"

"Yes."

"I'm here to walk you inside."

"Lovely." Not an ounce of sarcasm. No, not me. I followed him inside.

Oak Park Heights is an "earth sheltered" facility, built into a bowl in the ground to provide maximum security against escape. Just the idea the state had built a semi-subterranean bunker to contain its most violent inmates gave me the mental image of a hell on Earth. For many locked inside, it was probably exactly that. But having seen the absolute worst the U.S. prison system was capable of, I was taken aback at what was revealed to me that day. Nothing could have prepared me for it.

Walking inside, I was stunned by the sheer elegance of the place. It was clean. The lobby was well lit. Everything looked brand new. Even the walls looked like they'd just been given a fresh coat of paint. When we approached the visitor's check-in desk, the guard politely introduced me to the female officer behind the counter. She smiled at me like an old friend and asked me how I was. It took me completely by surprise.

"Huh? Oh. I'm fine, thanks." A little bewildered, too, but I didn't confess that. Meanwhile, that enormous chip on my shoulder – the one I'd carried with me into so many correctional facilities over the years – was starting to teeter.

After a quick set of formalities and a painless pass through a metal detector, I was handed off to another guard whose job it was to escort me to the visitor's area. This guy was enormous, about six-four, with a smooth, buttoned-down appearance that stood in sharp contrast to the long braid of hair that hung down almost to his waist.

"We've got a space reserved for you in the attorney-client area," he told me, "but it's a bit of a hike." He cast a quick glance down at my heels and back up at me. "You didn't happen to bring your sneakers, did you?"

I smiled in spite of myself. I hadn't been expecting to actually get along with the prison staff. It was a totally new experience for me. "Sure didn't."

"So you're here to see Chris Boyce, yeah?" He spoke in that unmistakable *Fargo* accent that had stereotyped all Minnesota and North Dakota residents. I had to suppress a laugh. Instead, I smiled brightly.

"I am."

"He's a great guy."

Another thing I hadn't been prepared for. "Do you know him well?"

"I wouldn't say we're pals. But I've talked to him plenty. Very nice. Smart. When you work in a place like this, you get to know the troublemakers from the ones that don't fit in. He's one of those. The ones who don't belong here. I hope he gets outta here soon."

We reached the end of an eternally long corridor and took a flight of stairs down. There was another metal detector waiting. I had to leave my handbag and my briefcase in a locker, but was allowed to take my pens and pencils and a single legal pad with me.

Past the metal detector and the wall of lockers was the visitor's area. The place was one large fishbowl, with glass walls all around and a central station where a team of guards stood watch. The attorney-client visiting room was also surrounded in glass, but it was private in that nobody else would be privy to our conversation. A huge sign, hung in a visible location for all to see, read NO CONTACT.

The guard led me inside and I sat down at the small conference desk. Before he left, he extended his hand. I shook it.

"Pleasure meeting you," he said. "We're having Chris brought up right now, so it won't be long." He motioned to the transparent walls, through which I had already noticed a handful of prisoners in the regulation visiting room. Most of them were staring in at me. It was probably the heels. "This is shatterproof glass and the guards are always in sight, so you'll be safe."

He was gone before I could muster up anything more than a weak "Thanks." That *Minnesota nice* really takes you by surprise.

As I waited, I began to study the behavior of the other inmates in the adjacent visiting area. I wondered how well that native *niceness* would translate to the prison population, if at all. In my experience, inmates never checked their attitudes before entering visiting rooms. If anything, they tended to amp it up for show, whether to assuage the worry of their family members or to not appear weak in front of other inmates who were also visiting their families. In comparison, everyone in the Oak Park Heights visiting room seemed remarkably... civilized.

My mind flashed back to an incident I'd had years before while visiting a client at Terminal Island in preparation for a hearing. Not five minutes after my arrival in the communal visiting room, I was cornered by an inmate – a wiry, five-foot-nothing heroin dealer straight from the slums of Bangkok who decided picking on me would improve his standing among the rest of the prison population.

The guard on duty, who was supposedly there to protect me, averted his eyes and looked in all directions except mine. So I took matters into my own hands. Literally. As the thug moved in to try to stick his face into mine – arching his back and stretching his neck out to try to bridge the height deficit – I grabbed the front of his orange jumpsuit and calmly said, "Back the fuck off or I'm going to pull your tiny little dick up through your nose."

His eyes filled with disbelief. I held him in that position until I felt him try to take a step backward. When I let him go, he staggered slightly and slinked away. A group of prisoners who had been standing around him burst into mocking laughter. They sounded like hyenas.

It was a stupid move. I could have been killed. But I wasn't going to allow myself to be intimidated. Looking out from my private glass enclosure in the Oak Park Heights visitor's lounge, I realized I wouldn't need any of that bravado here. I felt safe. I wasn't exactly ready to pack an overnight bag and have a sleepover with the boys, but at least I didn't have to worry for my life. And I was relieved that Chris had finally found a home in a place that didn't qualify as one of the nine circles of hell.

From the corner of my eye, I saw movement on the other side of the glass control booth. I turned my head and saw a flash of bright-colored clothing. It was Chris. He was dressed in jeans and an orange and blue striped shirt. His hair was cropped short and the whiskers of his neatly trimmed beard were graying. He looked at me through the glass door and smiled. The guard standing beside him opened the door and they both walked inside.

Chris wasted no time. He immediately threw his arms around me and planted a kiss firmly on my lips. I didn't fight it.

"Please don't kiss your lawyer," the guard said. His deadpan voice betrayed the look of sheer amusement on his face. Chris immediately let go of me and took a step back.

"Nice to meet you too," I said. We both laughed. Thinking back on it, I'm pretty sure the guard let out a chuckle of his own. But at that moment, all that I could see or hear was Chris.

***

It was time to get down to business, but Chris was like a school kid on sugar.

"You have very tiny feet," he said. He scooted his chair back from the table and leaned forward, staring down at my feet. For a second, I thought he was going to pick them up to examine them. When he only continued to stare, I cleared my throat to get his attention. It didn't work.

"Boyce." He looked up at me with a dumbfounded expression. I tapped the stack of papers in front of me. "We have a lot of stuff to get through," I reminded him. "I'm only in town for the next six days."

He smiled and leaned back in his chair. "Then we've got lots of time. Did I ever tell you there's a guy in here that put his wife in a wood chipper? Nicest guy, too."

I sincerely doubted that, but I didn't want to sidetrack what little progress we had already made. We had far too much to cover and there would never be enough time to satisfy his childlike curiosity.

"Can we get back to this?" I asked, trying not to sound impatient.

"Sure, sure." He scooted his chair back into position and folded his hands on his lap. "You want to know the first question they asked me when I got here?"

"Okay."

"As soon as I was taken to my house" – a curious euphemism for a prison cell that's widely used by prison inmates – "the guard asked me how I like my ribs."

"Your ribs?"

"Yeah. They barbeque here once a month. Not bad cooking, either. Lots better than the slop that passes for nourishment at other places. Are you really six feet tall? Because I'm only five-nine. I guess I was expecting you to be a lot taller. You know?"

I stared at him.

"Okay," he said, "back to business."

By the end of that first day, I was thinking a weeklong stay might not do the trick. But in the days that followed, Chris surprised me by putting his giddy passions aside and bringing his "A-game" to the table. If the appeal worked, there would be plenty of time for small talk.

***

"Let me ask you something."

"Ask away," Chris said. He looked like a kid getting ready to play a game of twenty questions, maybe truth or dare. What I had in mind was a little less fun than that.

"When you passed those top secret files to Daulton..."

"The Pyramider documents," he interjected.

"Yes. The Pyramider documents. Did you have any idea if they'd be worth anything to the KGB?"

His face grew serious and he squinted his eyes, as if trying to peer through the layers of years that had come and gone since. I hoped his memory was as good as I needed it to be.

"Not exactly. I mean, at the time I hoped they were. They paid for them, but I never found out. Why?"

I touched my pen to the sheet of paper before me. It was the notice of action rejecting the recommendation for parole. "Because one of the themes that keeps coming up is this whole concept of 'damage assessment.' As in, there's never really been an assessment performed to determine the amount of damage your Secret Agent Man stunt caused the intelligence community. It dogged Daulton's parole hearings and it's dogging yours. I never could figure out a way to address it before, and once I got Kelleher's support for parole I didn't need it anymore. But there's no way Kelleher will go to bat for you. Not after your escape. So we have to address it."

"You're telling me you want to get confirmation that what we sold the Russkies was useless information?"

"Bingo, Boyce."

"You can always call the KGB and ask them," he suggested, smiling. It was a joke, yet something about it made perfect sense.

"That's not a half bad idea."

The smile faded from his lips. "There is no KGB anymore, Cait. Not since the fall of the Soviet Union."

I gave him one of those *don't be stupid* looks. "Just because they're called the FSB today doesn't mean they're not up to the same old tricks."

The Federal Security Service of the Russian Federation was the agency that ultimately succeeded the KGB after it was dissolved in 1991. For a period of four years, it was called the Federal

Counterintelligence Service (FSK). Then Yeltsin pulled the plug and had it reformed. If you asked me, it was all the same thing.

"So what do you do? Pick up the phone and ask the operator to put you through to the FSB, formerly known as the KGB?"

"Yes," I said. "That's precisely what I'm going to do."

"Lady, you've got *cojones*."

"You're not the first person to tell me that."

***

The afternoon before my flight back to San Francisco, we did nothing in that damn visiting room except hold hands and look at each other. There's not a thing in the world that can make a moment more precious than the threat of an uncertain future hanging over your head. I had lived with it every day since my cancer diagnosis. It never left me. Chris could sense it, too.

"I love you," he whispered.

"I love you too," I replied. "God help me."

He didn't smile. "Daulton is in love with you."

The way he said it was matter of fact, as if he knew for certain. I suppose he probably did. When you know someone that well for that long, you know them forever.

"I know," I said. I thought of adding some levity by saying "What's not to love?" then decided it wasn't right. Not when a dear friend's heart hung in the balance.

"I want you to promise me something," Chris said. "If the appeal doesn't work, I don't want you wasting your energy on this anymore. I want you to focus on getting your health back."

"And if I refuse?"

"Then I won't participate in any further parole hearings," he said resolutely.

"You can lead a con to water but you can't get him paroled if he doesn't play ball?"

"Something like that."

Who knew if he was serious? The only thing I did know was that I didn't want our last conversation to end in a disagreement. So I lied.

"Okay. I promise."

***

The second I got home, I called my friend Vladimir. Vlad was a Russian Jew who had emigrated from the former Soviet Union in the early nineties. He was the only person I knew who might have the first clue about getting in touch with the former KGB. When I told him what I wanted to do, he became immediately concerned.

"Stay away from those people," he warned me in that wonderfully gruff accent of his. "KGB was bad, FSB is same." He sounded like a nineteenth-century peasant warning me away from Dracula's castle.

When I was finally able to convince him that I had no other alternative, he offered up one small but vital piece of information: "Old KGB headquarters in Kremlin Square is museum now. Maybe they help you?"

I couldn't find a fax number for the museum, but I did get an address. So, with the clock running down on the last month and a half before I had to have Chris's appeal turned in, I fired my Hail Mary pass. In my letter, I simply asked if there were any official files on record detailing the potential damages that Christopher Boyce and Andrew Daulton Lee had caused to the United States as a result of their dealings with the KGB in the seventies. At the end of the letter, I left my return address, my phone number, and my office fax number in the hopes I wouldn't have to wait an eternity for international mail delivery to get my answer – provided there would ever be one.

Three weeks later, the secretary at the law firm where I was working popped her head into my office and said, "There's a fax coming through from Russia... Is that for you?"

I probably scared the hell out of her the way I leaped out of my office chair and scrambled to the fax machine. What I saw come through caused my heart to sink. The entire response was in Russian.

After work, I called Vlad. No answer. I tried again the next morning. Still nothing. He was the only person I knew who could speak Russian and who could translate the message for me.

I considered roaming the downtown business district at lunch, asking random strangers if they knew Russian – but then a fabulous idea came to me. It was so simple that I almost slapped my forehead. I got in my car, took a drive up to 2790 Green Street, parked, and marched through the front doors of the Russian Consulate building.

Vague recollection tells me the place was ornately decorated, but at the time all I was interested in was having someone explain to me the contents of the fax I'd received. After showing the fax to a well-dressed Marina Oswald lookalike behind the front information desk, I was introduced to two "employees of the Consulate" who led me into a side office.

As the door closed behind us, I noticed that one of the two men was armed. He wore some sort of revolver in a shoulder holster that flashed itself for only a second.

Did he want me to see that? Or am I just that eagle-eyed?

I didn't want to know the answer. I handed him the two-page fax. "I received this from the museum in Kremlin Square and I was hoping someone here could translate it into English for me."

The guy packing heat – they probably both were, but I could only be sure of one of them – read the fax. Every few lines, he'd look up at me as if trying to figure out what a lanky American redhead like me was doing communicating with his Mother Russia. When he was finished reading, he said, "This is not from the museum. This is from KGB." Then, as if to clarify, he added, "Federal Security Service."

Whoa, momma.

"What is your interest in KGB documents?" His accent wasn't quite as harsh as Vladimir's and his English was much better, but there was no mistaking his place of origin.

I explained who I was, who I was representing, and why the information was so important.

He looked at me for a long time, sizing me up, probably trying to figure out if I was bullshitting him. Finally, he said, "This communiqué says no document exists on damages caused. There are no files on these men, as they were never considered valuable assets to the Soviet Union."

Oh, Bingo.

"It says all that in the fax?" I asked, just to be certain.

Without replying, he opened a desk drawer and pulled out a ballpoint and a pad of paper with the Russian Consulate letterhead across the top. He set the fax down beside the paper pad and proceeded to translate the entire text of the message in English. I watched him work, mesmerized by the precision of his bold block lettering.

Five minutes later, he held the small pile of papers to me and smiled. I'm pretty sure he was trying to look gracious, but there was a creepiness about him that gave me a chill. I took them from him and bowed my head appreciatively.

"Thank you," I said, and tacked on the only bit of Russian I have ever picked up: *"Do svidaniya."*

I was out of that place just as fast as my feet could deliver me.

WHERE THE RIVER MEETS THE SEA

Cait
(July 1997)

On the morning of July 22, 1997 – twenty years, two months and eight days after his conviction – Daulton Lee was released from FCI Lompoc.

He called me that morning from a pay phone at a Santa Maria coffee shop.

"It's a beautiful day in the free world," he announced when I answered the phone. He sounded like a different person.

"Who the hell is this?" I joked.

"It's your number one fan!"

We laughed together in acknowledgement of the long road we had traveled.

"So they finally kicked you out," I said.

"Yeah, but only because they got tired of hearing from you."

"They all do. Pretty soon, you'll probably do the same."

"Never." He cleared his throat and was quiet for a few seconds. Then he said, "I have you to thank for all of this, Cait. I'd still be in that place if it weren't for you."

He sounded as if he had so many more things to say, but not enough words to say them. I let him off the hook. "You're welcome."

"I wish you could be here with us," he said. "Would you believe this? I'm about to have breakfast with my mom and brother. I mean, to most people that's nothing. To me, it's everything."

He giggled. I giggled back. It was one of those perfectly unselfconscious moments usually reserved for little kids, or grown-ups who should know better but don't. At that moment, I didn't give a shit what category I fell into. It felt right and it felt good. Besides, I'd been through enough in the last eight months and I wasn't going to miss out on any opportunity to feel happy over something.

"Where to after breakfast?"

"Inglewood." He groaned, but despite his obvious distaste for the city were he'd be spending the next six months of his life, I could still hear the smile in his voice. "It's not exactly Palos Verdes, but it'll be a damn sight better than a prison cell."

The halfway house would be Daulton's first step into the real world after two decades of imprisonment. He would live and work there for six months. If he did well and stayed out of trouble for the duration of his stay, he would be able to go anywhere he wanted.

"We'll have to get together for dinner or something when I get my walking papers," he said.

"Absolutely."

"My treat."

"I'd expect nothing less."

"Enough about me," he said. "Are you well?"

"I'm still kicking."

"Not good enough. What's the prognosis?"

"I see a full recovery in the very near future," I lied. The truth was I had no intention of ever undergoing chemotherapy. Not even after submitting Chris's appeal. It was something few people understood. I knew Daulton wouldn't.

"When do you start chemo?"

"Just as soon as I've finished what must be done."

I hadn't told him I was representing Chris, but I knew he was aware. Word gets around fast in this tiny little sphere we call the world. He had avoided discussing it with me so far, but now it seemed we'd reached a point where it couldn't be put off any longer.

He started to speak, then stopped. I could tell he was grappling with something. Then he did something that completely surprised me. For the one and only time in all the years I'd known him, he mentioned Chris by name.

"Look, I know you're representing him. And it's no secret how I feel about that. I also know it's important to you that you do all you can to help Chris." He paused for a second, either to admonish himself for having said *that name* out loud or to swallow back the disgust of having done so. In my mind's eye, I pictured his face contorted in a grimace. Then he recovered. "But I have a stake in this, too. You're my friend and I owe you a lot."

"You don't owe me anything, Daulton."

"Please let me finish, Cait." He sounded frustrated. I shut my mouth and let him continue. "The last thing I want to see is you pissing your health away when you should be getting treatment. So if it'll help you finish sooner than not... remember these two names: Pitts and Nicholson."

My mind drew a blank. "Who?"

"Pitts and Nicholson."

"Who the hell are they?"

"You know who they are."

"I do?"

"Of course. Look it up, jog your memory. I think maybe you've been working too hard. It makes you blind to the obvious."

"Daulton, what the hell could you possibly be talking about?"

He didn't answer. He had the phone away from his ear and he was talking to someone in the background. When he spoke again, his voice had regained that insanely enthusiastic tone. It was just like someone had thrown a switch. Weird, but understandable. It was his birthday, Christmas, New Year's Eve and the Fourth of July all rolled up into one.

"I have to go, Cait!" he exclaimed. "Our table's ready, and I do believe there may be an eggs Benedict dish with my name all over it. We'll talk soon?"

"Yes," I said. He hung up before I had a chance to remind him not to choke on his *huevos*.

***

When I looked up the two names Daulton gave me, I kicked myself for not having remembered them.

This is why you don't work on parole appeals when you're sick and probably dying.

I shoved the invading thought aside and pushed on.

Earl Edwin Pitts was an FBI agent who had been arrested in 1996 for espionage. Between '87 and '92, Pitts sold intelligence secrets to Moscow for hundreds of thousands of dollars. Harold James Nicholson was a CIA agent who had gone to work in the early nineties as a mole for Russia's Foreign Intelligence Service.

A couple of spies. So what? Two more idiots who apparently hadn't heard of a guy nicknamed "The Falcon" and his estranged old pal "The Snowman." Or maybe they had and didn't think the same thing would happen to them. Either way, Pitts and Nicholson were old enough to know better. So what's your point, Daulton?

It wasn't until I read their sentences that the light went on over my head. Pitts was given twenty-seven years; Nicholson, twenty-three. With federal law requiring each to serve a minimum of eighty-five percent of his sentence before becoming eligible for release – and with the possibility of having another year shaved off for participating in the Bureau of Prisons DAP (Drug Abuse Prevention) program – this meant Pitts could be out in as early as twenty-two years, and Nicholson at eighteen.

I think I'm starting to see what you're getting at, Daulton...

Pitts and Nicholson had committed virtually the same crime as Chris, but received dramatically lighter prison sentences. The fact that these guys had been career intelligence officials – not just a couple of early-twenties kids living out a stupid spy fantasy, but grown men who knew the consequences for their actions – underlined the difference even more clearly.

My mental afterburner kicked on.

Back in 1984, Congress had passed the Comprehensive Crime Control Act. One of its purposes was to achieve uniformity in sentencing – to prevent the kinds of disparities that occur when one person is sentenced to life for stealing a loaf of bread, while another gets off with a slap on the wrist. Now I reasoned that if I could get the commission to see that Chris was being held to a totally different sentencing standard than Pitts and Nicholson...

Daulton Lee, I think you might just be a genius.

I pictured him inside that Santa Maria café with his mother and brother, shoveling down his first breakfast in the free world with a smile on his face to match the brilliance of the gem he'd just laid in my lap. In a single sentence, Daulton had given me the missing jigsaw piece to Chris's appeal.

***

I heard from Chris the night before I submitted the appeal. As usual, I had all of the documentation spread out on my dining room table. This time, there was nothing left to add. Every bit of ammunition I had was there on paper. I held the phone to my ear as we talked and surveyed the physical evidence of his last chance at freedom.

"I'm afraid to send this," I said.

"Why?"

"Because what if it doesn't work?"

"Then we'll figure something else out. Remember that promise I asked you to make? Forget it. I changed my mind."

"Good. Because I had my fingers crossed the whole time."

He laughed. It sounded forced.

"What, then?" I asked. "Another great escape?"

"Would you go with me if I did? You'd have to leave it all behind. Everything."

I thought about it. "Of course I would."

"Then there's nothing to worry about."

He was wrong. There was always something to worry about.

"I'm submitting the appeal tomorrow," I declared. "After that, it's out of our hands."

"Before you do, can I get you to add one small thing?"

"Okay... What?"

"I'd like a limo to pick me up when they let me out of this place. Think they'd pay for that?"

"Not funny."

"Oh well," he said. "It was worth a shot."

The following day, I packaged the appeal – all fourteen pages of it – inside an accordion manila folder and hand-delivered it to an overnight courier service four blocks from my office on Post Street. Then I went home, took the hottest shower my flesh could withstand, and was asleep before I could reach for the light switch. It was finished. I slept for twelve hours.

EXPECTING TO FLY

Cait
(September 24, 1997)

That's the bitch about real life. Whenever something wonderful happens, there's never any music to underscore the beauty. Only whatever you happen to have playing on your stereo in the background. If it's a shitty song, God help you – you'll probably be stuck with some ill-fitting auditory association for the rest of your life. On the day that Chris called to change my life forever, I had an old Buffalo Springfield record playing and Neil Young was singing about ending things with a cry. Thinking back on it now, I guess I could have done a lot worse.

It was September 24, 1997. By that point, I was used to hearing from Chris on almost a daily basis. He was still in Minnesota. Oak Park Heights hadn't transformed into a desirable place to live, but he had seen and survived far worse environments. I wondered – still do, in fact – just how many people could have pulled that off for as long as he did without completely cracking up.

OPH was populated with some of the most violent criminals in the state, but the controls the prison exercised over the inmate population were incredibly effective. Killings were rare. Fights were a lot more likely, but even those were out of the ordinary.

Occasionally, inmates with grudges were encouraged by the warden to settle their differences by donning a pair of boxing gloves. Nothing like the Earl Steven Karr attack had occurred in years. After more than two decades of struggle, life had finally begun to take on a peaceable rhythm for Chris.

This should have been a comfort to me, but it wasn't. The thought terrified me. Complacency is a dangerous thing. It can be a prisoner's worst enemy, more than loneliness, despair or the threat of violence. If he was in any true danger now, it was the danger of giving up hope.

I had done everything I could in the last two years to give Chris reason to believe there was a way out of the nightmare. But even that was getting harder. The parole commission's thirty-day deadline to render a decision on our appeal had long since passed without a letter of denial or even an unofficial "fuck you very much." If they had come back with a big fat NO, at least I'd know what recourse to take. Hearing nothing was far worse.

The night Chris called me to tell me the news, I almost didn't take his call. I knew it was him before I even picked up the phone – his calls were perfectly timed to my afternoon schedule – but I was worried that if he asked me for an update, I wouldn't know what else to say. After staring at the phone through a full three rings, I answered.

"Hey there, good looking."

The minute I heard his voice, I was glad I picked up. Something in the way he spoke, always so cheerful despite everything, had a centering effect on me. It was therapy a hell of a lot more appealing than any laid out for me by my doctors. Some days, it was enough to make me forget which one of us was free and which one of us was locked up.

"Hey, yourself," I replied.

As always, he wanted to know about me first. "How are you feeling?"

"I'm fine. Just a little tired."

In truth, I had never felt so weak in my life. The Tamoxifen, a cancer drug I started taking the week after filing Chris's appeal, had a slew of side effects so nasty it made me wonder just how much my survival was worth. There were headaches. Stomach aches. Insomnia. Hot flashes. Everything you can think of, and then some.

The medication, which supposedly treats breast cancer by lowering the body's estrogen levels, was also extremely successful at leeching all of the calcium from my system. This left me with deep, intense bone pains that made it a challenge sometimes just to get out of bed. Every time I wondered why the hell I was putting myself through it all, I thought of Chris. Even if he did eventually get out of prison, who would be there to take care of him if I wasn't around?

"I can call back tomorrow if you're not up to talking," he said.

"I didn't say that. Don't put words in my mouth. The last guy who tried that almost walked away with his pecker in his hands."

"There could be worse fates." Then, in a more serious tone: "But seriously, have you been doing everything the doctors tell you?"

There was an earnest concern in his voice that was always endearing, never nagging. Okay – maybe a little nagging. But it was laced with the kind of sweetness you only come across a few times in your life, if you're really lucky.

"Me? No way. I've found that just a little bit of denial is good for the body."

"Don't make me have to bust out of here to take care of you."

"Wouldn't that be something?"

There was an oddly wistful tone in his voice when he replied. "Yeah, it would."

"Don't worry about me. I'm just tired. The drugs kick my ass. How are things there?"

"Incredibly exciting. You wouldn't believe it. I finished that enormous Nietzsche book today and then went outside to win a few games of handball."

"Senior tournament?" I chided, knowing he could take it.

"Real funny. The kid I beat is half my age, but I'm twice as thrifty. Good thing he's not a sore loser. He's about three times my size."

And on and on. I talked about the weather in San Francisco and we argued about the genesis of the inaccurately attributed Mark Twain quote, "The coldest winter I ever spent was a summer in San Francisco." He told me what his family was up to; I told him the same about mine.

As usual, he asked about Daulton. I told him nothing had changed since the last time he asked, which was the night before.

"He's still at the halfway house in Inglewood. Still hating every minute. Still complaining that his neighbors aren't quite as high class as he is. Probably freaking out that he's the only one there who eats his fried chicken with a knife and fork."

"That's Daulton."

"Sure is."

"I guess he's still pretty pissed off at me." It was more a statement than a question, said more in jest than in sincerity. He knew damn well how Daulton felt about him.

"Put it this way," I said. "If you ever feel an inexplicable, excruciating pain in your crotch, that's probably a sign that he's taken up voodoo."

"That reminds me," Chris said. "I heard from the parole commission today."

My insides knotted and I fell silent.

"Cait, are you there?"

"I'm here. What do you mean you 'heard' from them?"

"I got a letter."

Somewhere in the back of my skull, a sleeping bear opened one eye. Then the other. They had sure taken their sweet time delivering their obligatory rubber-stamp denial, I thought. The bastards.

He began to speak, but by then my tongue was already in motion. "Sons of *bitches*! What the hell is wrong with these people? They had thirty days to give us their decision and it's been – what? Two months! If you ask me, I think we should sue the hell out of them."

There was a long silence on the other end of the line.

"Well?" I asked. "What the hell did they say this time?"

I could hear him chuckling.

"They granted your appeal," he said. "I get to come home."

I switched the phone to my other ear. "They did *what*?"

"Congratulations. As far as I know, you're the first person who's ever appealed a parole decision and won. When I get outta here, I'll take you to dinner to celebrate."

Now I wasn't sure if he was pulling my leg or being serious. "Don't fuck with me, Chris."

"I'm not! March 15, 2003. They approved the date." He laughed. The life in his voice when he did was all I needed to hear to know it was true.

I don't remember what I said after that. Whatever it was, I'm sure he didn't understand a word of it anyway. I probably cursed him for not having told me right away. I may have even accused him of having known longer than he was letting on. All I do remember is that for about the next week, the world was a sloppy, salty, snotty flood.

And when the sobbing stopped and the realization kicked in that there was nothing left to do, there came from my shoulders such a miraculous unburdening of weight that I'm convinced if I had tried, I could have taught both Mary Poppins and that skinny little Flying Nun a thing or two about aerodynamics.

THE FINAL MILE

Chris
(1998 – 2002)

Nineteen ninety-eight marked the beginning of a dark period in Christopher Boyce's life. What should have been a time of renewed optimism – of rejoicing over second chances and making plans for a future once thought lost – was overshadowed by the black cloud known as ADX Florence.

Located one hundred miles south of Denver within sight of the jagged spine of the Rocky Mountains, just the prison's nickname – the "Alcatraz of the Rockies" – was enough to send a chill down the spine of any federal inmate headed its direction. A name-check of some of the supermax prison's most well-known residents read like a roster of the damned: Oklahoma City bomber Timothy McVeigh; Terry Nichols, McVeigh's accomplice; 1993 World Trade Center bombing mastermind Omar Abdel-Rahman; Unabomber Theodore Kaczynski. All lived within its walls, where an eerie, unnatural silence prevailed.

Six months after having been assigned his parole date, Chris found himself bound for ADX Florence – returned, for the first time in a decade, to an environment where twenty-four-hour solitary confinement was enforced and where human interaction was all but forbidden.

Most inmates got to Florence by murdering prison guards, or displaying a host of otherwise incorrigible tendencies. Acting out violently, refusing to follow rules, repeated attempts at escape, or the commission of crimes that threatened the national security – all were the hallmark of the majority of Florence inmates. Chris was unique among them. His crime had been writing an article for the *Minneapolis Star-Tribune*.

By the time of its publication, he had already written more than a dozen pieces for the newspaper. Each article focused on some aspect of life behind bars, frequently painting Oak Park Heights in a positive light for its progressive approach to rehabilitation.

Readers of the *Star-Tribune* (which devotees called *the Strib*) seemed to have a love/hate relationship with the convicted spy and bank robber who'd been given a platform on which to express his personal views about life in prison. Some readers appreciated Chris's intelligence and candor and wished him well, even going so far as to write letters to the editor suggesting he should be a candidate for early release. Others relished the opportunity to see that Christopher Boyce was paying for his crimes the way they felt he should.

As far as the editorial department of *the Strib* was concerned, that was fine and dandy. Controversial bylines always sold more papers. Even the Oak Park Heights administration encouraged the endeavor, savoring the positive PR. That glow faded quickly the day Chris's article about Craig Dennis Bjork was published.

Bjork was a convicted murderer who had avoided his own death by virtue of the fact that Minnesota had abolished capital punishment in 1911, ages before the crime that landed him in prison for the rest of his life. While a prisoner at Oak Park Heights, Bjork had killed again, beating his cellmate to death.

Following the murder, Bjork embarked upon a campaign of terror, threatening the lives of other inmates with seeming impunity. This infuriated Chris. In addition to voicing strong support of the death penalty for repeat murderers like Bjork, the article also accused Oak Park Heights officials of doing nothing to protect the rest of the prison population from him. It was an accusation that didn't go over well.

Forty-eight hours after the article went live, OPH administrators contacted the Bureau of Prisons and informed them they were through with Christopher Boyce. His safety, they claimed, could no longer be guaranteed. Within a matter of weeks, his walking papers had come through. His next stop would be ADX Florence, the most highly controlled federal prison in the country.

Although he was no stranger to living in solitary confinement, the years he'd spent in round-the-clock isolation at USP Marion had left an indelible mark. The mere thought of returning to such living conditions, especially with his release date so close in sight, filled him with cold dread. He did what he could to fight the transfer, to no avail.

About fifteen years before, he had succeeded in improving his situation at USP Marion by leveraging the influence of sympathizers in high places. It was those connections that had been responsible for his transfer to Oak Park Heights in the first place. But by 1998, most of the senators who had championed for his humane treatment were gone, retired or promoted to bigger and better things. He had even fallen out of regular contact with Dave Jackson, who now had a family of his own to worry about. With a forlorn resignation, Chris faced a new reality. The fanfare of yesteryear was dead. Nobody could help him now.

The night before he was moved to Florence, Cait talked to Chris by phone and vowed to fight on his behalf. "They won't get away with this. You have your date, for God's sake! I'll get you the hell out of there, if it's the last thing I do."

"Don't say that. I'd rather have you healthy out there and me stuck in here than the other way around."

"Bullshit, Boyce." Cait had a habit of calling him that. He liked it, even though he claimed not to. "I didn't work my ass off on your parole to let this happen. You still owe me a backlog of legal fees and I intend to collect."

He tried to laugh, if only for her sake. He couldn't. That mechanism, whatever it was, seemed broken. Instead, he told her that he loved her.

"I love you, too," she said. The words were new enough between them that speaking them aloud still felt awkward. She decided not to linger on it.

"Just don't give up hope, Chris. Not now. You're almost there."

He sighed. There was something resolute in the way he did that reassured her. "Okay," he promised. "I won't."

"And you'll call me the first opportunity you have?"

"Yes."

She asked him to swear to it. He did. They were the last words she would hear from him for another two and a half months.

***

Sleep had become a stranger again. Even before everything – before TRW, before the Russians, before prison and the weight of the obscene shame – sleep had seldom stuck around for long. Nowadays, it didn't even bother to poke its head in the door for a quick hello.

Seventy-two hours after his descent into that cold, silent hell, he was still awake. He wondered how long he could last before simply passing out. Maybe he'd done so already and didn't even realize it.

The transfer to ADX Florence wasn't the minor setback Cait had made it out to be. Not to Chris, anyway. It meant much more than having to learn to cope again with the psychological battery of extreme isolation. If that was all there was to do, he thought he could survive it. Perhaps even easily, now that he had an end date to keep in his sights. It was the insidious nature of the transfer that he could not close his mind to.

The more he thought about it, the more an escalating sense of foreboding began to take shape in his mind. The gnawing sense of doubt he had been harboring ever since the parole commission's decision was at last evolving into a palpable certainty. He struggled desperately to turn his mind away from it, but every time he did it would only return again with a vengeance. It was the *other shoe*. And it was dropping.

I'll never get out alive.

Just voicing the words in his head was enough to scare the hell out of him.

They'll see to that. They never intended to set me free in the first place. And there are a thousand ways they can prevent that day from coming.

Terrifying scenarios arrived by night and played out before him, driving sleep even further. Death by mysterious circumstance certainly wouldn't be out of the realm of possibility, and he didn't think very many people would throw a fuss over one more dead ex-spy. Suicide in places like Florence – self-inflicted asphyxia or bleeding out of the radial artery – were not frequent, but not unheard of. Even a death at the hands of the guards themselves would be easily explained and just as quickly accepted by an investigating panel. Billy club-induced subdural hematoma inflicted while in the process of attacking a guard; accidental strangulation while resisting a textbook chokehold. Chris understood it all too clear. The variety of ways in which he could die between now and March of 2003 were limited only by the resourcefulness of those willing to see him dead.

And if they didn't want him dead? There were plenty of ways they could keep him behind bars forever. All they had to do was beat him and claim he struck first. Never mind that supermax guidelines required inmates to be cuffed behind the back and shackled with leg irons before their cell doors could be opened, making it virtually impossible for a prisoner to inflict any real harm on his jailers. In matters of one man's word against another's, the convicted always drew the losing straw.

He thought of Cait. Each vision of her brought more pain than the last. There was nothing he wanted more than to call her, yet the thought of doing so filled him with a paralyzing fear. Hearing her voice now would only serve to drive him deeper into despair. He knew he had to guard himself against that. He had seen far too many people lose themselves to that black hole. The only thing he knew to do was to close himself off to any emotional entanglements. No matter how much it hurt.

In the darkness of his prison cell in the belly of that vast, silent sepulcher, he squared off with the beast again.

***

The cell was a tomb with accouterments, a sterile 7x10 enclosure of poured concrete. Thick walls separated him from the other inmates. His bed was a thin foam mattress set atop a concrete block.

At the foot of the bed, an immovable concrete stool rose up from the floor like a rounded limestone stalagmite. His desk was a two-foot-wide, one-foot-deep slab of stone protruding from the wall. Several feet above that, a small wedge of concrete served as a shelf just big enough to seat a radio or small TV.

Each cell had a small shower stall that operated on a timer, and a combination toilet and sink that could be automatically shut off to prevent inmates from flooding the cell blocks. There was a polished steel mirror fastened to the wall with bolts, and the entire room was lit by a single electric light. The only view to the outside was through a four-inch wide, four-foot tall slit window that looked out onto the wall of the neighboring cell block.

The prison had no mess hall. All meals were served through a slot in the solid steel door that remained locked twenty-four hours a day. Inmates were allowed up to five hours of outdoor recreational time per week, but few took advantage of this since it was only offered early in the morning in near-freezing temperatures. It was a blatant action intended to discourage inmates from requesting recreation time, to which few complained. Nothing would come of it if they did.

The dehumanizing conditions of the rec area made it easy for most to decline. It was made up of a long row of individual enclosures that looked like dog kennels. The outdoor area where the cages were stationed was surrounded by twenty-foot walls. It was topped with steel girders and a thick layer of wire mesh to eliminate any remote chance of escape.

Chris called it his birdcage. On mornings when outdoor temperatures weren't unbearably cold, he would stand in the faint pre-dawn light and breathe deeply, sucking in the fresh air that blew in from the Rockies. Like a man breaking the surface of the sea for a quick breath before plunging down again into the abyss, these moments were some of the things that enabled him to survive the isolation. He longed to fly free, to feel the sunlight on his face again.

Communication with the outside world was heavily restricted. Inmates were allowed only one fifteen-minute phone call per month. He waived his telephone privileges for the first two months following his arrival, believing that taking a hard-line monastic approach to his immersion into isolation would strengthen his mind. Ten weeks later, he decided he could give a shit about any of that. All he wanted to do was hear somebody's voice. Cait's, if he could have his pick. But by then, he would have been happy just talking to an operator.

Finally, on the seventy-ninth day of his confinement, he called her.

As he began to dial, it occurred to him that it would have been the smart thing to do to have written in advance. At least Cait would know to expect his call. What if she was out? He decided to call anyway.

The phone began to ring. He shook his head at his stupidity. The old familiar dulling of the thought patterns was apparently back, that frightening but expected side effect of sensory deprivation. It had arrived shockingly soon. He referred to it as *solitary brain*. In the grave-like silence of his cell, making light of things – like what was happening to his mind as a consequence of the persistent isolation – was the only way to keep the panic at bay.

Cait's line rang a second time. A third. Then a fourth. He thought about hanging up, figuring maybe it was just as well. Would she still want to talk to him after not having heard from him in almost three months? Just as the fifth ring was relayed back across the continental divide, she answered. Her first words took him by surprise.

"Well, it's about damn time."

"Cait," he began, but stumbled over the rest of his words. He started again. "How did you know it was me?"

"There's this invention known as caller ID," she replied smartly. "And I don't know anyone else who'd call me from the 719 area code. Although I was starting to doubt you ever would."

He didn't bother trying to defend himself. Not because he thought she wouldn't understand, but because he felt he had earned whatever she had to throw his way.

"It's good to hear your voice," he said.

"Where the hell have you been? Wait, don't answer that. I know *exactly* where you've been. Why haven't you called? Did you get my letters?"

He told her that he had, every single one.

"How are you?"

"I'm okay," he lied. "How's your health?"

"Forget all that. Listen up. While you've been vacationing in Club Purgatory, I've been working on trying to get you moved. So if you thought avoidance could get you out of paying me back for all these years of legwork, I have news for you. The bill just got higher."

Chris smiled for the first time in months. Maybe longer. The action felt strange yet comforting. "How good's my credit?"

"Maybe not that good. If we can transfer you to a medium security prison, we could get you kicked off the federal teat six months sooner in trade for going into a halfway house. You can't go that route from the supermax. I'm thinking FCI Sheridan or Lompoc."

"*Lompoc?* You might be crazier than I am."

"Not as crazy as they'd be to accept you back," Cait conceded, "so I'm pretty sure that idea's cooked. I'm liking Sheridan, though. Sounds like a hotel. If we can get you there, we might be able to get you paroled early to a halfway house in San Francisco."

The federal penitentiary at Sheridan, Oregon, was a medium security facility just fifty miles southwest of Portland. Chris's parents had moved to Oregon in the early nineties, making it an ideal location for him to wait out the remainder of his time before parole.

It would be close enough for them to visit frequently, giving them all the opportunity to begin rebuilding their strained relationship.

When he said nothing, Cait spoke again. "Did you hear what I said, Boyce?"

"Huh? Yes."

"No you didn't. If everything goes right, you're looking at 2002 instead of '03."

Four more years.

Chris didn't know if he could make it another four days, let alone four years. He began to turn the idea over in his head. Considering it. The more he looked at it, the more feasible it became. With the exception of thirty days in the wild and eighteen months as a free man in Bonners Ferry, Chris had spent the last twenty-one years of his life in prison – a great chunk of that in solitary confinement. If he could hold on to his sanity for as long as it took Cait to negotiate the red tape, there might be hope of escaping alive after all.

"Chris?"

He jumped. "Sorry. Yes. That's a hell of a lot better than the year 2046, or whatever it was before."

"You're damn right it is." She sounded cocky and full of fire. He drew strength from that. Despite everything Cait had been through in the year and a half since her cancer diagnosis, he had never seen her falter.

"I'm sorry that I didn't call. It's just this place..." he sighed. It was like the sound of a man trying to expel a demon that had been plaguing him for far too long a time. "This place."

"I understand."

It was all she needed to say. They spent the remainder of the short fifteen minutes speaking softly to each other.

The next day, he submitted an official request for a notepad and a set of pencils. He had some cobwebs to clear out.

***

Square one, again.

The voluminous collection of books Chris had amassed over the course of the last seventeen years since his recapture was not allowed to follow him. As a result, he had lost some of his most precious belongings. The beautiful leather bound Lord Tennyson book his father had sent him. Gone. All those books on falconry, probably parceled out among Bureau of Prisons employees as souvenirs for their private bookshelves.

Even his typewriter, which had remained with him as a constant companion and an outlet for his creativity, had to be left behind. In his last few years at Oak Park Heights, he had taken advantage of the growing availability of computers to do most of his writing. Yet he'd still kept a place in his cell for that old noisy clatter-box, a dinosaur from a bygone era that represented more to him than just ink impressions on a blank sheet. A small part of him grieved that he'd never see it again. It had gotten him through a lot.

He had to get his writing hand back into shape. He practiced by writing letters to his family and to Cait, frequently commenting on his hideous penmanship, which had never been good to begin with. Nowadays, his handwriting resembled something akin to chicken-scratch. He thought maybe an actual rooster with a piece of graphite strapped to its dominant claw could have done better.

The months rolled past. The blisters on his fingers came and went, then finally disappeared as rigid calluses began to form. He liked them. They made him feel useful for a change. The thought of sketching again came to him. He even toyed around with a few tentative scribbles drawn purely from imagination, but stopped short of asking for drawing materials. He wouldn't risk their ire or call attention to himself.

And so he sat and wrote, and read letters from Cait and his family repeatedly. Some nights, he would take all of Cait's letters and unfold them, laying them down beside him as he slept. He knew it was ridiculous. It definitely felt that way. He made his mind up that he didn't care. How ridiculous could it be if it made her feel so much closer than she really was?

On rare occasions when sleep eventually did find him, he dreamed of falcons. Only this time, he wasn't alone. There was always a tall, beautiful red-haired creature standing just a few feet away, looking on.

***

I walk a narrow path. Speak only when spoken to. Make no eye contact. That's important. A closed mouth keeps words locked away, but the eyes always have a way of speaking a lifetime's worth of language in a single glance. I cannot risk it.

If they tell me to jump, I will. Without even bothering to ask how high. I'll simply jump with all of my effort and hope that it is good enough. If told to lie down, I will do that as well. The risk of giving them any ammunition to use against me, the smallest comment, even the slightest twitch at the wrong moment, is too dangerous.

I have come too far to risk everything now. If my freedom means having to swallow whatever pride I have left, I have resolved that I will gorge myself and ask for seconds.

Mister Jailer Man, you can have my body but you cannot have my mind and soul.

P.S. Just read this back to myself. If I walk out of this place with a single marble left in my head, it'll be a miracle beyond all miracles.

***

There was something trying to get into his cell through the slit in the wall that passed for a window. Lying perfectly still with his head resting at the foot of his foam-padded cement bed, Chris watched.

It happened every two or three minutes. A dark shadow would cross in front of the window, blocking out the light, then disappear again. Perhaps it was the rescue party. They had to be crazy to think he could squeeze himself through that tiny, four-inch space. Chris rebuked himself for not having practiced his shrinking skills in advance of their arrival. Then he realized he was slipping back into that no-man's land between reality and madness, and forced himself to sit upright.

He threw his legs over the edge of the bed and stared down at his bare feet, trying to will the cobwebs from his mind. From the corner of his eye, he saw it again. A quick black flutter dancing for an instant on the other side of the reinforced shatterproof glass. Chris drove his palms into his eye sockets and rubbed vigorously. Blotches of gray and black danced against his eyelids.

He opened his eyes again and picked himself up off the bed. He approached the window and pressed his face against it. Cold. It was always cold here, no matter what it was doing outside. The forced air circulation played hell on the sinuses, dried everything up, caused you to wake up in the morning with a backlog of phlegm. It was even worse if you slept with your mouth open. Mornings felt like getting over the last strains of strep throat. Just like everything else, he had learned to live with it.

There was nothing to be seen outside, except for a sliver of sky above the adjacent cell block wall. He moved his head up and down, then left and right. Still nothing. He was about to turn back to his bed when a black mass suddenly slapped at the window. He jerked his head backward and in the flash of an instant before it vanished again, Chris found himself staring into the eyes of a crow.

His heart leapt. A gasp escaped his lips and turned into a short, shrill laugh. The sound startled him. You didn't hear such things at ADX Florence. Instinctively, his eyes shot to the closed door of his cell, half expecting it to fly open and for men with clubs and face shields to come charging in. When that didn't happen, he turned his head back to the window.

"Where are you?" he whispered aloud. His toes were pumping, lifting his body up and down like a child at a pet store window. He thought this had to be the greatest thing to ever happen to anybody, anywhere. "Come on back here, buddy. C'mon back."

It did. This time, it flew down at him from beyond his field of vision and brushed viciously against the triple-paned glass. It lingered there only for a moment, suspending itself in midair with a wild, frenzied burst of wings, trying vainly to gain purchase on the slick flat surface with its talons.

"Hey!" he exclaimed, keeping his volume level to no more than a hoarse whisper. "Get me outta here, will you?"

He laughed again, then cut himself off abruptly. It wasn't the slightly manic tone of his laugh that caused him to stop – although if he hadn't been quite so preoccupied to notice, it would have scared the hell out of him to hear it. He just didn't want to call attention to himself. The last thing he needed was for some sadistic guard to peek into his cell and radio one of the gun towers to pick the bird off the building with a single shot.

The crow disappeared again. He waited with his face pressed to the narrow glass and his hands braced against the wall as if to keep himself from falling through. A minute passed. Two. Then it was back again, flapping and scratching and beating its chest against the invisible barrier.

"You crazy damn avian!"

It flew away and dove back in for another try. When that didn't work, it tried again. And again. It went on like this for ten minutes. Maybe longer. Then it stopped, just like that. He assumed the crow had either worn itself out or given up. It had been a valiant effort.

He continued to watch the window for the rest of the day until the light outside faded. Then he slept on his bed with his head at its foot so he could watch the window. All the next day, he lay in bed and waited for the crow. It never returned.

***

It was a bottle of the finest, most expensive champagne he could find. On the label was a name he couldn't quite see. Not even when he closed his eyes and concentrated. Normally that wouldn't matter much, but tonight was special. It was New Year's Eve. The last day of the century. Last century of the millennium.

Chris tried to see the label again. Now he could almost make out the letters. It looked like *Don Drysdale*, but he was pretty sure it was supposed to read *Dom Perignon*. He shrugged. It was the *solitary brain* again, putting holes where there once were none. He left it at that and began dreaming up a pair of finely-crafted champagne flutes. Maybe he'd even throw in a picturesque setting for two. Who cared? It was New Year's '99 and the sky was the limit.

It was a month ago when he'd seen Cait last, sitting across from him in the penitentiary visiting room with that atrocious Plexiglas partition between them. She had wanted to visit sooner, but he asked her not to. Her persistence finally wore him down. With the exception of a call every other month and the occasional message in a bottle – sometimes to Cait, sometimes to his folks – he had not seen or spoken to anyone in close to two years.

Cait's arrival had been like a bolt of lightning to his senses. Anyone else would have despised having to speak through telephone receivers to communicate, but Chris was glad the barrier was there. Any closer and it would have been too much, like touching a raw nerve with the tip of a razor.

She looked great. Her hair had grown out longer and her summer surf tan was still there, even in late November. He asked about her health and she shrugged it off as she always did – only unlike times before, she looked confident in the way that she did.

"Minus my left side, I'm back on the road to being myself again."

"You're still beautiful," he told her. His voice was sincere.

"Considering you've only had yourself to look at for the last couple of years, I'll take that as a minor compliment."

She told him all about what she had done, about all that was still left to be done, to save him from this place. Chris listened to every word, content in the knowledge that she knew what she was doing and miserable with himself for putting her through it all.

"When I get out of here," he told her, then stopped to correct himself. "When *you* get me out of here, I'm going to take care of you for the rest of your life."

He meant every word, even though he had no idea how he'd ever be able to live up to that promise. Cait was the one who had spent her life building a successful career while he lay wasting behind locked steel doors and unscalable concrete walls. The bachelor's degree in history he'd earned through correspondence at Oak Park Heights would probably be meaningless in the real world. Especially considering the gravity of his crimes. What was more likely was that she would wind up having to take care of him.

A darkness fell over him, visible as a shadow.

"Hey," Cait said. "What's wrong?"

He thought about it. "What's wrong is that you're here with me when you ought to be out there enjoying your life. I don't mean to sound ungrateful. I hope it's not coming off that way. I just... I wish we could have met under better circumstances. You know?"

"I know. But that didn't happen, did it? Look, I'm forty-five years old. I've been living my life. I've had the opportunity to do everything I wanted. You're next, Boyce."

"Don't call me that." His voice was deadpan but the ghost of a smile lifted the edges of his lips. It was amazing how she could do that. Even amid the awfulness of their surroundings.

"You love it," she said and smiled.

There was a vaguely dizzying sensation as Chris slid back into the here and now. "I love *you*," he said. His voice was rough from lack of use. He realized he was alone again and felt ashamed for having spoken out loud. The bird at the window was one thing. Talking to an empty room, that was another.

He realized he'd lost track of himself between dreaming up the champagne flutes and trying to remember if mistletoe was a Christmas thing or a New Year's Eve thing. Unstuck again, only his fate was far worse than any character ever dreamed up by a writer. No matter where or when he traveled to, he would always return here in the end.

He checked the wind-up clock seated on the edge of his cement desk. Two minutes to midnight. Almost time. The second hand counted away the remainders of the century, ticking him closer to the verge of a moment he never dreamed he'd spend in an isolation chamber.

Somewhere in the back of his mind, a ten-year-old boy named Chris – after St. Christopher, his mother's idea, what a laugh that was – stood watching.

There will be people living on the moon in the year 2000, the boy said. An awestruck expression formed on his pure, unblemished face. *We'll all be riding rockets to the stars. And me, too.*

The countdown began. *10... 9... 8... 7...*

He held his breath as he watched the tip of the second hand. He held the imaginary bottle of champagne in one hand. With the other, Cait's hand. He snatched a quick glance sideways and saw that she was smiling.

6... 5... 4...

No cities on the moon, he told the boy, *but when you grow up you will know that there are things in this world more beautiful than that. More beautiful than you could ever imagine.*

3... 2... 1...

The silence all around was deathlike. The bottle of champagne vanished with the flutes. Cait was gone. He laid back on his thin foam mattress and stared up at the concrete ceiling.

"Happy New Year," he whispered.

***

June 30, 2000
Dear Chris,
First, the good news. They should have already notified you, but since shit moves so slow in this system there's no telling. The Bureau of Prisons, in their infinite wisdom (and only after two years of badgering by yours truly, thank you very much), has decided to grant you transfer to the federal prison in Sheridan.

Hallelujah, praise Allah, and all that good stuff. Pick your deity of choice and insert here. We've also been successful in our bid to get you cleared for an early release to a halfway house in San Francisco. I've been hammering out the details with the people there to make sure it sticks. If everything goes according to plan, your last day at Sheridan should be in mid-September, 2002.

Now for the not-so-good news. Okay, it's downright bad and it hurts me to have to tell you on paper. But I know that if I wait until you get around to using that damn monthly fifteen-minute call to ring me up, you may never find out.

I fainted in my oncologist's office during a routine checkup last month. I'd had a headache for five days solid and thought it was just stress... or too much coffee... or not enough, maybe. Right before I passed out, it actually felt like someone had beaned me with a baseball bat. The long and the short of it is, my test results came back and it looks like some form of brain cancer. Left temporal lobe, the size of a pea. The cancer, that is. Not my temporal lobe. Sorry, I know desperate attempts at humor are probably not appreciated right now but it's the only way I'm going to get through this without losing my mind.

I have to talk to you. Call me. I wish I could call you but in case you hadn't noticed, the federal government's idea of rehabilitation for people in your neighborhood doesn't exactly lend itself to the ability to leave messages for inmates.

The doctor told me that surgery isn't an option because the cancer is in the part of the brain where the mental process of comprehension takes place. In other words, one false move and I could spend the remainder of my life as a zucchini in diapers.

They put me on Taxol, that shit they gave Lance Armstrong. While he's out peddling his skinny ass around town, I've been vomiting into any receptacle I can find. I don't know why I'm telling you this. I shouldn't be. But I am terrified that everything we've worked so hard for could be gone by the time 2002 rolls around and I want to tell you again with my own voice how much I love you. Call me.

Yours,
Cait
P.S. I stopped wearing my Manolo Blahniks because the treatment makes me piss myself. I can't ruin those shoes, they cost me a fortune. As a consequence, I no longer "tower" as much when I stand beside people. You'd appreciate that, I'm sure.

***

Sometimes, God smites. Other times, he smiles. And all we are left with is to wonder why. A little girl dies crossing a street she's crossed a thousand times. Meanwhile, at that very same moment somewhere far away, another child escapes the wheels of an oncoming car by the skin of her milk teeth. Is there reason there? Purpose? Or are we all simply the victims of a God who can't tell his Ls from his Ts?

Cait believed it was the latter. She had known too many good people who had suffered unkind fates to think there was anything to it but chaos and random order. The only other option was to believe in a dispassionate God.

Finding understanding was the hardest on Chris, who had been raised a devout Catholic but had given up his faith long ago. In the days and weeks following the letter from Cait, he found himself fighting the urge to pray. It was a reflex so deeply rooted in his being that resisting it was like trying to defy instinct. Often when he sat in helpless contemplation, he would look down to find his hands clasped together in the ritualistic manner of prayer. Sometimes he would curse disdainfully and pull his hands apart. Sometimes he wouldn't.

The news had one positive impact: it forced him out of his self-absorbed despair. It gave him something else to focus on beside his own situation and made him remember something he had long ago forgotten – that there were fortunes far worse than confinement. His world had become a concrete cocoon. In it, his mind and body lay dormant – but alive. Cait's world had become a perversion of nature, where the very body she inhabited was revolting against her. When he meditated on the alternatives, he could no longer say his situation was worse.

He began to write her on a daily basis. The letters became more than just words on paper. They became his conduit to her – a symbolic transfusion of every last ounce of positivity he could muster within himself. Professions of love; words of encouragement; sketches of falcons in freedom and mountainous ranges that imagined worlds where sickness and disease had no place. She had reminded him of how much she needed him and he swore he would never forget again.

After his transfer to Sheridan, he was finally able to call with more frequency and he took advantage of this. Once again able to walk in the sun and converse with other inmates, his mood altered dramatically. Cait sensed this – it was unmistakable when they spoke, and even palpable in the tone of his letters, which had previously strived for positivity but were now actually brimming with it.

At home in San Francisco, Cait went on with her life. She continued to surf. She continued to work. She decided that what little quantity of time she had left would be made up for in quality. Time passed, sometimes slowly, sometimes far too quickly. Then something inexplicable happened.

Seven months after the diagnosis, the cancer arrested itself. Just like that. The lump, which had deposited itself in Cait's brain with the malicious intent of an undetonated bomb, simply stopped growing.

God had smiled. Or maybe the random hand of death had landed somewhere else. Who could say for sure?

She sobbed as she told him over the phone. And for the first time in what felt like a thousand years, the former altar boy lifted his head upward and mouthed the words *Thank you*.

***

September 15, 2002
To Whom it May Concern,
The time has come at last to bid FCI Sheridan a fond farewell. I've kept my cell as clean as possible for you, its next tenant.

Good luck to you. May your stay be as pleasant as my own. You probably think I'm nuts to be leaving this place behind with good feelings, but you have no idea where I came from. Never forget this. No matter how bad your situation, there's always someone out there who's got it worse and who would love to trade places with you.

The toilet works fine, you just have to jiggle the handle a few times to get the water to stop running. The sink backs up sometimes but if you just let it be, it'll eventually drain.

There's a well-fed mouse that lives in the cell block. His name is Leftie. He got that nickname when he survived a bait trap by chewing off his own left foot. You'll recognize him by the unique way he limps when he scurries. Don't hurt him – otherwise, the rest of the guys on the block will be extremely upset and might even take their grief out on you.

Stay away from the meatloaf in the mess hall if you can help it. Or, if you're brave, give it a try. Just make sure you head for a toilet the minute it hits your system. You don't want the guys in here making up some horrible nickname for you.

Me, I've got a lady on the outside and I hear that she can cook. Is there anything else in this world that could be better than that? I didn't think so.

So long,
Chris

THE FALCON AND THE BRIDE

Chris and Cait
(October 19, 2002)

A cool breeze blew, rustling the high branches of the giant redwoods. Two hundred feet below, in the thick wooded canyon where the redwoods' trunks rose from the earth, a crowd of people had gathered. They sat in folding chairs amid the fallen leaves of autumn and faced an oval-shaped wooden platform where the groom stood, waiting for his new life to begin.

Chris shifted his weight nervously and straightened his bow tie. The tuxedo felt more like a costume than an outfit – having worn prison-issued clothes for half his life, his body hadn't yet re-accustomed itself to the physical discomforts of fashion – but he figured he could bear it for another few hours. After all, it was only one of the most important days of his life.

At the top of the path that led down to the clearing, Cait appeared. Her wedding gown trailed behind her as she walked with her brothers, one on each arm, to stand by Chris's side.

She looked at him and her eyes grew wide.

Are we crazy?

He smiled and nodded as if acknowledging her unspoken thought.

We absolutely are.

Chris gazed out at the faces of the people who had come so far to be there and thought of the long road he had traveled. His family was there – his mother, his father, brothers and sisters and their children – as was Cait's. Surely nobody present had expected things to turn out quite like this. Least of all, him.

One month and three days earlier, on the morning of September 16, 2002, Chris walked out of the Federal Correctional Institution at Sheridan a free man. All of Cait's work had finally, really paid off. Life was no longer a promise to be kept at some future date. It was here.

He left the penitentiary with nothing but the clothes on his back. All of his belongings – including the books he had collected and the random keepsakes he'd acquired during his stay – he had given away to other inmates. It was part of an age-old tradition when a man left to begin his life anew. There would be no place for the reminders of his imprisonment.

Stepping outside through the front doors, unaccompanied and unrestrained for the first time, he was instantly overcome with a sensation of panic. It flashed through every sense like some strange neurological misfire, lasting only long enough for him to wonder what the hell he was supposed to do now. He took a deep breath and closed his eyes, telling himself this must be what all inmates experience when they've been in lockup far too long.

Easy does it. One step at a time.

The words took him back to the last time he had tasted freedom, just past the free side of the razor wire fence at Lompoc. This time, there would be no need to look over his shoulder. He held his eyes closed and waited for it to pass.

When he opened his eyes, he saw a car enter the small parking lot. He recognized the faces of his parents immediately. *They look so old,* he thought as the car drew nearer. He realized the mental image he'd carried of his parents was woefully out of date. Seeing them now, and how much they'd aged, was a painful reminder of just how long he'd been away.

How must I look to them? Like Rip Van Winkle on his waking hour.

They came alone, just the two of them, at his request. They had wanted to bring everyone along – a Boyce family reunion right there in the parking lot of FCI Sheridan, onlookers be damned – but he'd asked them not to. Emotional overload was not something he wanted to experience on his first day of freedom.

"Let me ease into it," he had asked, not really believing there would be any way to do that, but willing to give it a shot nonetheless.

Chris raised a hand and waved. The car pulled to a stop. In seconds, he was in the arms of his mother again. It was a little like being reborn. Only this time around, it was a different bottle he craved.

He let go of his mother and turned to face his father. Chris extended his hand in the manner of greeting that had always been the way between them, for as long as he could remember. Instead of returning the handshake, Charlie Boyce put his arms around his son and embraced him.

"I've been waiting for this day for so long," Charlie said, his voice muffled against his son's shoulder.

They held each other for a long time. When they parted, tears were streaming down both men's cheeks. Noreen Boyce stood watching, weeping softly.

"Figure you can give me a ride out of here?" Chris asked, trying to lighten the heaviness of the moment.

Charlie looked at Noreen. "We don't normally pick up hitchhikers," he said, "but I think today we can make an exception."

The three of them climbed into the car and drove slowly away. Chris sat and stared out the window the entire ride to Portland, trying to believe it was true, afraid to wake and find himself dreaming in his cell. As the miles ticked off on the odometer and the prison was at last far behind him, he began to relax. But as tired as he was, he never once closed his eyes.

At Portland, they drove straight to the airport. Chris's next stop would be San Francisco, where Cait was waiting. He regretted having to leave his parents again so soon after seeing them, but there was nothing he wanted more than to hold her. Their time together would be fleeting – he had to be checked into the halfway house by four p.m. – but after so many years spent waiting for this day to arrive, he decided he would gladly take every second that he had.

He spotted her right away, standing alone at the bottom of the ramp leading down into the baggage claim area. The last time he'd been through an airport, security measures had been lax. The fact Cait couldn't be there to greet him at the gate seemed insane. The world had changed, alright, and not all for the better.

There were bombs to worry about, guns, people with horrifying intentions. He supposed it was not much different from the world he'd left behind. Only now, everything felt like it was on fast-forward. He noticed people everywhere with portable telephones attached to their ears like appendages. He wondered what everyone was talking about that was so important it couldn't wait for a face-to-face conversation. As he closed the distance between himself and Cait, everything around him receded until it was just the two of them.

She attacked him with a hug before they even said hello and he reciprocated, lifting her off her feet. Before he put her back down, their lips met. The last time had been at Oak Park Heights, five years before. It had been awkward then. This time was different. There was nothing to come between them now – no watchful prison guards, no leering inmates, no cameras, no bars, no walls – and the only thing that kept them from losing themselves to the moment was the fact they were in public.

"Did you check a bag?" she asked him.

"No. What you see is what you get."

"Then let's get the hell out of here." She took his hand. "I've got something in the car that'll cool those jets of yours."

He followed her lead eagerly as they left the terminal and hopped onto an escalator. He stood behind her and looked her over, head to toe. How many times had he dreamed of this moment? Now that it was here, he realized the reality was nothing like the fantasy. This was infinitely better.

Cait turned around to smile at him and discovered his stare had migrated. "Are you checking out my ass?" she exclaimed.

He laughed bashfully and looked away, but his eyes were immediately drawn back. "Of course I am!"

She grabbed his hand and pulled him up alongside her. "Eyes front."

In the parking garage, she led him to a cherry red Jetta that chirped like an electronic bird when she pressed a button on her key fob. Chris observed, curious. Everything was louder in the free world. Even the cars talked back.

Cait threw open the backseat door, still holding his hand, pulling him close. "I hope you're hungry."

"I could eat," he replied.

The smile she gave him was devilish. "Climb in back, soldier. I bet it's been a long time since you've had any of this."

Here? Now? Okay, he thought. *I'm game.*

He moved past her and slid into the backseat. Immediately, his hand stumbled across a package wrapped in plastic. It was the size of a shoebox. He turned his head and saw that the entire backseat compartment was stacked with similar packages.

"Fresh out of the oven," she announced, trying to hide her laughter.

Chris picked one of the boxes up and set it on his lukewarm lap. It was adorned with a purple bow that held the plastic covering in place, reminding him of Easter baskets from ages long since passed. He tore the ribbon loose and lifted the lid.

"Cookies." There was a tone in his voice that screamed utter dismay. He caught it before she had an opportunity to react, rephrasing the word, feigning an amused lilt. "Cookies!"

He placed one of them in his mouth whole. When he smiled at her, his teeth were black with chocolate chips.

"For God's sake, Boyce, don't choke on it!" She motioned to the miniature mountain of boxes stuffed with a bakery's worth of confections. "You've also got macadamia nut cookies, sugar cookies, brownies, and a shitload of other stuff to put you into a diabetic coma."

"This is almost better than sex," he quipped.

She rolled her eyes. "I picked you up some clothes, too. They're in the trunk."

It was something that hadn't even occurred to him.

"Thank you."

She walked around the car and climbed into the driver's seat. Chris grabbed two of the cookie boxes and hopped out of the backseat, into the front. "You drive, I'll feast."

They reached the halfway house in a depressingly short amount of time. It was in the San Francisco Tenderloin district. The place looked like a flophouse. Dangerous looking men with prison tattoos and eyes that warned away the leery milled about on the sidewalk in front of the sagging building, which looked like it had stood since the early part of the century.

"It beats prison," she offered, but Chris wasn't looking at the halfway house or his soon-to-be neighbors. He was looking at her.

"Do you want to get married?"

She laughed. "I don't think you'll be able to find an ordained minister here. At least not one that still has a license to practice."

"I'm serious."

"I'll just bet you are."

"Do you love me?"

The smile faded from her face. "You know I do, Chris. I think I've loved you since the first time I laid eyes on you. If that's even possible."

"And I've loved you ever since I saw you in that beach parking lot."

It was the closest thing to a confession she ever got out of him, the nearest they ever came to discussing what had been lying dormant in the back of her brain for twenty-one years like a great, big unexplained mystery. She almost spoke the name aloud – *Guy Blake* – and then decided against it. Some things were better left unsaid. It was easier that way. It kept things uncomplicated, clean. Maybe even a bit less frightening.

"And here I thought all that love at first sight bullshit was just that," she said.

"Let's get married."

He had never been this forward in his life. It was a new experience for him and he appeared to be relishing it. Cait shook her head and stared down at the emblem on her steering wheel.

"I'm forty-eight years old, Chris."

"And I'm forty-nine. We'd make the perfect couple."

She raised a hand and touched his cheek. "Let's just make sure this is you talking and not your freedom."

They kissed.

"Is it Daulton?" he asked her.

It had been a long time since he'd last spoken the name.

"What do you mean?"

He shrugged. "I don't know what I mean, exactly. I know you two were close."

"It's different with you."

"I know it is. I believe that. I also know he probably cares about you a lot more than you realize. I don't need intuition to tell me that."

She sighed. It had been four years since Daulton's release from prison. In that time, they had done their best to maintain their friendship. It was even easy, for a while. He spent Thanksgivings in San Francisco with her family, and she visited him on numerous occasions in southern California. But his jealousy over her relationship with Chris was always there, bubbling beneath the surface. The nearer Chris's release date came, the further Daulton drifted, until eventually she decided that maybe it would be less painful to simply let him go.

"Daulton has nothing to do with anything," she said. "I haven't talked to him in almost two years."

He looked relieved to hear that. Not because he considered Daulton a threat, but because he thought he had already brought enough pain to his old friend's life to last an eternity.

"Look," he said, "I've wasted enough time. I don't want to waste any more. I want to marry you. I know you have your doubts. I have mine. The longest and most meaningful relationship I've ever had was with a goddamn pillow in isolation."

The words caught her by surprise and she burst out laughing. He laughed, too.

"I may not ever be the best husband in the world, but I'll try."

There was an almost childlike sweetness in the way he spoke to her. She had no doubt his intentions were true. What she doubted were her own abilities to share her life and her home with another person – a husband – after living alone for so many years.

"I'll tell you what," she said, nodding her head in the direction of the halfway house. "You get your ass focused on what you have to do here and I'll consider your proposition."

He smiled. "I love it when you talk legalese. You make everything sound *dirty*."

She thought she would have to think it over longer than she did. But before she even pulled into her driveway that afternoon, she had the answer.

They didn't see each other for another week. The halfway house imposed strict limitations on the comings and goings of its new arrivals, and that extended to social time with friends and family. The only allowance was for work. At the first opportunity he had to leave for the afternoon, she picked him up early and brought him to her home.

It was in her kitchen over homemade espresso that she turned to him and said, "Oh, by the way? Yes."

They forgot about the coffee. After all, it's only coffee.

Three weeks later, on the morning of October 12, they were married in the small living room of her San Francisco home by a justice of the peace who was on his way to a Star Trek convention. He was costumed in full Vulcan regalia, but agreed to remove the Spock ears for the exchanging of the vows. The full wedding ceremony would take place October 19 in the backyard of Cait's good friend, Patrick Miller.

Patrick was also Chris's first boss. All he could offer him was minimum wage, working as an assistant at his stonework facility on a turkey ranch overlooking Dillon Beach, but it gave Chris the job he needed to secure his stay at the halfway house. It also gave Chris the opportunity to spend his lunch breaks staring out at the beach, watching marsh hawks and red-tails and the occasional golden eagle fly overhead. Most of the time, the two men ate lunch side by side in silence. Sometimes, Chris would talk about falcons.

On the day of the wedding, Patrick picked Chris up from the halfway house and drove him to his home in Occidental. The house had been built over a running creek at the bottom of a canyon, surrounded by first- and second-growth redwood trees. It was one of the most beautiful places Chris had ever seen. As they pulled to a stop in the driveway, a group of people who had gathered at the bay window of the home turned and looked out.

"Oh my God," Chris said.

"See anyone you recognize?" Patrick asked him knowingly.

"My brothers and sisters." Tears brimmed in his eyes. He made no effort to stop them.

Now the group of people, who had been waiting for this moment since one awful day in January of 1977, began to come out of the house. Most of them had not seen or talked to their big brother in more than twenty-five years.

Patrick nudged him with his elbow. "Don't just sit there. Come on, you've got some family to see."

It was a beautiful day.

***

The newlyweds spent the night apart. Chris had to be back to the halfway house before curfew. It would still be at least another month before he would earn the privilege of taking weekend trips.

Rather than spend her wedding night alone, Cait brought her parents, Tom and Pat, to spend the night at her house. She gave them her room and took the spare room for herself. Just as she was pulling back the covers to climb into bed, she heard her mother's voice.

"Cait?"

Tom was already in bed, but Pat was standing in the middle of the room. There was a yellow sticky note in her hand. "I found this on your pillow." There were tears in her eyes as she held it out to her daughter.

The note was written in Chris's handwriting. It simply said *Now we finally get to see what it's like to spend our life together. I love you.*

THE HARBINGER OF WINTER

Cait
(May 2004)

I knew something was terribly wrong when Chris suggested going to see the ducklings. He'd been giving me *that* look all weekend. The one that says, "I'm memorizing every inch of your face because you're not going to be around much longer." At first I thought it was my imagination. But the morning I awoke from a restless sleep to see Chris standing in the doorway of our bedroom watching me, there was no question.

There are just some things that subterfuge can't hide. Bad news is one of them. Some people make great bearers of ill tidings. Like the military guy in the immaculate black uniform who shows up at the door of every newly widowed soldier's wife. That's a solid pro through and through, if ever there was one: the soundless arrival on the curb outside the house with the little white picket fence; the somber stride up the walk that tells everyone who lays eyes on him precisely what his business is; the gentle rap on the front door to announce his arrival; the perfect expression of sympathy as he informs another young wife that she will be raising her children alone. Every bit of it rehearsed for minimal devastation and maximum compassion. Chris, on the other hand, had absolutely no practice delivering bad news. Especially news that wasn't about him.

It was May, 2004. We were still living in San Francisco. After months of careful consideration and the meticulous weighing of pros and cons, I had decided – against the protestations of Chris, who told me he would love me even if I were built like a surfboard – to have reconstructive breast surgery. I loved him all the more for that, but it was a decision I made for myself and nobody else. It had been far too long since I'd felt like a whole person. I'd been through enough. It was time to reclaim that piece of me which had been taken away.

So I met with Dr. Loren Eskenazi, a Stanford-educated plastic surgeon with a reputation to match her infinitely kind nature. Loren got it; she understood where I was coming from. She had the heart of a healer and the hands of an artist. After a series of consultations, the date was set.

I had the surgery on a Thursday at St. Mary's in the Haight. When it was all over, I was sent home with my newly installed silicone sacks and two sets of drains poking out of my breasts like appendages. The drains were small rubber tubes about five inches long, paved below the muscle wall and stitched into place around the insertion area.

The next few days were some of the most miserable of my life. Pain pills were of no use whatsoever. Sleep came in short bursts that were interrupted every few minutes by racking pain. The bandages and drains made sleeping on my side impossible, so I was left with no other recourse but to lie on my back like an upended turtle.

My first post-surgical check was scheduled for the fifth day. By then, the pain had begun to subside to the point where I'd regained some of my ambulatory capabilities. I wasn't quite ready to sashay down Broadway on the hunt for a new purse – I still needed help hoisting myself out of bed – but at least I'd be getting out of the house.

An hour before we were supposed to leave for Loren's office in Pacific Heights, Chris suggested leaving early so we could stop by Golden Gate Park on the way.

"I don't know that I'm up for a hike today," I told him.

Chris wasn't having any of it. He grabbed a pair of sneakers from my shoe rack and set them down on the floor in front of me. "No, let's go. The baby ducklings should have hatched by now."

"There's no such thing as a baby duckling," I shot back listlessly. My voice sounded like shit and the old tank was on E, but even at my worst I can still be sharp as a tack. "You're either a duckling or a duck."

Chris tried to smile. It wasn't working. His face just contorted into a poor imitation of joviality. "I know. I think I'm the one who told you that."

"I knew all about Donald and his kind long before you entered the picture."

"Come on. Let's go. It'll be good to get outside for awhile."

He was right. I had spent the better part of the last five days in bed. Besides, that time of year was always the most beautiful in the park. The air blowing in from the coast was never warm – it never has been and probably never will be – but the sky outside our front bay window was just right. I didn't want to say no. I also had the feeling he wasn't going to take anything but yes for an answer.

"Alright." I motioned to the tennis shoes. "If you do the lacing, I'll do the walking."

Five minutes later, we were in the car. No sooner had the engine kicked to life than something in Chris's mood darkened. There was a defeated slouch about his shoulders as he drove, and his hands clung limply to the steering wheel.

I asked him if he was okay and he responded with four words that have always been a dead giveaway to me: "What do you mean?"

"I mean are you upset or sick or something?"

"I'm okay."

"You're acting strange."

Chris looked at me and for the first time, I noticed that his eyes were bloodshot. "Just tired, that's all."

My mind went everywhere. Had he been fired from his job? Had he gone and robbed another bank? Was he leaving me for another woman? By this point, I should have been terrified. I should have barraged him with a dozen questions. Maybe forced him to pull to the side of the road and not let him drive another foot until he spilled it. But I didn't. A cool calmness was descending over me. As if I'd already seen the outcome long ago and was simply along for the ride as it unfurled in real time.

We hit Sunset and drove north toward the park in silence. Through the open passenger window, I watched the city recede and the green unfold. I breathed it all in, every moment, unaware that for the first time in days I wasn't thinking about the pain.

We drove into the west quarter of the park closest to the coast. Chris wound the car slowly through narrow, curving roads to the duck pond where we often took the dogs. It was a favorite place of theirs, and I felt a momentary pang of guilt that we'd come here without them.

He parked the car and began to walk around to my side, but I beat him to the punch and let myself out. I needed to start doing things for myself and now was as good a time as any to start.

We walked to the water's edge and looked out across the pond. Chris pointed to a spot in the middle of the pond, where a school of ducklings were paddling furiously after their mother.

"You see them?"

He had moved around behind me. Suddenly I felt like Lenny in *Of Mice and Men*. George standing off to the side, making pie-in-the-sky promises about rabbits while retrieving the revolver from his jacket pocket.

The family of ducks drifted in and out of glades and lilies as they crossed the water. It was warm enough that even the turtles had come out. A cool gust blew in the aroma of the salty sea and I let it fill my lungs.

"They found a lump during the surgery, Cait."

I turned around to face Chris. He had driven his fists deep into the pockets of his jeans and was shifting his weight from one leg to the other. He had his head hung low, like a child who's been forced into some horrible, guilty confession. Or a man who's just had the duty of informing his wife she is probably going to die.

When he raised his head to look at me, I saw that he was crying. Or trying not to. Whatever he was aiming for, he was missing the mark by a long shot. His face looked like a dam on the brink of complete collapse.

"What kind of lump?" I asked. My voice was calm and even. "How big?"

"Big."

That was all he managed to get out before losing it. Tears flowed freely now and he made no effort to stop them. He told me everything, his words coming like spasms between sobs, never once looking at me as he spoke. Doing so would have been too much like pronouncing my fate.

"The doctor removed it. She sent it down to the lab right away. They said it was cancer. She tried to get it all, but she isn't sure she did. She told me about it when you were still in recovery. We both figured it would be better to wait a few days to tell you."

Chris wiped the tears furiously from his eyes and let out a huge sigh. The look of relief on his face was clearly visible – color had already begun to flood back into his cheeks where that old familiar pallor had lately taken up residence. Yet something still remained, an expression that I can only describe as looming dread.

I closed my eyes and tried not to think about what lay ahead. The news was dreadful, but it wasn't all that big a surprise. A shock, yes. A kick in the gut, absolutely. But not a surprise. Anyone who's ever had cancer more than once will probably tell you the same: there's not much to compete with that first diagnosis. It's like your first broken heart. Nothing that comes after can compare. And the fact was, the last time big bad C and I had crossed paths in 2000, I knew it wouldn't be our last dance.

Chris, though. Poor Chris.

"You've known since the day of the surgery?" I asked him. He nodded. "How the hell did you keep all of that in for five days?"

"I'm sorry," he said, and his voice broke again. "I wish it could be me, Cait. It should be me."

He shook his head once, then twice, like doing so could magically stop the torrent or alter the reality of the situation. When that didn't work, he turned away.

I walked to him and leaned my shoulder against his. It was the only part of my upper body that I knew could take the pressure, even though at the moment I was feeling no physical pain. Just numbness.

I could sense his almost animalistic need to grab hold of me, to clutch me tightly against him, but the tenderness that I had recognized in him so many years ago prevented him from doing so. Gently, he put his arm around my shoulder and stroked my hair with his hand.

We stood that way, in the beautiful light of that horrid summer day amid the ducklings and the turtles and the random passers-by, until I knew that it was time to go and start the fight again.

***

Death is a bastard. He grins at you from behind the veil while his minions do his bidding. It's never enough for him to see his victim simply pass away like a leaf dropping from a tree. When Death has it out for you, he makes sure the plunge is eternally long. And if he can inflict as much pain as possible in the process, he's only more than glad to oblige that impulse.

In the summer of 2004, I found myself facing off with that devil again in a fight that drove me to the brink of my physical and emotional endurance. Death had returned with a vengeance, and this time he would take my breasts again, destroying all of Loren's work and causing me at times to question if it wouldn't be simpler to just throw in the towel and call it a battle well fought. In those quiet moments I would think of all that Chris and I had been through together and all we had yet to experience. We hadn't even been married two full years. I decided I wasn't willing to cry uncle just yet.

My oncologist determined that there would be no chemo necessary, just drugs. Hideous, powerful drugs with side effects I wouldn't wish on my worst enemy. On the bright side, I got to keep my hair. To celebrate that fact, I ceremoniously dyed it a bright shade of blue. Ultramarine. Chris said I looked like a walking lollipop. I said that was quite a compliment coming from a guy who looked like the "before" photo for a men's hair color product ad.

I continued to surf. Two months after Loren's discovery of the lump, I competed in a surfing competition in the Bay Area and won. Death sat watching the entire time, seething from the sidelines. I clutched that trophy to my chest as evidence that even with the hounds of Hell nipping at my heels, I was capable of so much more than lying down.

When August came and my first round of drug treatments was over, Chris and I decided to leave San Francisco. It had been my home for twenty years and I had come to love it more than any other place in the world, but in my heart I knew it was time to move on. I also knew that it was time to give Chris something he had longed for ever since that fateful day in January, 1977 – a home that he could call his own, removed from the constant noise of city life, surrounded by wide open areas where he could fly his falcons in silence and in peace.

Death, that omnipresent son of a whore, is not through with me yet. Nor am I through with him. My life has become a miraculous balancing act, an attempt to strike an impossible equilibrium between the desire for a "normal" life (whatever the hell that is) and the constant need to look over my shoulder and gauge my distance from the beast that would have devoured me whole if I had only let him.

Day by day, one step at a time, I tend to the flowers in my garden and I continue with my life's work. I love my dogs and dote on them like the children I never had. I care for my ailing parents with the same love and compassion they gave so selflessly to me when I was a child, and as I watch their steady decline into Alzheimer's I am reminded once again of the preciousness of memory and of the fact we're really only here for a flash of a moment.

I love my husband as well as I know how, and often marvel at his ability to love me in return when the realization that we are two fiercely independent people rears its ugly head. Yet I know I couldn't live without him and I shudder to think how in the world he would ever get along without me.

I do all of these things because I can, and because I understand that every moment of my life – every fraction of an instant spent fending off the inevitable fate that awaits us all – is a treasure beyond material value. So I fight for every breath, and negotiate every hurdle, and steel myself against the worst this world can throw me. And every chance I get, I thumb my nose at Death and let him know he has already lost.

ABSOLUTION

Chris
(October 2005)

Chris slowed the old Ranger to a crawl as he approached the bank. He peered through the passenger's side window and tried reading the hours of operation printed on the door. Too small. Just as he was about to circle the block again, he saw an old cowboy swagger up to the entrance and waltz inside. Still open. He glanced down at the digital clock on the dashboard and figured he still had at least twenty minutes.

He picked up speed, breezed past the main parking lot entrance, and rounded the corner. He pulled to a stop on the curb and turned off the ignition. The engine sputtered and spat and the front end lurched violently as the engine slowly died.

Chris ignored it. The truck had been a steal and it got him where he needed to go. Half a lifetime ago, he might have been moved to take it to the shop. He might even have been able to afford it then – amazing how far $140 a week got you in the early seventies – but these days, money was harder to come by.

The two-and-a-half-decade gap in his work history didn't help matters, either. Nor did the fact that he was obligated to disclose his prior convictions to all prospective employers. Strangely enough, few had a grasp of what the word "espionage" really meant, but there was no ambiguity when it came to the words "bank robbery." Once, when reviewing his application for a pizza delivery job, the hiring manager had actually laughed out loud at what he mistakenly presumed to be a bad joke. When Chris didn't laugh along, the manager's smile melted into a mask of concern. The job had gone to someone else.

Not every opportunity played out the same way. Sometimes providence would smile at just the right moment. Like the time not long after his release from prison when the hiring manager of a Petco in downtown San Francisco had recognized the name on the job application and exclaimed, "Oh my God! My baby sister played your baby sister in *The Falcon and the Snowman*!" Thanks to that minor miracle, Chris was hired on the spot.

The jobs didn't always pay well, but they satisfied one of the principal conditions of his parole. He made up for the rest by being thrifty. And by driving the Ranger, which Cait hated, but it was still one hell of a step up from where he'd been just three years earlier.

Several times, Cait had offered to pay for an upgrade. Each time, Chris refused. He had paid for the battered pickup with his own money and that was important to him. Cait didn't like it, but she understood.

When he was sure the engine had finished its death dance, Chris lifted the emergency brake into place. He touched his forehead with a slightly trembling hand. He was sweating, even though the temperature outside was only fifty-five degrees. Beyond the Ranger's mud-splattered windows, autumn was breathing its last dying breaths as winter stood poised to pick up where its predecessor left off. Just around the bend, 2006 loomed impatiently.

Concentrating, Chris tried to slow the racing of his heart. This was normal, he reminded himself, but it didn't make getting out of the pickup and walking into that bank any easier. The last time he'd been in a bank was twenty-five years ago, and he had exited running.

He mopped the beads of sweat from his forehead and wiped his hand on his lap. He considered his options. There was no other way but to do it; he had no choice. He reached into the breast pocket of his windbreaker to make sure what he needed was still there. It was. He drew the zipper up until the tab rested just inches below his chin. Then he angled the rearview mirror to see behind him. The street was deserted, except for a small delivery truck that sat idling outside a furniture store a block away.

He tried to swallow, found his saliva reserves had been tapped out, and almost called it off. But then he remembered how far he'd come and decided to get it over with.

The driver's side door let out a scream of protest as he threw it open. From behind and to the left came the sudden blast of a horn, followed by the whinnying screech of tires against asphalt. Inches away from the tip of the pickup's open door, a late model sedan cruised past. Its driver was waving a single fist in the air, mouthing what was no doubt a stream of obscenities. Chris reflexively jerked the door closed, but by then the threat had passed. Now his adrenalin was really pumping. He threw his head backward and stared up at the burned-out dome light until his breathing slowed.

I'm going to get myself killed before I even get inside.

This time making sure the coast was clear, he cracked the driver's side door open and stepped out. A tow truck was lumbering its way toward him down the street, but he was out of the way and onto the sidewalk long before it reached him. He waited until it had driven past to begin walking in the direction of the bank.

Halfway to the corner, he realized that he'd left the key in the ignition. Twenty-five years earlier, he might have been able to get away with that move – but these days, leaving a car unattended, even in Tinytown U.S.A., was asking for trouble.

He retraced his steps to the pickup, opened the passenger door, and snatched the keychain from the ignition. The trembling of his hands had begun to subside, but not quite enough to prevent him from losing grip. The keychain bounced once on the floorboard and disappeared.

A hissing curse escaped his lips as he rested his belly on the bench seat so that he could feel around underneath it. As his fingers closed around the keychain, he exhaled a short sigh of relief – one small crisis averted.

How the hell did I ever do any of this before?

He stood, closed the passenger door, turned and headed for the bank. He was okay until he reached the corner. The moment the building came into view, he was overcome with a swimming sensation.

Fuck this. I can't go through with this. And then he remembered what Cait had directed him to do and he knew it had to be done. Today. Right now. He sucked in a deep breath. This time, he held it for a few seconds before letting the air seep slowly from his pinched lips.

The inner voice spoke again. *Onward,* it said. *You have business here.* He began to walk.

He reached the entrance of the bank just as the door was about to swing closed. There was a young lady with a gorgeous head of long dark hair approaching from the opposite direction on the sidewalk, and Chris pulled himself aside to hold the door open. She walked past him and entered the bank as if he weren't there. No eye contact. No thank you. Not even a dirty look for his trouble.

I've pointed guns at people with more manners than that, he reflected. The observation was amusing enough to make him forget the rude sleight, but not enough to calm his nerves. The moment he was through the door, he was struck by a wave of anxiety so strong it almost commanded him to run the other way. Only the fact that he had a stated mission to carry out prevented him from doing so. He was locked in; there was no turning back.

His eyes swept the inside of the bank from left to right and found the security guard almost immediately, stationed just past the entrance. The guy wasn't much older than Chris himself. Sixtyish. Late fifties, at best. He wore a holstered revolver and a uniform that looked about one size too large for his slight frame. The hat perched on his head sat at a slightly askew angle that gave him an almost cartoonish quality, and he was leaning comfortably against a waist-high stool with his hands folded in his lap. Surely not at attention the way he probably should have been, and certainly no deterrent to anyone desperate enough to enter with less than honorable intentions.

Just beyond the security guard, in plain sight for all entering patrons to see, was a placard that read PLEASE REMOVE ALL HATS AND SUNGLASSES. This was a new one on him. Chris assumed that this was now the standard, and wondered if any of his own exploits all those years ago walking into banks disguised in low-brimmed hats, dark sunglasses and full facial theatre beards had had any influence on its enforcement. After a moment of pondering, he decided he would think about it later. He walked past the sign and took his place in line.

Eleven people, including the brunette with the great hair and lousy manners, stood between him and the tellers' counter. Eleven transactions that could each take up to five minutes apiece to complete, depending on how complex they were. With three tellers on the job, the amount of time he would have to spend in line was already far longer than he'd counted on.

He turned his head and eyed the security guard again. One of the bank employees, probably a loan officer or maybe even a manager by the neat look of her business suit, had stopped to shoot the breeze with the old rent-a-cop. The two were discussing something of interest. Chris could tell by the way the uniformed man leaned in and the way the lady kept gesticulating with her hands, probably talking about the weather or this week's reality elimination show. Not about the ex-bank robber who had just walked undetected through the door and was now slowly inching his way toward the front of the line.

One of the customers at the counter stuffed a printed receipt into his pocket and walked away. The teller waved another customer forward. As the line continued to shorten, Chris's stomach began to fold into knots. This was a bad idea.

He struggled to occupy his mind with other thoughts, but nothing would stick for more than half a second before falling away. The moment had hijacked his attention. He could feel the past and present colliding in a dizzying patchwork of images and sounds. He tried to channel it into a single, cohesive thought but found himself incapable.

He tried to recall the name and location of the last bank he had robbed, but his brain wouldn't comply. All that was coming to him now were flashes of moments long past – faces, mostly, every single one of them brought back now in disturbingly vivid detail.

He blinked and saw the face of the little old lady with the trembling lower lip. How long ago had that been? Ages. He hadn't meant to pick her – it was just the way the cards had been dealt that day, and if he'd had the opportunity he would have aimed the business end of that damn gun at someone else instead, maybe someone who didn't remind him so much of his own grandmother. The confused expression on her face as she regarded first the pistol in Chris's hand, then him, then the pistol again, had never seemed so vivid to his mind's eye. He felt as though he were seeing it now for the first time, an instant replay delayed by almost three decades.

How terrified had the teller been that day? Did she think her number had been called and that she'd be dancing on a cloud any moment with her long-dead relatives? The robbery had only lasted a minute, no more – just enough time for the contents of the cash drawers up front to be emptied into a money bag, since Chris never stuck around long enough to direct the tellers to the vault – but that was certainly long enough for her to have pondered how her family might react if the man behind the fake beard and the sunglasses suddenly decided to pull the trigger.

Less than ten paces ahead, another customer finished his business and left. The line shuffled forward.

Alice, that was her name. Or no – maybe Alma? He had learned it years later, only after Cait had tracked her down as a part of the parole brief preparation when Chris was still in lockup at Oak Park Heights. The retired teller had agreed to be interviewed by Cait, and during their conversation had referred to him as "the nicest young man." The words had blown his mind; they'd been almost too difficult to comprehend.

"I interviewed every one of those bank tellers you held up," Cait had told him. "Not a single one of them had anything bad to say about you."

The absurdity had caused Chris to laugh out loud, but only for a moment before his face grew serious again. "But I held them up. At gunpoint." Then, as if to underscore his point, he added: "The gun was loaded."

"I know it was loaded. So did they. And they all said the same thing. They never felt in danger. I guess nobody expects a polite, soft-spoken bank robber."

He had shaken his head in disbelief, then uttered something he'd never told another living soul. "If there's anything I regret more, it's that. I wish I could take it back."

But it wasn't the stealing of money that he wished he could erase – the banks themselves had been picked first by location, second by FDIC affiliation to minimize the potential financial blow – and it wasn't getting caught that eventually brought him around to wishing he'd never had the stupid idea to begin with. It was the people, plain and simple. Most of them had been women, some verging on elderly. Like Alice. Or Alma. Anne? He wished he could remember her name.

A young guy in a Seahawks hoodie brushed past Chris on his way from the teller. Seconds later, a middle-aged mother followed. There were now only three people left in line. He had to calm himself or he was going to cause an incident.

He considered the faces of the tellers on the other side of the counter only feet away and wondered how they would react if they knew what he had done and the person he had once been. Would they call the security guard over and have him thrown out? Would they run? Or would they merely size him up and determine him a non-risk?

He began to study their faces, moving slowly from left to right: the twenty-something blond girl with the fake tan; the overweight bald guy with the clean-shaven face… and that's when he saw her. Alice. Or no – maybe Alma. Anne? Only this time, the name plate read something totally different. He was still too far away to see it clearly without his glasses, but when he squinted the letters solidified into a word that looked like Charlotte.

The Falcon and The Snowman: American Sons

The line before him shrank again, and now he could see with certainty that the third teller – the one on the far right with the graying hair and reading glasses in a flower print blouse that looked exactly like Alice (her name had been Alice, he remembered now) – was, indeed, somebody else. But the resemblance was uncanny. So much so that he looked away, afraid of being recognized.

Behind him, the security guard had ended his conversation with the bank employee and was now scanning the lobby with a bored expression. The rude brunette had made it to the counter and was talking to the male teller like he was her subordinate. And somewhere, someone was saying the word "sir" over and over.

A gentle tap on the shoulder from the man in line behind him brought Chris out of his daze. The teller, whose name was Charlotte and not Alice, beckoned him toward her.

"Sir, I can help you here." Her voice was kind.

He stepped up to the counter. For a moment he only looked at her, studying her features, noting the way her eyelids curved softly down at the edges and the way she wore her glasses on the bridge of her nose. She could have been Alice the bank teller's twin sister. But that was impossible. That was more than twenty-five years ago.

"How can I help you?"

His mind drew a blank. He felt like he was standing on the arc of a bridge between two realities – the world of today and the world of long ago. Then he remembered, and he reached into his breast pocket. He pulled out the envelope Cait had given him and set it on the counter.

"I need to cash a check," he said, and the act of speaking those words aloud was like a panacea that rocketed him back into the here and now with forceful clarity. He almost repeated himself – might have, in fact, if the teller by the name of Charlotte hadn't spoken.

"Not a problem." Her reply was bright. Almost too bright.

She took the envelope and removed its contents. It was a personal check in Cait's name, made out to "cash" for $17,000.

Charlotte read the amount on the check, then looked up at Chris. The moment of truth, which was really no moment of truth at all but only a casual glance, seemed to last an eternity. Then Charlotte said, "Paying off your bookie?"

Chris smiled despite his nervousness. "No. My wife is paying off her car. I'm headed to Western Union right after I leave here to take care of it."

Too much information, he thought. *Why don't you tell her about your criminal record while you're at it?*

"Take the money and run," Charlotte joked.

Something inside crashed against his stomach and he felt suddenly nauseous. His face fell, but just at the moment when the flight or fight instinct should have kicked in, he recovered. "No way. My wife would have my hide. She's the one who makes all the money."

Charlotte laughed. "It's the same in my house. Not a problem, I just need your ID. I'll get my manager to approve this and get you on your way."

Three excruciatingly long minutes later – there wasn't enough cash in the till for that large a withdrawal, so the money had to be removed from the vault – he watched Charlotte count out $17,000 in hundred dollar bills as her manager, a guy in an expensive tie and matching suspenders, looked on. The manager had the stuffy look of a U.S. marshal, which only added to the surreal sensation of panic that nearly overcame Chris when the pile of money was slipped into a thick envelope and handed to him.

He thought about asking for larger bills, then canceled it. He didn't want to be here any longer. The moment was far too much like reliving a past he wished he'd never lived. So instead, he stuck the envelope into the breast pocket of his windbreaker, muttered the words "Thank you" – *That's exactly what I said to Alice all those years ago, "thank you"* – and took off at a brisk walk for the door.

He nearly broke into a run when he heard a male voice behind him call out – but as previously pointed out, it had been years since Christopher Boyce had run from anything. At the sound of the words "Hold it!" Chris stopped dead in his tracks and slowly turned around.

The bank manager gestured him back to the counter. Charlotte had something in her hand and was waving it at him. It was his driver's license.

"You'll probably be needing this."

Chris took the card and stuck it absently into the front pocket of his jeans, his fingers now far too shaky to even consider trying to slide it back into place in his wallet. He looked at Charlotte and shrugged his shoulders, almost sheepishly. It was an act that made him look far more lost than any man of his age should have rightfully been.

"I'm sorry," he said.

"You're forgiven," she replied.

Charlotte smiled then, and the look on her face when she did was so sincere that it bypassed Chris's senses and struck like an arrow in his core. That sensation, the one of being in two worlds at the same time, came rushing back. For a brief moment, he felt like Vonnegut's own Billy Pilgrim. Wherever and whenever he was, he was grateful to have the moment.

"Thank you," he told her. It was the only kind of absolution he was going to get, but he took it. Before walking out of that bank for what he hoped would be the very last time in his life, he added: "It means a lot coming from you, Alice."

The woman whose name was not Alice – nor Alma, or Anne – considered the curious man before her with the sorrowful blue eyes. Then he walked away and she never saw him again.

When he was gone, Charlotte turned to her manager and raised her eyebrows quizzically.

"They're getting weirder every day, Ned."

Ned responded under his breath. "No shit, Char."

TAMPING THE DIRT

Chris and Cait
(October 2005)

Chris came home to find Cait already there. These days, the presence of her car in the driveway at any hour before sunset was an anomaly. He parked behind her and shut off the engine, eyes surveying the house for some sign of a disturbance. He had no idea what he was looking for, but he had some inkling that whatever the cause for her early return couldn't be good news.

He got out of the car and walked cautiously toward the front door. Usually, his first order of business would be to walk around back and check on Zeke, make sure he was still in his mew. It wasn't that he expected to find the falcon gone. It was just a force of habit. Zeke always reminded Chris that he was free. Even after three years back in the real world, it was still good to touch the bird's feathers and lay hands on the evidence of his liberty.

When he walked through the front door, he found Cait in the front room with a piece of paper in her hands. Her brow was furrowed and she had a look on her face that reflected belated relief.

"What's up?" he asked. He was still standing in the doorway, afraid to enter.

She looked up and held the piece of paper out to him. "It's a letter from the sheriff's office. About the bones."

"What about them?" He wasn't eager to take the letter. If it was disturbing news, he'd rather hear it from her lips than in the language of the local bureaucracy.

She set the letter down on the coffee table and sighed.

"Whatever the bones were," she said, "they're not human. As to what they are... they're not sure. But as long as that wasn't a person someone buried back there, it's no longer their concern. Case closed."

He put his hands in his pockets and stood staring down at the crisscross rug pattern at his feet. This wasn't the sense of relief he'd anticipated. Was this it? Was it over now? And if it was, did this mean things were supposed to go back to being the way they were before? Something told him they never would.

That auger had unearthed a lot more than just bones in a bag. The sleepless nights he'd experienced since were testament to that. The circus of cops that had descended like marionettes in some mad Gestapo play hadn't helped, either. He had hoped that a resolution – any resolution – would have brought some sense of closure. But the emotions he was experiencing were not those of relief.

"You look tired," Cait said.

He rubbed at his eyes absently. "I didn't get much sleep last night."

"Why don't you go lie down and I'll wake you up in an hour?" She sounded worried. The look on her face only emphasized that. She had hoped that once the matter was cleared up, he would be able to sleep again.

"Good idea." He sauntered down the hall into the bedroom.

He kicked off his shoes and lay on the bed in his street clothes, knowing Cait hated it when he did, too troubled and preoccupied right now to care. He closed his eyes and tried to sleep. When he did, it was like drawing the blinds with the TV on. The absence of light only made the images in his head play out with more vivid clarity.

In the beginning, it was easy enough to try to forget the past and move on. Newfound freedom is a rollercoaster ride, even for those who want nothing more than to slow down and live a quiet life. There had been family to see; places to revisit; joys to rediscover. Even the things he hadn't wanted to do – taking any job he could just to satisfy the requirements of his release, making obligatory visits to his parole officer – these things hadn't troubled him because they served to focus his mind on the here and now. But ever since the bones on the property line out back were unearthed, sleep had become a stranger again.

The dreams were back, too. They were rarely cohesive, with little more than the suggestion of a narrative he might have followed to uncover their meaning. Not that there was anything about them he couldn't understand. This was an old-fashioned haunting. Only in his dreams, he was the ghost, doomed to relive his fate for an eternity.

Sometimes in his dreams he was back at Florence. Sometimes, Marion. Always, he was doing the same thing – pacing aimlessly, without even the ability to let his imagination take him somewhere else. In one dream, he was back at Lompoc, surrounded by a gang of knife-wielding inmates. They attacked him and beat him and plunged their weapons into him. In another, it was Daulton who dragged a jagged blade across his neck, leaving Chris to bleed out on the floor of his prison cell.

He tried not to let Cait know, but even on nights when he didn't wake her up with his moaning and his thrashing, she could always see it in the dark circles under his eyes the next day.

I have to get rid of this.

He opened his eyes. Suddenly, his mind was filled with a sense of urgency, as if the thought had given voice to something critical he should have done long ago.

The hole. Chris sat up. For the past six weeks, the gouged plot of earth had been surrounded by police tape. Even the neighbors had given up hope the cops would ever wrap up their investigation and shifted the location of their fence. Which meant that damn hole now officially belonged to him.

He stood and put his shoes back on, then left the house and walked into the garage. There was a shovel hanging from two screws in the wall. He took it and walked back outside. Cait followed him.

"What are you doing?"

He raised the shovel with one hand and pointed in the direction of the hole with the other. "I'm going to take down that damn tape and cover that hole."

"Right now? Why don't you get some rest first?"

He shook his head. "I have to do this now."

She didn't argue. There was a look about him that told her whatever was driving him couldn't wait. He turned and began marching in the direction of the property line. Cait watched him go.

The police tape was still there, a bright yellow barrier encircling the upturned earth. The warning POLICE LINE – DO NOT CROSS screamed out in bold black lettering to anyone approaching. Chris snatched it all down and tossed it aside. The auger and its horrifying discovery had been taken away long ago, leaving only the hole. It stared up at him like an unblinking eye.

Piles of soft earth lay all around. He began to shovel them back into the ground, his motions slow and methodical at first, then gaining speed as the hole in the earth began to disappear. His mind flashed back twenty-five years to another hole, one similar in size – only back then, he had been digging it out. Sweat poured down his face. He thought if he turned his head, he would see Billy once again, standing beside him in his Lompoc-issued jeans and work shirt, dutifully holding the wheelbarrow in place, risking his neck for the sake of a friend.

I give you one in ten odds this'll work, Billy chided.

Chris stopped shoveling and looked around, convinced the voice he'd heard was real. He was alone. When he turned his attention back to the hole, it was gone. The earth had been filled in and all that remained was a scar where the natural growth had been disturbed. He stared at it for a long time, wondering how long it would take for that scar to fade and for things to regain their natural balance.

Then he realized something.

It's not right. It's not finished. There's still one thing left to do.
He set the shovel down and mopped his brow. Then he turned and walked back toward the house.

* * *

Dinner was on the table when he came back inside, but Cait could tell right away that Chris hadn't finished what he'd set out to do. Not yet. The dogs ran to greet him as he walked in, but he moved past them and went straight into the back study.

It was a small room with a rollup desk and a bookshelf stuffed with old atlases and history books. He sat down at the desk and tore a sheet of paper from a spiral notebook, rummaging around until he found a ballpoint pen.

He stared at the blank sheet of paper for a few seconds – long enough for him to ask himself what the hell he was doing and what he thought this would accomplish – but then the first words came and he surrendered to them.

Daulton,
I've always heard that time brings perspective. They never told me it would be this clear. Who'd have thought that after all these years, after so much water and so much shit, after everything we heaped upon ourselves, the picture I see now when I think of you and me isn't of a couple of graying ex-cons. It's not even us as stupid twenty-somethings, drunk off our asses and plotting the first steps of that irreversible road I wish we'd never taken.

These days when I think of us, I see a couple of dark-haired little twerps, running around on the hillsides of our tiny Palos Verdes world, watching birds fly overhead and dreaming of the day we'd be big enough to catch and fly our very own.

Our dreams were big back then, and so was the world. Now it feels like everywhere I go, I'm in danger of stepping into some mess of my own creation. I wish the world was big again so that I could lose myself in it. I bet you feel much the same way.

If I could go back in time and find those kids we used to be, I'd take them aside and try to talk some sense into them. Although who knows if that would have done any good? I think the movies and the books have it all wrong when it comes to that sort of thing. It takes a lot more than a single push or a mouthful of words to change the course of a life. And maybe everything that happens, happens because it's supposed to. I don't know.

The only thing I do know with any certainty is that despite it all – the bad choices that we made, the mistrust that got between us, the arrests and all the years of our lives we lost as a result – the greatest tragedy of all was the death of our friendship, and the loss of that short, funny-looking kid I loved so much when we were boys.

Kids don't ever speak that four-letter word to each another, especially boys. And grown men aren't allowed. Especially a couple of fuckups like you and me, whose only real accomplishment in life was to give our trust over to the one and only person in the world who could ever have saved us from that awful place we got ourselves into.

I know you never want to hear from me again. I respect that and I understand. All I can do is hope you find your peace, just as much as I hope I find mine.

Your friend always,
Chris

When he was finished, he set the pen down and folded the letter into his breast pocket. He pulled open the desk drawer and found a matchbook. Then he stood and walked down the hallway into the front room where Cait sat.

"I'll be back in a little while," he told her.

"Are you okay?"

"I'm fine. I just have one more thing to do. I won't be long."

He turned and walked out the front door. The sun was starting to sink on the horizon and the air was cold, but there was still a long way to go before winter. He marched across the front lawn and through the chain link gate, out into the sagebrush, back to the spot where the hole had been.

When he got there, he stared at the scar in the earth for a long time. The years unfurled before him like some great and terrible tapestry. From out of it all came the names of the two people he had cared for most.

Daulton.

Cait.

There was room for only one of them in his heart now. The choice had been easy to make.

He pulled the letter from his breast pocket and read it again. A bittersweet smile formed on his lips as he thought again of the boy with the dark, brooding face he had befriended a half century ago.

The smell of sulfur hit his nose as the matchbook burst to life. He held the letter to the flame and watched as his words were consumed. He bent to one knee and dropped it on the freshly laid dirt. When it was no more than a smoldering ball of ash, he stood and tamped the earth with his feet.

"Goodbye to all that."

***

Night had settled in by the time Chris returned. Cait was waiting for him. She noticed there was something different in his expression and his body language, a lightness that was refreshing to see. He looked like a man who had just come home from an exhausting journey.

"Everything taken care of?" she asked.

"It's all done," Chris said.

He crossed the room and stood beside her. This was important right now. To let himself know he wasn't alone.

"I know five a.m. comes early," he said, "but I was thinking I'd take Zeke flying in the morning. And I was sort of hoping you might want to come along. Maybe bring the dogs. A real family outing. We haven't had one of those in a long time."

Cait smiled. The light behind her eyes – still vibrant, still kicking, even after everything she'd been through and all that was yet to come – lifted his spirits. "I'd love to."

He took her hand in his and squeezed it.
Thank you.
She squeezed back.
You're welcome.

EPILOGUE

Christopher Boyce was officially released from parole in July of 2007. He and his wife, Cait, have been married since 2002. He continues to be an avid falconer.

In 2012, Cait Boyce announced that her cancer had gone into full remission. She continues to work as a legal professional and is a vocal supporter of LGBT and prisoner rights.

Andrew Daulton Lee worked briefly as a personal assistant to Sean Penn after his release from prison in 1997. He is alive and well and living in southern California.

Calvin Robinson was arrested in May of 1988 for attempting to smuggle forty-five tons of marijuana and hashish into the United States. He was convicted and sentenced to life imprisonment.

Gloria White, who was sentenced to five years imprisonment for harboring Christopher Boyce during his stay as a fugitive in Bonners Ferry and for allegedly helping him plan several bank robberies, died on February 23, 2011. She was sixty-nine. To this day, Boyce maintains White took no part in the robberies.

Christopher John Boyce in 1955, age two.

Cait Mills in 1961, age seven.

The Falcon and The Snowman: American Sons

Chris, age 12.

The Snowman and The Falcon in simpler times. Andrew Daulton Lee and Christopher Boyce, 1968.

Chris and falcon, 1969.

Cait's senior class photo, 1971 (age 17).

Chris and his VW Beetle, 1971.

Chris outside the Black Vault at TRW in the mid-seventies.

Chris, age twenty-three, with prairie falcon shortly before his arrest. He is wearing the same sweater that would appear in his mug shot.

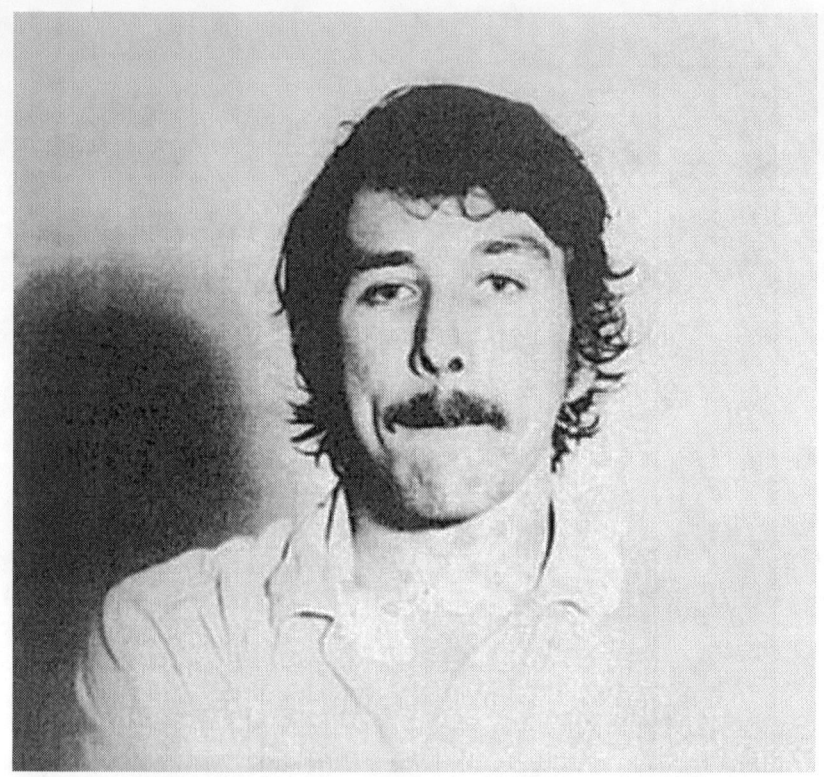

Andrew Daulton Lee mug shot, January 6, 1977.

Christopher Boyce mug shot, January 16, 1977.

Chris at Lompoc Federal Penitentiary, just before his escape.

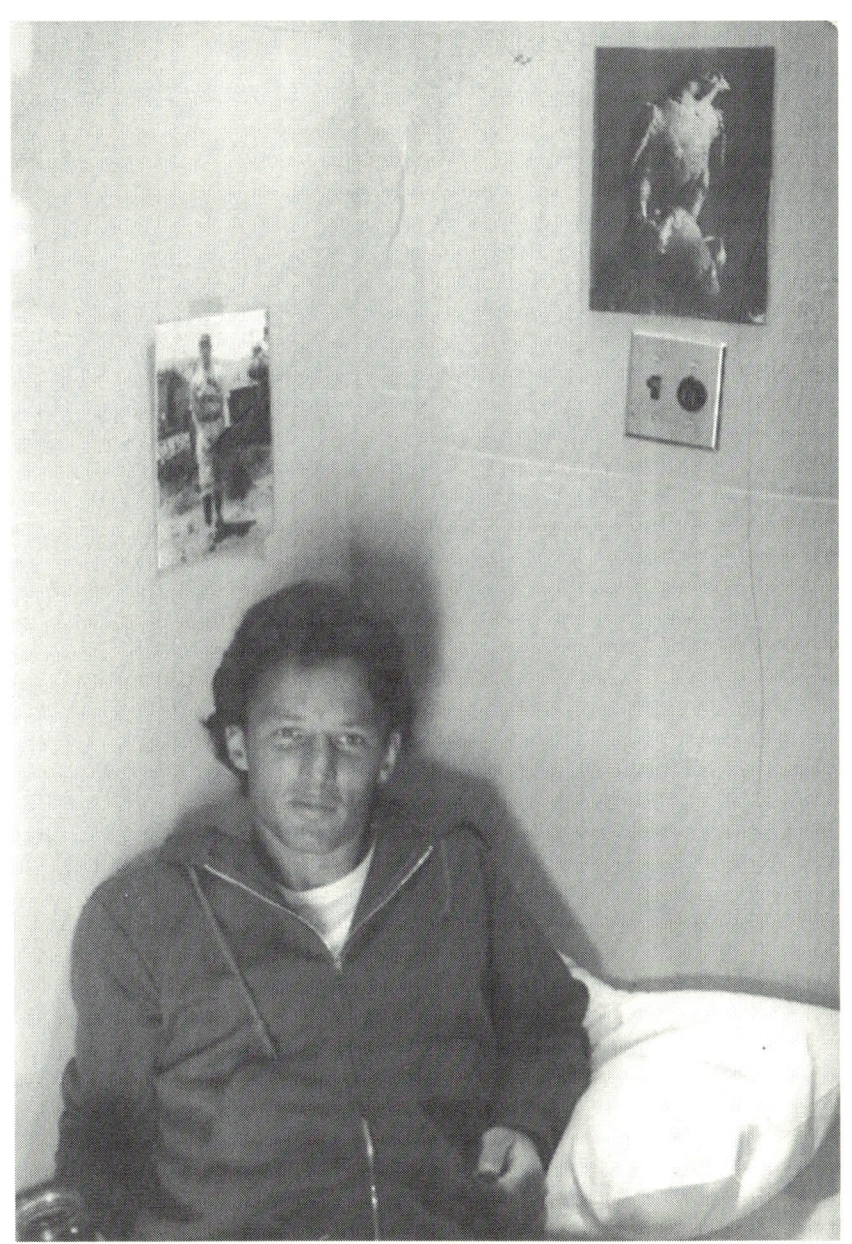

Chris in his Lompoc cell, days prior to his escape.

The Falcon and The Snowman: American Sons

Outside in the yard at Lompoc.

Chris, with Lompoc Federal Penitentiary in the background.

Scoping out the perimeter fences at Lompoc.

U.S. Department of Justice
United States Marshals Service

WANTED
BY U.S. MARSHALS

NOTICE TO ARRESTING AGENCY: BEFORE ARREST, VALIDATE WARRANT THROUGH NATIONAL CRIME INFORMATION CENTER (NCIC).

UNITED STATES MARSHALS SERVICE NCIC ENTRY NUMBER: (NIC/ W224966144).

NAME: CHRISTOPHER JOHN BOYCE
AKA(S):

DESCRIPTION:
- SEX: MALE
- RACE: WHITE
- PLACE OF BIRTH: SANTA MONICA, CALIFORNIA
- DATE(S) OF BIRTH: FEBRUARY 16, 1953
- HEIGHT: 5'9"
- WEIGHT: 160
- EYES: BLUE
- HAIR: BROWN
- SKINTONE:
- SCARS, MARKS, TATOOS:
- SOCIAL SECURITY NUMBER(S): - -
- NCIC FINGERPRINT CLASSIFICATION: 16 04 TT 10 03 16 54 TT 04 05

ADDRESS AND LOCALE:

WANTED FOR: ESCAPE   T 18 USC 751
WARRANT ISSUED: LOS ANGELES, CALIFORNIA
WARRANT NUMBER: 19347-148
DATE WARRANT ISSUED: JANUARY 21, 1980
MISCELLANEOUS INFORMATION: BOYCE was convicted of ESPIONAGE in LOS ANGELES, California on June 20, 1977. Sentence to 40 years. Escaped from FCI Lompoc, Ca. 1-21-80.
VEHICLE/TAG INFORMATION:

IF ARRESTED OR WHEREABOUTS KNOWN, NOTIFY THE LOCAL UNITED STATES MARSHALS OFFICE. (TELEPHONE _____).
IF NO ANSWER, CALL UNITED STATES MARSHALS SERVICE COMMUNICATIONS CENTER IN WASHINGTON, D.C.
TELEPHONE 703-285-1100 ; NLETS ACCESS CODE IS DCUSM0000.
(24 Hour telephone contact)

FORM USM-132
(EST. 5/79)

The Falcon and The Snowman: American Sons

ESCAPED FEDERAL PRISONER

Originally Sentenced For Espionage (40 years)

NAME: BOYCE, Christopher John
DOB : 2-16-53
SEX : Male
HGT : 5'9"
WGT : 160
EYE : Blue
HAR : Brown
POSSIBLE HOBBY: Falconry

SMT : Mole left jaw.
POB : Santa Monica, CA
DOW : 1-21-80
RAC : White
SOC :
FPC : 1604TT10031654TT0405
NCIC: W224966144

IT IS ANTICIPATED BOYCE WILL USE AN ALIAS AND ATTEMPT TO CHANGE HIS APPEARANCE.

REQUEST ALL POSSIBLES BE THOROUGHLY CHECKED AND THEIR FINGERPRINTS COMPARED WITH THE ATTACHED FINGERPRINT CARD.

IF CONTACTED, NOTIFY UNITED STATES MARSHAL, SEATTLE (206) 442-5504/0290 OR UNITED STATES MARSHAL SERVICE HEADQUARTERS (703) 285-1100.

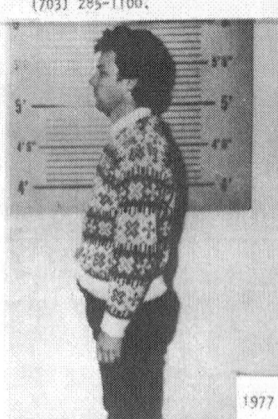

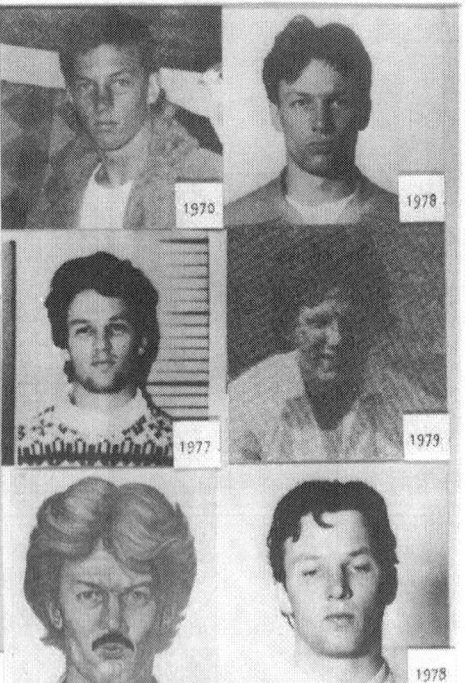

The Falcon and The Snowman: American Sons

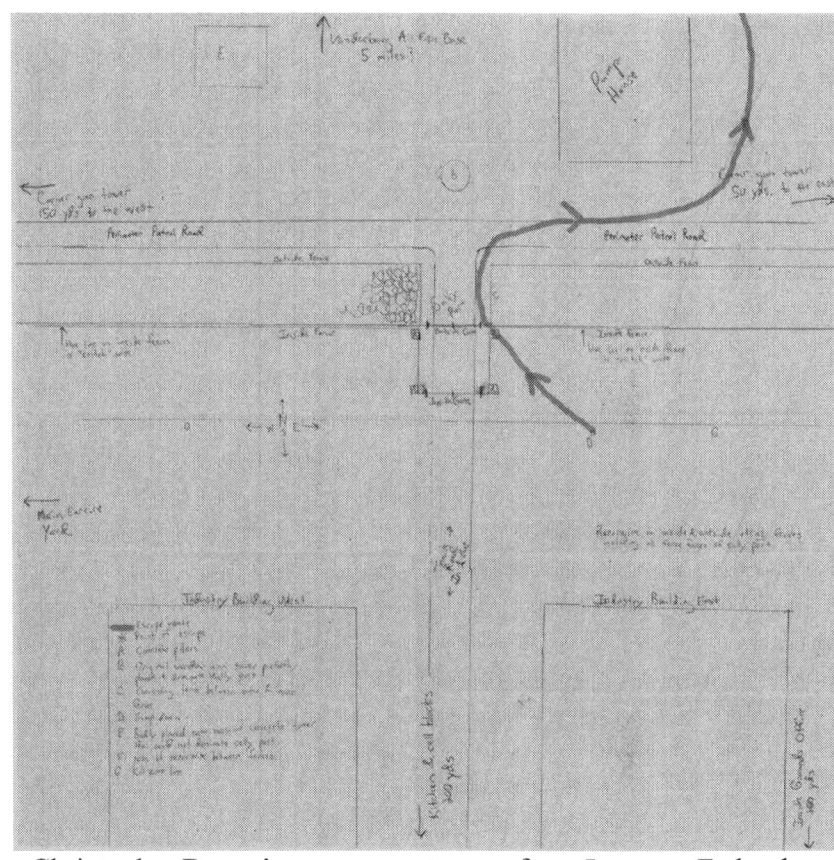

Christopher Boyce's escape route map from Lompoc Federal Penitentiary.

The Falcon and The Snowman: American Sons

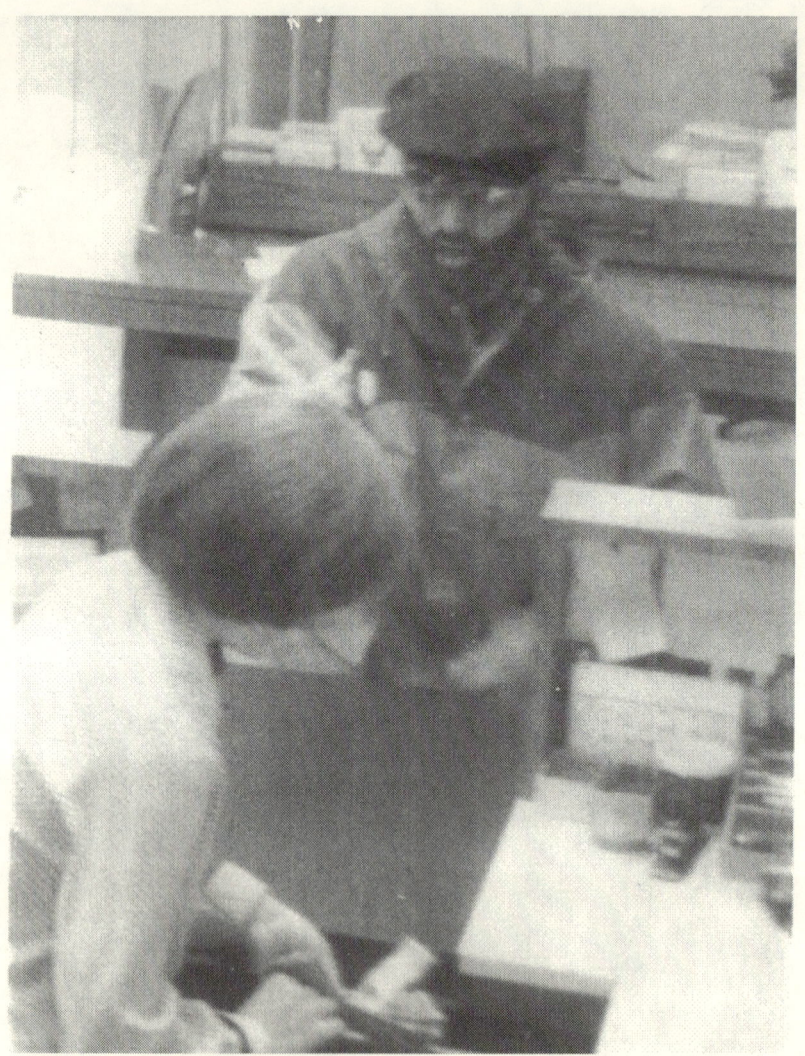

Photo used at Christopher Boyce's trial for bank robbery in Idaho, 1982.

Daulton Lee at Lompoc in the eighties.

Chris, giving his testimony before the U.S. Senate Subcommittee on Investigations, April 18, 1985. His attorney Bill Dougherty is seated to his right.

Christopher Boyce self-portrait, 1990.

The Falcon and The Snowman: American Sons

Chris as a beaten down boxer. Self-portrait, 1991.

Daulton Lee, Cait and her brother Tim Jones at Lompoc Federal Penitentiary, 1996.

The Falcon and The Snowman: American Sons

Cait and Chris at Oak Park Heights Prison, May 1997.

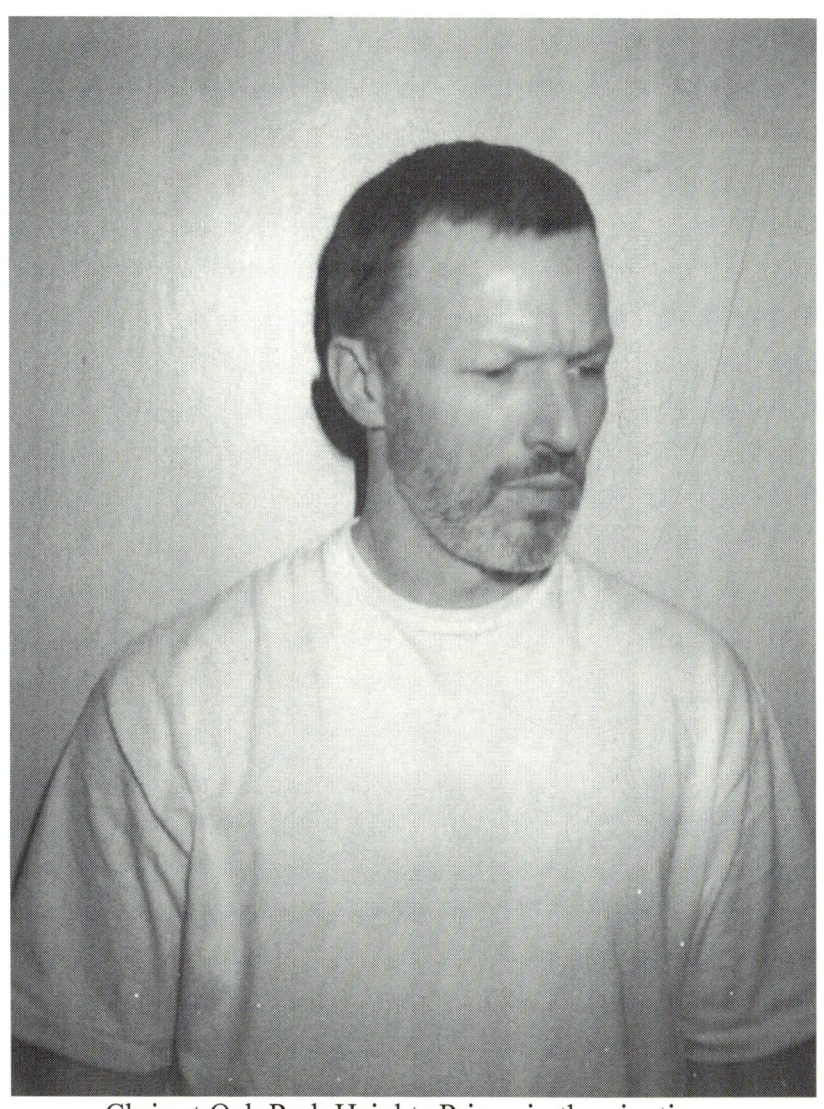

Chris at Oak Park Heights Prison in the nineties.

Chris graduating with his bachelor's degree in history from Oak Park Heights Prison.

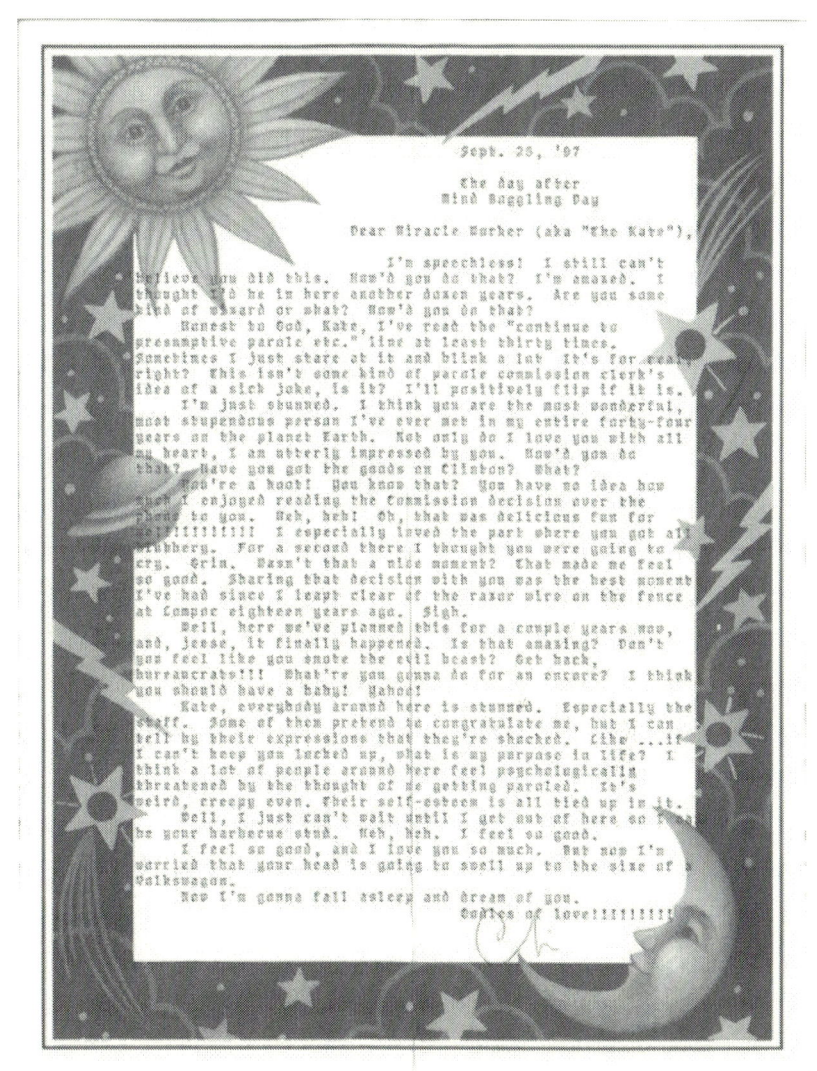

Letter from Chris to Cait, September 25, 1997.

The Falcon and The Snowman: American Sons

Cait and Daulton, San Francisco, 1999.

Helen Mills (Cait's mother) and Daulton, San Francisco, 1999.

Living room wedding, October 12, 2002. (Photo courtesy Matt Kramer)

Wedding ceremony with friends Sandra Hess and Matt Kramer, October 19, 2002. (Photo courtesy Matt Kramer)

Cait and Chris watching peregrines at Half Moon Bay, 2003.
(Photo courtesy Matt Kramer)

Cait, with dogs Theo and Lola, 2003. (Photo courtesy Matt Kramer)

Chris and Joachim, the Harris' hawk, 2003. (Photo courtesy Patrick Miller)

Cait, Joachim and Chris in San Francisco, 2003. (Photo courtesy Patrick Miller)

Chris, Theo and Cait, 2004.

The Falcon and The Snowman: American Sons

Chris and falcon, 2004.

Hawking on the grasslands, 2013. (Photo courtesy Vince Font)

Cait and her brother Tim Jones at an event for the San Francisco AIDS Foundation, 2013.

The authors: Cait Boyce, Vince Font and Christopher Boyce, 2013. (Photo courtesy Jane Font)

Thank you for reading *The Falcon and The Snowman: American Sons*. We hope you enjoyed it. If you did, please recommend it to a friend. If you didn't, recommend it to an enemy. We also hope you'll share your opinion of the book by leaving a brief review about it on Amazon. You don't have to write a book report – just a simple blurb will suffice. Leaving feedback is a great way to help boost the book's visibility on the Amazon market and beyond. It also helps other readers discover books they may be missing out on.

To contact us or to find further supplemental material, including frequently updated blog posts, photographs and video, please check out our blog at www.thefalconandthesnowman.com. All you nutty social media enthusiasts can also follow us on Facebook (facebook.com/thefalconandthesnowman) or on Twitter (@CodenameFalcon).

Thank you,
Chris, Cait and Vince
(August, 2013)

Made in the USA
Lexington, KY
29 November 2013